Journal of a
Walden Two Commune:
The Collected Leaves
of Twin Oaks   Vol. 1

Issues 1-15

Library of Congress Catalogue Card Number: 72-84005

Printed in the United States of America

• Typesetting by WALDEN THREE

• Distributed by the COMMUNITY PUBLISHING COOPERATIVE
(Yellow Springs, Ohio 45387)

Table of Contents

Introduction

Here are the first four years of Twin Oaks Community, in the form of newsletters that were written along the way. Newsletters don't tell the whole story, of course. They were intended to be partly historical record, partly letters to our friends, and partly propaganda organ to advertise the benefits of community living. So we mostly left out the quarrels, frustrations, and discouragements; those are told about in another volume.* The *Leaves* has always been kept deliberately cheerful. That doesn't make this running account a false one—just perhaps a little one-sided.

Anyway, the facts are here, from the day we laid our sleeping bags out under the apple trees because we couldn't find the keys to the farm house, to the day we held a summer conference to try to get another community started. That's June, 1967 through July, 1971. This volume doesn't end the story, either. Twin Oaks is very much alive, getting bigger, stronger, and happier all the time. Barring major accidents (like nuclear holocaust) there will be a Volume Two, and Three, and Four.

Part One we've called "Heads in the Clouds." Many of you will have been through this stage. Maybe you're there now—lots of theorizing, while you continue to work at your old job or stay in college. Not every community starts with theories, but ours did. Rudy and Dusty published a paper called *Walden Pool*, and they printed articles of anybody whose thinking remotely resembled either Walden Two or any other kind of community. During the same period, George, Josie, and I were at Walden House, trying (not very successfully) to save up money to buy a farm, while running a cooperative city house and putting out a newsletter about it. The house was a dismal failure, but the newsletter turned out to be a help, eventually, by attracting the attention of people who later joined Twin Oaks. *Walden Pool* and the *Walden House Newsletter* between them show the background thinking for Twin Oaks and tell about the Ann Arbor conference where we met each other and began to commit ourselves to each other and to a rural commune based on *Walden Two*. Part One is roughly chronological, alternating between the two publications and reprinting those sections that turned out to be relevant in the long run.

Part Two contains reprints of the *Leaves of Twin Oaks*. They tell their own story, but perhaps I should comment on the authorship. Most of it was written by me. Where I have said "we think" or "we feel," it was either that the Community did indeed have consensus on that opinion or else I thought it did, or that enough of us agreed to make the plural form legitimate. Although we have never had complete unanimity of opinion on any issue, the point of view expressed in the *Leaves* has usually represented at least a majority opinion. Generally speaking, anything I didn't write myself is signed by the author. These articles, too, usually represent majority thinking, for they were written by the people who influenced our thinking; though an occasional minority protest did get aired in the *Leaves*.

We haven't used many names in the *Leaves*, especially in the early issues. There were a number of reasons for that. Rudy wanted to avoid any kind of hero-worship or cult of personality. After all, we weren't trying to talk people into joining Twin Oaks because of certain interesting people who happened to live here; we wanted them to join because we have a sane social system that makes a good life. Then, there was the turnover problem. If we wrote about our individual members in one issue, would those members still be here when the next issue came out? In the early years we couldn't count on it.

*A Walden Two Experiment, with a foreword by B.F. Skinner, a book to be published early in 1973 by William Morrow and Company. Copies available direct from Twin Oaks Community, Louisa, Virginia 23093.

Another interesting aspect of community that may be apparent in reading through the *Leaves* is that communities have to solve and resolve some problems over and over. Many subjects are discussed several times, from slightly different points of view. In case anyone wants to read everything we ever printed on the subject of, say, labor credits, or government, or fruit trees, or pigs, we have made an index for this volume for ease in locating articles dealing with some particular subject.

In the appendix you will find our Behavior Code, which in some respects is borrowed from *Walden Two*. All of it, except Paragraph Four, was written in 1967. We added the "no-bitching" paragraph in 1969. The Code is meant as a guideline and as a goal. As such, it indicates some specific behaviors that we, as individual members of the group, are trying to establish or trying to eliminate. Although noncompliance is not punished by any legal sanctions, social sanctions can be—and naturally are—brought to bear on each of us, shaping our behavior toward the desired ends.

We haven't bothered to correct what now are, in some instances, old errors in the *Leaves*. Thus, you will note in one issue that we intend to pound the last nail in the new building by Hallowe'en, and in a winter issue we are still wishing we could move out of the barns. Community is like that. Things seldom work out quite the way they were planned. Our excitement about the filmwinder and TOPIC industries was ill-founded. Neither came to anything. We have learned not to publish articles about industries until we start making money from them.

But, in general, the *Leaves* gives a good picture of what life is like at Twin Oaks. It is a fair guess that during periods when few issues were published, things were not going very well here and I, for one, didn't feel up to putting out a newsletter. When the publication rate steps up, it usually means life is interesting here and there is progress to report. These days issues go out regularly. You can take that to mean that life at Twin Oaks is very good indeed and getting better.

Kat (Griebe) Kinkade for the Community

Twin Oaks, June, 1972

Part One:

HEADS in the CLOUDS

Chapter One: The Genesis

December, 1965

WALDEN HOUSE

Walden House is a seven-bedroom house in Washington, D. C. It is old, in need of certain repairs and painting, but comfortably livable. It is capable of housing perhaps ten people, with a little crowding. At present there are seven living in it.

Economically, Walden House operates as a cooperative, everyone paying an equal share and doing an equal amount of housework and general maintenance. Work is allocated on a labor credit system much like that described by Dr. Skinner.

In terms of long-range plans for a rural, self-sufficient Walden Two community, Walden House serves several purposes: It gives us practice in group living; it provides a communal shelter for us while we work and save money to purchase a piece of country acreage; it serves as a recruiting center.

Walden House is a place for impatient Walden Two enthusiasts. It is the scene of necessarily limited but determined action toward the founding of a society like the one Dr. Skinner described. (Walden House has no direct connection with Dr. Skinner.)

February, 1966

WHAT IS A LABOR CREDIT?

If you've read *Walden Two* you probably think of a labor credit as a means of exchange, or possibly a unit of work. It is both of those things. But seven months of daily experience with the labor credit have given us a sharper definition. A labor credit is a Degree of Unpleasantness. Now most utopians would be shocked at that statement. Work can and perhaps ought to be satisfying or enjoyable, or at least inoffensive. One of the most appealing aspects of the system as described by Skinner is that no one ever has to do what he doesn't like to do—unless for a very short time. The difficulty with the cooperative house approach to utopia is that about 95 per cent of the necessary tasks are considered by almost everybody to be unpleasant. To determine the precise value of any job, therefore, becomes the task of determining which jobs are considered most unpleasant by most people.

Consider the difficulties. First of all, most of the tasks are clearly "women's work." Given that a division of work along strict sexual lines is outmoded and ridiculous, we still must face that prejudice in the minds of most of the men who are interested in Walden Two. "Why should I do women's work when there are women around to do it?" asked a prospective member just the other day. "True man's work," says another in a recent letter, "is involved with nature—building, planting, harvesting, brewing, fighting, arguing, and management." No comment.

Setting sexual arguments aside for the sake of sticking to our subject matter, the fact is that there is much work to be done at Walden House, and nobody really wants to do any of it (except, perhaps, the fighting, arguing, and management).

Skinner understood all of this perfectly, as did Bellamy before him; and that is why the labor credit represents, not a unit of time or a degree of effort or a reward for talent or initiative, but a degree of unpleasantness.

Everybody seems to agree that cleaning the oven is unpleasant. It takes about forty-five minutes and rates 5 credits. Grocery shopping, considered a white-collar job in spite of the driving and sack-lugging involved, rates only 6 credits, and it takes at least three hours.

One of the things one speculates about regarding the system of labor in the book *Walden Two* is just how the different values were ever fixed upon in the first place. Here at Walden House we think we have at least one possible answer. We know how we are doing it. Oddly enough, we started with the *laissez-faire* system of bidding! Initially we all sat around in a circle, and the jobs were called out one by one. Each person named the number of credits he considered he would do the job for. Theoretically, the jobs would go to the lowest bidder. Theoretically, too, by the end of the bidding, everyone was to have an equal number of credits' worth of obligation. There is not space enough to describe the difficulties we encountered in this. Math majors among you will understand instantly why we were up until 1:00 a.m. Those who have ever tried to live in the same household with people from different parts of the country, different financial and cultural backgrounds, and different systems of values will not be surprised that at the end of this bidding marathon no one understood the system except its inventor, no one was sure whether he had a bargain or had been cheated, and no one was at all satisfied that this was the best way to spend every Sunday evening. Nevertheless, that first week's work got done. As has been *laissez-faire's* fate in other times and situations, this system was quickly found to require controls. Otherwise, how could one stop a member from bidding a job at three times its worth, just because no one happened to feel like bidding against him? (Remember, there were only five members all together.) And how could one justify that Tuesday dinner went for 1.2 credits, while Wednesday dinner went for 0.75

because two people (who both happened to have Wednesday free) were bidding against each other? We instituted a "ceiling bid" that eventually turned out to be a fairly fixed value. In fact, though we retain the term "bidding" to the present day, the actual procedure is much closer to "choosing" or "signing up." The oral sessions rapidly gave way to a sign-up sheet; the weekly equality rule proved awkward and was replaced by a system of surpluses and deficits that can be carried over from week to week. (One member consistently does all his work for the month in two or three days, then slides on his surpluses; another gets further and further behind each week until her deficit begins to look dangerous, then works desperately hard all one week and puts herself at par again.)

Least popular of all chores has proved to be dishwashing. When the credit value of dishwashing reached the ridiculous figure of 8 and still lacked volunteers, we reached into our pockets and bought a used dishwasher. Dishwashing is now rated at 2.5.

A couple of problems we have not yet solved. Most pressing is the matter of making labor less painful. Also, what do you do if a member gets too far behind? So far we just nag. If anybody has any bright suggestions involving positive reinforcement, we'd like to hear about them.

THE WORD FROM SINAI

Among the amazing things one discovers in associating with other Waldophiles is that it is perfectly possible to see Walden Two from several distinct and quite incompatible angles. A friend of ours, for instance, swore that Skinner intended that the Walden Code should include the Ten Commandments. We laughed at him and he became quite adamant. "It's in the book," he kept insisting; and sure enough, he found it for us, right on the bottom of page 162. We still laughed and told him what to us was perfectly obvious — that Skinner had been employing a metaphor. Our friend had no use for metaphors. All that was required, he said, was rewriting the famous commandments a bit so that they were relevant to Walden Two living. Finding that we could not take him seriously, he took the job upon himself. When we left him, he was composing, "Thou shalt have no other Goods before the Good Life. . ."

DEAR MR. FRAZIER:

I don't understand why you have such a complicated labor credit system, just to make sure everybody does an *equal* amount of work. I am sure I don't care if somebody works less than I, as long as I feel they are contributing something. People who are so particular about *counting* the hours they work are not the best kind for community.

— Freesoul

Dear Freesoul,

Sounds good. The last fellow who told us he didn't mind being exploited by lazy people stayed here a month and left with a deficit of 44 credits. It seems *he* was the one that he wanted people to make allowances for. We are now somewhat wary of people who *talk* generously about labor.

From WALDEN POOL

March, 1966

INTRODUCTION

Since Gerald Baker began advertising last July, hundreds of people from all over the country have expressed an interest in planning and building a real Walden Two community. In an attempt to keep inquirers informed of current developments, Baker tried to organize "circular letter" groups. This didn't work out too well, and a process of general correspondence and forwarding of letters was used to circulate ideas and information. Still everyone couldn't be kept informed, especially those who were interested but not enough to devote the necessary time for letter writing.

As letters continue to come in, Baker and the Regional Directors of the project find less and less time for general correspondence. Needless to say, there are numerous problems and ideas that need to be discussed. This newsletter is an attempt to present such discussions not only to the Walden Two activists but, more importantly, to those who prefer to remain uninvolved at this point.

NATIONAL NEWSLETTER, ET AL.

This being our first newsletter, I feel it appropriate to state some of the goals of the social science division.

First is the provision of a sounding board for criticism, worries, praises, and general emotional reactions to all facets of the social science aspects of developing a Walden Two-style community. Second is the furnishing of a medium through which all members can share pertinent ideas and information.

Finally is the actual development of a society that the members preplanned and are continually wishing to improve.

April, 1966

MEMBERSHIP QUALIFICATIONS

At the last meeting of the Atlanta Walden Two Committee, the topic of membership qualifications arose. There are several important considerations that all those interested in the community should be aware of. Should people applying for membership be screened, and if so, what are to be the criteria for accepting or rejecting prospective members?

For instance, should the community accept homosexuals or others considered by outside society to be "odd" in their behavior? What specific kinds of "oddballs" do we keep out, considering that the outside considers *anybody* who would join a community slightly strange?

If, in starting the community, we begin with a very small group, such as a national headquarters staff, it will be possible to grow slowly, allowing each new person to integrate himself into the community easily, or else decide that he doesn't want to stay. In this case, screening, or anything of that sort, could and would be minimal.

If, on the other hand, we begin with a larger group, we may be forced to develop some sort of criteria to weed out those who would be a detriment to the community. If we had a large group of people, even a few of whom were extremely incompatible, our chances for success would not be good.

Given the possibility that screening might prove to be necessary, what qualifications should be set up? Those of us seriously considering beginning the community should express ourselves on this subject. Should homosexuals be allowed? What about standards of mental health? Moral, political, or religious (or anti-religious) standards? Do we admit people who have a history of financial irresponsibility? Let us know your opinions on this matter, so that we can discuss them in the next issue.

BASES FOR COMMUNITY

As a general outline for the community I propose the following generals, as a basis for further discussion.

1. A cooperative farm and industrial commune.
2. Communal child rearing.
3. Maximum use of all psychological and social science in helping each individual to understand himself and to learn means for self-actualization and to understand all others in his social environment.
4. Use of psychology to train children social skills helpful in cooperative living.
5. Continuous experimentation with possible improvements in social organization and individual training.
6. An otherwise Summerhillian framework of education.
7. Fluid communication between administration and members.
8. Consciously accepted behavioral engineering rather than unconscious control.

Problems to be considered:

1. Type of work-payment system (Skinner's labor credits?);
2. Methods by which members may gain money for use in the outside world or for purchases of special value to them;
3. Any bylaws that may be necessary (as for severance payment to any member who may leave);
4. Structure of administration and requirements for this service position.

From WALDEN HOUSE NEWSLETTER

April, 1966

DEAR MR. FRAZIER:

"I don't want to join a community; I want to start my own. Can you tell me how to go about it?"

— VIP

Dear VIP,

Yes. First get a Ford Foundation grant; then gather together a thousand persons of all different professions, a team of professional psychologists, and a lot of pretty girls. We are pretty sure this is the way to go about it, because this is the advice everybody gives *us*.

"Dear Mr. Frazier: I am going to do a term paper on intentional communities, and I want to use Walden House for my research. Please let me know when I can come and inspect you."

— Freddy Frosh

Dear Freddy,

There are more freshmen wanting to do term papers on us than there are members here. Why don't half of you join us, and the other half can write term papers on them.

June, 1966

PROPOSAL FOR GOVERNMENT

During a recent meeting in St. Louis, the problem of democracy arose; and the question of just how much freedom the planners are given and to what extent the other members control planned social changes.

The argument against democracy is that it allows the unqualified to place restraints on the experts. This retards the possibilities of constructive social change and experimentation.

The argument for some degree of democracy is that it keeps the non-planners from having a feeling of helplessness in relation to their daily activities. This would be especially disastrous in the early formation when most of the members will want an active part in the social planning. Many potential members would be scared away by a fear that the planners might become selfish dictators. This is a primary point raised by most of the people I have talked with who are new to the idea of Walden Two. This fear does have what I consider a rational counterpart in that no matter how much we like to think about planners as experts in community planning who will work for the general good of the community, there are decisions that depend on the preferences of the other members and on their general readiness to try certain changes.

Keeping all of these arguments in mind, the following system is proposed.

1. The planners constitute experts in community management and social change whose job it is to coordinate the activities of the community as a whole. When a problem arises or an experimental change is to be tried, the planners discuss it with those in the various areas that the changes will affect. The planners then draw up a plan agreed upon among themselves.

2. Prior to its instigation, the plan is posted on a bulletin board.

3. A high percentage (75%) of signatures on an attached sheet would effectively VETO the proposal.

4. If not enough members sign, the proposal is put into effect for a previously specified experimental period. After this period, another proposal is put on the bulletin board suggesting that the system be maintained. A lower percentage (majority) of signers is then needed to effectively veto the proposal completely.

This technique has the advantage of giving a feeling of representation to the nonplanners while also favoring experimentation. It also provides a measure of the satisfaction of the members with the changes being tried. By having votes necessary to veto rather than to support, a trend toward less and less nonplanner influence is built into the system. If the planners do a good job, then the bulletin board and voting will soon become less used and in effect there will be a democratic form available but without restrictions from the unqualified members.

BACKGROUND INFORMATION CONCERNING THE MOVEMENT

Presently there are at least four groups of people working somewhat independently toward a community such as Walden Two. One group is Walden House in Washington, D. C. . . .another group is Living Research, of which Robert Erdmann and Efraim and Enid Gugel are a part. Living Research is concerned with educating and preparing prospective members for community life.

A third group began last July when Gerald Baker began advertising intensively, inviting people to write him if they were interested in the idea of a Walden Two community. Since then almost a thousand people have written him expressing their interest in communities. Some of the inquirers set up Walden Two Committees, the Atlanta Walden Two Committee, which publishes this newsletter, being one of them.

The fourth group was formed by Jim and Annette Breiling, who met with Skinner last fall and arranged to compile a list of all the people who had written him about *Walden Two*. The list has continued to grow and now includes more than 170 names and addresses, representing 254 adults and 95 children. The current undertaking of this group's activities is the National Convention, also described in this issue, which is probably the greatest present need of the moment.

NATIONAL CONVENTION

The much-needed National Convention is to be held August 28-31 at the very appropriately-named Waldenwoods Conference Center near Hartland, Michigan. The Center, complete with Walden Lake and three stately colonial-style lodges that are surrounded by sixteen hundred acres of private estate, should provide an ideal environment for productive, exciting, entertaining, and successful convention.

The objectives of the conference are to: become acquainted with conference participants; review the position of *Walden Two*, psychology, and behavioral engineering; conduct workshops in all phases of community founding and functioning; prepare a schedule for community development; establish permanent committees in all areas essential to community development; establish a formal organization to coordinate the founding of a successful community; and establish communication and dissemination procedures.

The seven workshops will deal with the following fields: community membership, community social structure, community economic structure, community location, community construction, community financing, and community development.

From WALDEN HOUSE NEWSLETTER

June, 1966

EXPERIMENTAL COMMUNITY

Since we have repeatedly stated that we are interested in living in a community "like the book," we are fairly accustomed to being told that we are rigid, and that our attitude is "not experimental." Now that is an interesting question to speculate about.

I confess that I try in vain to imagine what a completely experimental community would be like. Suppose ten people got together and decided to determine, using purely experimental methods, the best pattern for family structure. How long would it take for each pattern to be tried? Or suppose that each person or couple experimented with his own pattern. I am not sure what you would have, but I don't think it would be a community.

When you experiment, you have to start from some base, some generally-understood agreement of a working arrangement. Now for a starting point, we like the Walden Two idea as described by Dr. Skinner. Failing that (and for economic reasons we cannot literally start there) we would like to *aim toward it*, and use that as a common base.

People who call this idea "rigid" do not usually mean that. What they often mean is that they disagree with parts of it and have their own equally rigid ideas about where to start. Quite often, oddly enough, their starting point is right where they are now — with the values of our lush, competitive society.

"Oh, I like the Walden Two idea very much, all except the sharing property; I wouldn't go for that" or "Walden Two would be great, if they just had democratic government" or (most common of all) "Walden Two, yes, but not common nurseries; I want to raise my own kids."

So what we would end up with, if we took the advice of all these people, would be a little community just like the big one, with a little added social security and a trifle higher intellectual level, perhaps. Thank you, but we are not interested. If we have to compete for food and shelter, we'll do it in the big society; if we have to stick to the same old tyrannical family structure, we don't need a community to watch us do it; and if democracy is the best available answer to good government, we are all straightway going to go into local politics. Why piddle around with a handful of people when there is a world to conquer? We are not looking for a smaller puddle, so that we can be bigger frogs.

Not all of our critics are conservative. There are also those who feel that Skinner did not go far enough. They feel that it is our obligation to experiment with, for example, group marriage or psychedelic drugs. We will grant that an experiment in, for example, group marriage, is as valid and interesting as our experiment in equality of labor. And we do not deny that choosing one and not the other for a starting point is somewhat arbitrary. Nevertheless, we are using Walden Two for a rallying cry, and it is not even ethical (to say nothing of sensible) to cry "Walden Two" and have something else in mind. We submit that the marital arrangements Skinner had in mind were loosely monogamous, at least for a starter, and that drugs did not come into the picture at all. We'll go along with that. We are interested in Walden Two. Is anybody else?

LABOR CREDIT "PROBLEM"

Nothing we have ever written in this newsletter has elicited more response than our remarks about dishwashing. Evidently this is a matter on which nearly everyone has an opinion. The suggestions range from "everyone wash his own" to "hire a maid."

What is interesting in this flood of helpful mail is that the writers are unanimous in thinking that Walden House has a problem getting the housework done. That is not what we meant to say.

Just what is the difference between the way we get things done and the way they get done in your household? Simple. In your house someone is forced to do that work, either because it is his "role" or because economic or other levers are used, or because no one else will do it. In your house, the work gets done, because *someone* is exploited.

At Walden House we take a dim view of exploitation. The object of the labor credit system is to divide the work evenly. Labor credits are not a problem; they are a solution.

In the process of applying the solution, little difficulties come up, and we try to entertain our reading public by reporting them. But the main problem has been solved.

August, 1966

SUMMER CONFERENCE

Quite a lot of people have told us that they could be quite serious about Walden Two if it had a better head start than our small effort can give it: some financial backing, a larger group, a staff of competent personnel, etc. We can understand this attitude readily enough, and we share in the hopes for a community closer to our ideals.

In an effort to find out how many people across the country are serious about this, and what our combined resources might be, there is being planned a Walden Two National Conference. Some of us from Walden House are going to attend. If you don't make it yourself, you may expect a report on it in our next newsletter. But we would rather see you there!

WHY COMMUNITY PROPERTY?

The holding of property in common at Walden House is not an article of dogma. We don't do it because it was recommended by Jesus or Marx. We do it because it saves money and makes sense. Where it ceases to have these functions, we cease to practice it.

There are clear advantages to private ownership, and on the day when Walden House can afford a separate and equal *x* for every member, then *x* shall cease to be community property. But that day is not yet. In the meantime, we have a principle that says all members should enjoy equal advantages. (That *is* an article of dogma.) As far as we can see, the only way to manage this is to have a great deal of common property.

We do not deny that group ownership makes problems (Who left the saw out in the rain?). Careless handling of fine equipment will reduce its usefulness and beauty considerably, and any rule you can make is at best a compromise. As we tread carefully among the destructive alternatives, we try to keep two principles in mind: that property well cared for is a basic requisite for economic growth; but that the human being is in all cases more important than the property.

From WALDEN POOL

September, 1966

NATIONAL CONVENTION

Eighty-three people attended the national convention held August 28-31 at the Waldenwoods Conference Center near Hartland, Michigan. Conference participants conducted workshops in all phases of community founding and functioning, prepared a time schedule for community development, established permanent committees in all areas essential to community development, and made first steps towards establishing a formal organization to coordinate pre-community activities.

A TAPE-RECORDED MESSAGE
FROM DR. B. F. SKINNER

There has never been a time in the history of the world when a conference of this sort would be more timely. Something must be done and soon to discover how men can live together without destroying themselves. It ought to be done at the level of the national government. The United States, as the strongest nation in the world, could set a pattern by refusing to perpetuate international violence and by insisting on a careful investigation of all other alternatives. It has not. Instead, it has held steadfast to the traditional patterns of aversive control. If someone does something you don't like, knock him down. If a nation differs with you in its form of government or its ambitions,

bomb it. Worse than that, the United States is supplying to half the world the munitions that will be needed to maintain those practices for decades to come. So it must be done at another level, and perhaps you are taking the first step.

Undoubtedly we don't know all there is to know about human behavior, but we already know a lot. It can help. The science of behavior can be applied to the most pressing problems of today—to design of culture, to solving the problems of economic production, as well as leisure, and so on. It can't be done on government grants or foundation grants. It's got to be real people leading real lives. That is the pattern I had in mind when I wrote *Walden Two*. I think it is a viable pattern, and a very promising one. In many ways the successful design of an intentional community might be the most exciting and encouraging achievement in the latter half of the twentieth century. I don't know whether the pattern I drew up in *Walden Two* is the right one, of course. The book is fiction—I had to assume that I knew the results of a ten-year experiment and, of course, I didn't. But perhaps you will try the experiment and come up with the real results. If *Walden Two* helps to suggest some way to start, I shall be very happy.

SOME THOUGHTS ON THE CONVENTION

At one of the sessions of the Convention, we were led in a discussion on *Strategy and Tactics*. This was explained as meaning the determination of the objective and the means of gaining it. Some of us didn't see the relevancy of the discussion at the time, maybe it was the unfamiliarity of the words. But now that we have had time to think about it, it is important. We need to spell out the purposes or goals of the community, and then determine how to achieve them.

THE GOALS

The philosophers have described the best society variously as "the good life," "the fulfillment of the needs of man," "the maximum enjoyment of life," "liberty, equality, brotherhood," and "a society in which one man cannot be used as a means for the purposes of other men."

These are broad terms and we have to know what qualities of life and what actions are included in the meaning, and what are not. Knowledge of what constitutes the real needs of men should be the subject of a Walden Two study; however, among the goals that I saw in the book, important to me are:

- The placing of the purposes of the individual above property or profit, and also above the purposes of any technology. People are ends in themselves, not means.

- Equality among all members—no elite or hero or personality cult.

- The use of behavioral science with its emphasis away from negative reinforcement or punishment, to raise children to be loving human beings.

- The emphasis on cooperation, not competition.

- The expansion of community to provide for the people of this country an alternative to the corporate state.

- The use of experimentation to chart the path to fulfillment of the needs of men.

The goals that we arrive at must be the primary purpose of the community for they provide for the needs of the individual person. The purposes of the college, of behavioral engineering, and the constitution and its organizational structure must serve the purposes of the community, not vice versa. The constitution must be drawn to perpetuate the goals, not the structure. The organizational structure must preclude a tyranny of the majority—the purposes of each individual should be spelled out and guarded.

HOW DO WE GET THERE?

Behavioral science or engineering is heralded as the technology by which people are to be conditioned to want to be decent human beings. However, technology is a tool, and tools are amoral. The morality of the wielder of the tool determines the morality of the product.

For this reason, we need measures or yardsticks to be able to determine to what extent people are being used for the purposes of others, and further, to what degree they are being conditioned to want to be used for the purposes of others.

There was some feeling (at the Convention) that the *first* purpose of the behavioral technicians might be to develop the techniques of the technology, with Walden Two coming second. However, the development of the technology is necessary; what all of us have to do is to make certain that it is used for the right purpose.

There was some difference of opinion on how closely the book should be followed. In general, the difference was in three areas: *1)* apprehension that if the book is followed too closely it might become a bible or dogma, *2)* the possibility of the formation of a planner-manager elite, and *3)* the amount of democracy to be used.

I am not worried about the first because of the degree to which experimentation is being emphasized. As for an elite forming, we will just have to be sure that the planners and managers get no special privileges and that their authority does not go outside their areas of technology. The amount of democracy or consensus to be used is a problem and needs study. Generally speaking, there should be consensus in matters of opinion, and direction in matters of technology. The control of human beings is supposed now to be a technology; however, I don't know whether it is that far along yet — further, I question its efficacy among people who are not products of Walden Two. So much of what we are thinking and discussing at this stage is in the area of philosophy, and philosophy is not a technology.

As for the mechanics of getting the community going, the money raising is all-important and that is why the grants seem to be necessary. There is some difference of opinion as to how necessary. If we can get them, fine; but there must be no strings attached. It would be better, in my estimation, to start with one million dollars and create our own wealth from there, than to start with five million and have to compromise any of the purposes of the community.

The first thing to do is to get the piece of land, get the agriculture going, build the housing, meeting houses, and the basic production shops. The production shops should include food processing, wood working, metal working, automotive and equipment repair, construction, electrical-electronic, printing, arts and crafts, and research and development. When we have food and housing and basic shops, we would be ready for people with skills. The general policy of production would be to become as self-sufficient as is reasonable so that we wouldn't have to pay the exorbitant overhead costs of the corporate state.

To pay for raw materials and the products of heavy machine tools and some food that we couldn't produce ourselves, we would start by selling the goods and services that we've developed for ourselves, then develop allied products. Market development could include mail order, consumer co-ops, health food stores, etc.

All this does take time and does need planning, but if we can stick together I think we have a good chance of succeeding; there were a lot of good people at the Convention.

October, 1966

CONFERENCE REPORT

We promised you a full report on the Walden Two conference held in Michigan the last of August, and we are embarrassed to tell you that we cannot possibly give you anything of the sort. The Conference was a full, busy, dramatic, and confusing three days; and if we chose to report on it fully, it would take us easily twelve issues, or two years. We expect that within that time other exciting things will be happening that we will be wanting to talk about. So we are going to have to be satisfied with a very selective report on the Conference. There will also be an official report coming out, which you will hear of when it is ready. But we have no fear of duplication — what the newsletter prints is strictly the unofficial report!

IN GENERAL

The Conference was well worth attending. Eighty people showed up; if you subtract a few small children and curious bystanders and add a few absent wives and husbands, you still come up with about eighty people. Although almost all age groups were represented, the majority of the group was between 19 and 30 years of age. Mostly they were good looking, intelligent, good-humored, and likeable people.

The setting for the Conference was well chosen. The facilities were appropriate, and the prices reasonable. There was a large and lovely lake and a number of recreational facilities for our use. Most of us, however, used these very little. We had gone to Walden Lake to talk, not to swim — and talk we did.

The talk commenced at 8:30 a.m. at the breakfast table and moved from there to the workshop groups. (Breakfast had been planned for 8:00, but participants who had spent until 4:00 a.m. in discussions just couldn't make it that early.)

THE WORKSHOPS

The idea of the workshops was to break the community planning into sections, dividing responsibility. Each of us chose the group in which he was most interested — social structure, economics, membership, location, finance, etc. Tentative decisions on important matters were supposed to be reached by group discussion and then presented to the Conference as a whole. There were four sessions of three hours each to get this accomplished.

In the writer's opinion these workshops were failures in most cases, and quite unnecessarily so. They might have been dynamic group productions of thought and tentative policy; instead they were monologues by the workshop leaders, reminiscent of college classrooms, group participation being treated in some cases as if it were an interruption to the lecture (which indeed it was, and a welcome one). Nevertheless, the workshops were not classrooms, there were no grades or prizes for good behavior, and attendance was not compulsory. Frustrated with lack of progress in their own groups, the greater part of the Conference attendees drifted from workshop to workshop, looking for vital activity in which they might take part. The second day saw attendance at the workshops halved, with perhaps 20 per cent of the total attendance being the same people as the previous day. This made it doubly difficult to get serious business accomplished, and frustration compounded itself on all sides.

One workshop escaped the general fate. The committee on finance was well directed and used its human resources reasonably. Among other things, they came up with an interesting survey on financial resources of the Conference attendees. Though few conclusions can be drawn from the figures this survey produced, it was encouraging to note that the greater part of the group fully expects to put their own finances behind the community, if they have any confidence that it will succeed, and that most are prepared to join such a community if it has as many as fifty members.

If the workshops did not generally produce very much, this does not mean that nothing was accomplished at the Conference. On the contrary, a good deal of work was done. One of the profitable alleys of activity was the contribution of ready-laid plans by certain of the leaders. These individuals had already given much thought to the foundation of the community before the Conference, and the group showed keen interest in knowing what ideas they had produced. Foremost in importance is their plan for acquiring large amounts of money through grants. Their confidence in their ability to do this was encouraging. Most of us know nothing of such matters and had assumed that we would have to get money by working for it; but these gentlemen assure us that grant money can be available to us if we go about it right. There was some minor opposition to this plan, as well as some skepticism, but most seemed to think that it was a good plan, provided only that it works.

Less popular was the idea of coordinating the community with an experimental college. Though the idea seems sound enough (our most obvious resource is an abundance of Ph.D.'s), there was a strong feeling expressed by some people who thought that a college would not be profitable. Be that as it may, the idea has been placed on a back burner for the time being, but we have not heard the last of it by any means.

The main source of discontent with the pre-conference plans was the inescapable fact that they involve a great deal of time—an estimated 3½ to 5 years before we can actually set foot on community grounds and begin to call it home. Many of us are impatient to begin. There was evidence that the majority of the group at the Conference wanted to begin sometime in 1967. Grant money cannot be obtained in such a short time, nor can much careful, detailed planning be done. But there were some who thought that planning was less necessary than hard work, and that Walden Two would be the better for depending entirely upon its own resources.

Compromise prevailed, however, in the form of planning for summer camps every summer between now and the time when the community is actually established. It is not very clear just what will take place at these summer camps, or how long any of us will be able to stay at them, or what can be accomplished by the in-and-out sort of attendance that is likely to occur. The camps were explained as "training" camps — training, evidently, in behavioral engineering. We are not at all sure what that means. If it means attending classes in psychology, we are declaring ourselves dropouts in advance. If it means learning to be nice to each other, we submit that people are always nice to each other at camps. Only real community living will teach us anything. Personally, we think the camps will be extremely exciting and valuable, but we remain curious about the "training" that will take place.

THE GENERAL SESSIONS

Whereas the workshop sessions had frustrated the group at large, the general sessions frustrated the leaders. There was no meeting of the larger group that did not result in at least a small rebellion. At one session the group refused to hear the planned lecture. At another there were impassioned impromptu speeches and shouts of "hear! hear!" And at the last session the question of internal government was raised —but not answered.

GOVERNMENT

That question of government is one in which we take great interest. Dr. Skinner made it pretty clear that Walden Two would be better off not being a democracy. His idea was that it would be essentially an oligarchy, carefully appointed by those deeply involved in the community's workings, and controlling—inasmuch as it controlled at all— by use of behavioral engineering techniques.

The difficulty at the Conference arose from the fact that nobody knows quite enough about behavioral engineering to step into a group of eighty people and control it. The method substituted, ludicrously enough, was to take to the podium and scold us for not "behaving" properly. "You

see," explained a desperately sincere and dedicated leader after a particularly senseless minority demonstration on the subject of democracy, "what happens when you don't use behavioral engineering!"

Yes, we see. We see, as well, what happens when a group of highly intelligent, articulate people are brought together and asked to accept a plan without being told what the form of the plan will be. We might be willing to submit with faith to a Grand Plan by a Great Mind, if we were sure that God, or Skinner, was behind it. Lacking these deities, we are thrown upon our own resources; and all of our conditioning calls out for some sort of plebiscite, some form of democratic check on power. There is no suggestion here of any abuses on the part of those who are presently leading the movement. On the contrary, their personal integrity is very evident. Nevertheless, we stand for some system that does not depend on personal integrity for its functioning. And we were not alone—the murmur was loud enough and insistent enough so that a constitution committee was appointed, and this document is now being written, over the protests of those who shouted "behavioral engineering" until the meaning of the term became lost, and the very words themselves became a form of punishment to inflict upon the rebels. . .

THE GOOD THINGS

But along with the conflict and the frustration came two bright stars that made the Conference overwhelmingly worthwhile. The first is our delight in finding the group compatible. At no other convention, in no other activity, have we ever met so engaging a group of people. On all sides were those who piqued our interest and whom we didn't have enough time even to become acquainted with. Here, a gentle-spoken man who plays jazz piano; there, a man who looks like a carpenter and teaches art; here, a family who has raised a baby in an air crib; there, a subtle mind hiding behind a southern accent. It was like walking for the first time into a well chosen library. We didn't have time to open many of the books, but we can already feel the delights of acquaintances to come.

The second great joy was the almost certain knowledge that a Walden Two community will be established within the next few years. Having met each other and seen the seriousness with which other people from all over the country regard the Walden Two idea, there is no longer any doubt that we will form a community. If we get those big grants, it will be a prosperous community. If we don't, it may be a struggling one. But the movement is launched. The difficulties are clear; but the goal is worth the effort, and we shall overcome.

January, 1967

The national convention held in August 1966 was an encouraging step for most Walden Two enthusiasts. It was encouraging that so many people were committed enough to the idea of an experimental community to travel so far to participate in planning a community. It was encouraging to learn that for the most part these people were warm, creative, intelligent, and interesting human beings. The purpose of the Conference, however, was by no means merely to meet and react with the participants, but to investigate all phases of community founding and functioning and to establish a formal organization for coordination. In the process of accomplishing the main purpose of the Conference, many people voiced different ideas about the meaning of a community, the goals that a community should attempt to reach, and steps that should be taken in establishing a community. The basic differences were first expressed, perhaps, in the community development workshop, of which four of us from Atlanta were members. The proposal involved summer training camps, an experimental college, and a 500-member community — all to be financed with foundation grants. The time required for all this was expected to be five years. The objections made to the proposal were:

1. Too much depended on the grants. If attempts at getting the grants failed, years of work would be wasted.

2. Five years is far more time than necessary for planning and financing a community.

3. One major goal of a community is *community*, an experience to be had by working together, sharing, and actually building the community with the labor of the members. The big money approach called for "hiring it done," an approach that might sacrifice *community* for *a* community, a community more expensive and professional, but one which could not provide its members with a real community experience.

These issues plagued not only the members of the community development workshop, but many of the participants of the Conference in general. Some alternatives were proposed; and by the time the Conference came to a close, a few modifications had been made in the original plan. The experimental college was deleted from the plan and the time for establishing the first community was set at an earlier date. Also another committee was formed to investigate the possibility of extending one of the summer camps into a small starting community.

Most people left the Conference feeling that it had been a success despite the disagreements that had not been satisfactorily settled. As issue 6 of *Walden Pool* said, "Among us are trained, competent, and very practical people; and the direction of this project is largely in their hands."

As time went on, however, it became apparent that the training, competence, of some of the leaders might well be appropriate for the classroom or laboratory but not very appropriate for solving the problems of organizing people for an effective cooperative endeavor. Lack of communication between official and unofficial leaders was a major problem. Another problem, even less excusable, was a communications difficulty between several official leaders. To know that such problems had developed was discouraging for many people, but to know that these problems were being resolved in a most unadmirable way was reason for alarm. Members of the Atlanta Group wrote a letter to the leaders in which they described the situation as they saw it and proposed a meeting during the Christmas holidays for the purpose of resolving interpersonal problems, formulating a few policies, and doing some work on a constitution.

As it turned out, the leaders had been exploring the possibility for a Christmas conference for some time. A grant from the Johnson Foundation to finance the conference had been arranged. Participation at the Christmas conference was by invitation, however, and only members of what appeared to be an "in group" were invited. One purpose of the conference, then, was not to resolve interpersonal problems.

The conference was held as scheduled on December 28, 29, and 30, 1966, in Racine, Wisconsin. Prominent psychologists, architects, and behavioral engineers attended to deliver speeches to the participants. For some time this was the only information any of the non-participants had concerning the activities of the conference. The decision made at the conference to withhold any but official statements—which were slow in coming—about other activities, served to complicate the suspicions and hostilities that had developed among the non-conference participants.

To split or not to split, that became the question for those who felt left out. Many believed that the conference had served to answer that question, but others wanted to watch and wait until more information was made available. Members of the Atlanta Group began investigating the feasibility of a get-together in Atlanta to discuss recent events and the possibility of establishing a small starting community. The idea was found to be feasible and a meeting was held January 28, 29, and 30, 1967. Fifteen people attended, most of whom were from Walden House and the Atlanta Group. Everyone at the meeting agreed that serious mistakes had been made by certain leaders, but that these mistakes would immediately lose their significance as soon as some indication had been made that such mistakes would not occur in the future. The discussion about a small starting community was highly encouraging. Funds and members for a community were available and certain phases of the initial planning were set into motion. When the meeting was over, the general feeling was to work within the framework of the national organization as much as possible. Everyone was tired of just pussyfooting around and eager to get a community started.

March, 1967

TWO CONFERENCES

RACINE

During the Christmas holidays a conference of Walden Two people took place at Racine, Wisconsin. Attendance was by invitation only; those invited were chiefly behavioral scientists, other professional people, and certain other selected persons who are involved in the Walden Two movement. This group evidently bore no relation to the group appointed to leadership at last summer's Conference, since several committee heads were omitted from the invitation list.

For two months we have had to go on rumor for information on this conference. However, a report has finally been released and was published in *Walden Pool.*

ATLANTA

In the meantime, something less formal took place in Atlanta, Georgia at the end of January. We can tell you more about that one, because we participated. This meeting was by invitation, too, which consisted of four long-distance phone calls saying, "Hey, let's get together and talk about Walden Two."

Ten of us gathered in Rudy's apartment, together with several sympathetic outsiders, and discussed ways of making our community dreams come true. All of us are watching the doings of the national committee with great care, but we all felt that it might not pay to put all of our hopes in the national committee basket, and that we had best be making "meanwhile" and "if not" plans of our own.

There was great rapport among the people gathered, and this in itself stirred greater hopes of a successful cooperative effort in the direction of Walden Two.

Two things seem clear from our get-together: that we all are interested in a community that is rural, independent, and equalitarian; and that we are willing to do the work that such a project requires on a limited budget.

In order to make the plan feasible financially, one friend has offered the loan of the necessary funds to purchase a farm, located in the farm belt around Washington, D.C. This means that Virginia is the probable location. The terms on which the money is being loaned are utopian, indeed, and include a provision that the first three years of occupation of the land by the community will be free of any rent or payments.

We feel that this is head start enough. From there on it is up to us. We are confident that hard work and good sense, plus our personal savings, will see us through the difficult "getting started" period, and that there is enough ability among the group to see us safely into a state of financial security.

THE LAND

As this newsletter is being printed, we are just about to begin looking for and at property that would suit our purposes. The weather has not permitted this activity before now. We need about 100 acres, several buildings, some farm equipment, adequate water supply, and plenty of privacy. We will keep you posted on what we find.

COMMUNITY PLANNING

Of course planning is going ahead at full speed. We are restricting participation in this planning to persons who give evidence of serious intention to become members of this community, and who have a lively interest in the planning work.

MEMBERSHIP

We are not at this point ready to receive applications for membership, since requirements have not been fully decided on, nor dates set. Walden House, of course, remains open in the meantime to people who are ready to move before we can actually begin operations on the farm. Walden House will be sold and the city operations closed at that point. We will be making a general announcement within a few months when we are ready to solicit membership for the farm community. Correspondence on the subject in the meantime is perfectly welcome, however.

May, 1967

EQUALITY

We mentioned in our last issue that any community we are involved in will be "equalitarian." After some thought on the subject, it occurs to me that this word requires some explanation. Equality can mean a lot of things, and most of them are not what we intended by that statement.

For instance, equality in our community doesn't mean that if you buy one member a $600 clarinet, you have to buy everybody a $600 clarinet. This is pretty obvious. The desire for clarinets isn't distributed equally, and the instruments won't be, either.

But does equality imply that if you buy one member a clarinet, then every member should have some possession of equal financial value? I think not. The desire for expensive possessions is not distributed equally, either. One person needs some possession to make him happy, and another needs nothing at all except a few books and a good friend.

Can we say then that every member should derive an equal amount of "happiness" from community living? Happiness is hard to quantify, but even if you do that (and some people are working at it), you would still be up against the fact that some people have a greater capacity for enjoyment than others, more energy, a better musical ear, a higher sex drive, a keener intellect, and so forth. So you can't really distribute happiness equally, either.

We could try, perhaps, to see to it that every member had an equal opportunity to fulfill his needs as far as his capacities will allow. This is closer to what we have in mind. But the question is: how do you know when you have succeeded? *Can* you know? Probably not.

But you can know this: you can know whether every member of the community feels contented with what he has and is, or what he expects to obtain or attain, in relation to the opportunities available, or whether he feels that somebody else has unfairly usurped his share.

Equality in a community is a relationship so structured that no member envies another. Simple.

At this point we are far from the mathematical or even dictionary definitions of the word *equality*. It may be asked why we bother to use the word at all. Part of the answer is that there doesn't seem to be another word to use in its place unless we go into jargon, saying "non-envy-behavior." But a stronger reason is that we are trying to make a clear stand against deliberate inequalities, such as are the rule in society at large. We have grown up in a culture that puts a premium on selfishness, that applauds the person who successfully exploits his fellow men, and that honors most of all those who receive riches in exchange for doing nothing at all. We are trying to create a miniature society in which every member considers his neighbor's needs equally with his own, where exploitation is unthinkable, and where it is assumed that every member is doing his share of the necessary work.

The contrast is so great, and the scope of the problem so far-reaching, that we find it necessary to make a clear statement about it. We do not intend, if we can help it, to permit inequalities of the type where one member has something that another member would wish to have but is denied for no fault of his own. At least we intend to minimize this kind of conflict as much as possible. What we end up with won't literally and technically be "equality." But it will, we hope, be a general feeling of fairness, a logical first step in the pursuit of happiness.

WE LOOK FOR PROPERTY

Searching for the right farm turned out to be an interesting and enlightening experience. The first thing that happened is that we learned to read ads correctly. For instance, we found out right away that "Fireplace in every room" means no other heating is available; "Water in kitchen" means there is no indoor toilet, and "Thirty acres cleared" means the other eighty acres are in useless brush. Because if there were central heating in the house or usable timber growing, the ad would say so. The rule to go by in ad-reading is: "If it isn't mentioned, they don't have it."

We saw ten farms before we decided on one, and we learned a little about farm living while we were at it. Many farmers do not have plumbing; a few do not have lights. One family we met is still dipping its water from the spring, 200 feet from their house, and bringing it in with pails. Wood heating is the rule everywhere, presumably because the fuel grows right on the property.

We also discovered that many rural people do not farm but work in town; those families who do farm often sell their vegetables, fruit, and dairy products to their neighbors. We met one family who have a cow but buy their milk in bottles from the A&P. Their reason: their teenagers won't drink raw milk.

WE CHOOSE A FARM

Right in the heart of Virginia lies a 123-acre spread that we decided we wanted to live on. This is a farm that has been going for many years and is being sold because the owner is getting too old to handle it. Among the ten farms that we looked at and the four that we seriously considered, this was the only one that has a thoroughly dependable water supply for the number of people who might be living there. This is a serious consideration in a state that has had three consecutive years of drought.

Two creeks and a river border the place, and it also has a spring and a well. About a third of the land is wooded, and the other two-thirds is cleared. There are several small barns that will serve us for many years, and a small house. We regret that we were not able to find, within our price range, a farm with a large house on it, in order to make life easier in the first year or so. We did look at big houses, and we were strongly tempted by one in particular that was over 150 years old and had fifteen rooms. But in the long run we had to decide between a big house and a big water supply. We know that we can build a house—but only God can make a river.

The land has varied contours that make a pleasant view, and an excellent site for a large pond. It is close enough to town (Louisa, Virginia) for any emergency purposes, but isolated enough that we will have a feeling of privacy and space. We didn't hear a single airplane in any of our visits to the site.

Along with the farm purchase was included a big tractor, a seed drill, and several smaller pieces of farm equipment. All of this is in good condition. The house, likewise, has been kept up, and the soil has had the benefit of fertilizer and crop rotation.

THIS SUMMER'S PLANS

Next month at this time, if things go as scheduled, nine of us will be living on the farm. We will be sleeping in barns and tents and using all of our daylight hours to care for the crops and put up a building to house us in the following winter. There will be no attempt to limit our work to the four-hour day or even an eight-hour day; there will be little emphasis, even, on the Good Life. Those of us who are going know what the good life means for us this year — it means working fulltime at the most meaningful project any of us has ever tackled. Material shortages and discomforts do not seem very important in comparison. Nevertheless, the material facts of our existence have influenced our approach. Aside from a questionnaire that most of you will have received by now, we have not attempted to recruit large numbers of members under the banner *"Walden Two."* For we know well that readers of Dr. Skinner's book envision the community as possessing a great deal in the line of physical comfort and leisure, and we are far from being able to offer it. Insofar as we advertise for members at all, it is in the hope of finding others like ourselves with a strong interest in the pioneer aspects of community and a relatively small commitment to their present style of life.

THE COUNTRY AIR, ETC.

One of the things that strikes me about the farm that we are to occupy is that all of the bucolic cliches that I have become familiar with in two decades of fiction reading have suddenly come to life. The bees *do* indeed hum in the apple blossoms; the smell of fresh hay *is* pleasant; and a quiet walk on the leafy carpet of the silent woods *does* refresh the spirits. I want to tell all of our readers about the birds calling over our heads as we pat seeds into the warm, brown soil, and about the wheat standing and waving in the breeze, and about the majestic oaks spreading their boughs over our heads. But I am stopped by the knowledge that every writer who has ever loved the country has already written all about it, and those who dwell in cities have become inured to the sound of the words. Just as they no longer really hear the cars passing on the street, neither do they respond to the sound of rural description. So I leave the subject regretfully, for I am full of wonder at its reality, and I tell our readers only this: that every lovely line ever written about fields and forests is true, and that for once, life is better than art.

PLANTING BEGINS

Farmer Jones, the present owner of our land, has been helpful and cooperative about letting us put in our garden crops this spring, even though we don't legally take possession of the farm until June 15. He has, in fact, plowed up our garden space for us, a big help to us in our effort to get everything done on weekends. As a result, we have been able to plant at least one seed package of every vegetable offered in the seed store, except the very early vegetables that we are already too late to plant. We have a long row of something called celeriac, and another of a root named salsify, which some of us never heard of before, in addition to the more usual carrots, cabbages, and beans. We also

planted 115 pounds of seed potatoes, which ought to supply our table adequately for the year. We also made an attempt to plant corn for animal feed, but our weekend-only schedule has limited this project severely. We did manage to plant about two acres of seed corn, which might feed our chickens or ducks, but we will have to buy corn for any pigs or other animals we decide to raise.

FARMING HELP

We have two good friends who are more than willing to help us learn the farming techniques that we need for our first year. One of them is Mr. Jones, who is not moving very far away and plans to keep in touch with his place and help us to develop it agriculturally. We like Mr. Jones very much—he is tactful and considerate and never makes us feel like fools; and we in turn never try to pretend that we know anything that we don't know.

The other good friend is the United States Government, in the form of the local County Agricultural Agent. This agency is most active in aiding farmers, and we are particularly in need of their pamphlets and advice. So when people ask us "What makes you think you can farm?" our answer is simple. We have these two friends who are encouraging and helping us. Between Mr. Jones and the Department of Agriculture, we shouldn't fail out of sheer ignorance, at any rate.

THE FARM VEHICLE

Every farm needs a truck. But a community farm needs a special kind of truck. Not only should it serve to haul watermelons to town and fertilizer back to the farm, but it ought to be covered, so that we can use it for hauling furniture when new members move in. Furthermore, it ought to seat several people, so that a good-sized group can be taken for moving or harvesting, or for going into town to see a movie.

We figured the most economical means of meeting all of these requirements would be to buy a school bus. So we sought, found, and purchased a used bus and removed most of the seats. At present it is being used to take busloads of personal belongings from Walden House to the farm, where they are being stored in a barn. In a few weeks, the bus will go to Atlanta, where it will pick up the Atlanta group and their household effects, plus a beehive and a hydroponium that those ingenious and impatient people have begun.

Last week the bus was stopped by a state policeman, who wondered why a school bus would be running around the country at midnight. But our license is in order (it is licensed as a truck), and he let us go, with advice to paint out the words *School Bus* from the side of the vehicle as soon as possible. We mean to do this, but we have to get together first to decide what color to paint it. Suggestions range from slate blue to yellow-and-red paisley.

WATERMELONS

There is a certain portion of land that Mr. Jones has kept in the soil bank but has obtained permission to plant watermelons in. It is a pretty big patch that Mr. Jones plowed up for this purpose; but we didn't want to waste it, so we put in as many hills as the patch would take, using five different varieties of seed. Mr. Jones calculated that the patch should yield 240 watermelons this summer! Just how nine people are going to eat 240 watermelons I am not sure. I have in mind supplying the Jones family and our other neighbors; the local stores can absorb a few; and they tell me the deer sneak out of the nearby woods and nibble at them. But I remain dismayed. Watermelon doesn't freeze or can. Pickles are made only from the rind, and even the pigs can eat just so many. Does anybody have a recipe for watermelon sherbet?

VISITING

Several persons have written asking for permission to visit us, either at Walden House or at the farm. Our hectic schedule at present will not permit us to have visitors at Walden House. However, after we are moved in and settled on the farm, we should be able to find time to talk to those who want to take the trouble to look us up. However, visitors should be warned *not* to try to find us without writing first for detailed instructions on how to reach the farm. We are not known in Louisa. We will at first have no telephone. So anyone planning to visit must necessarily write in advance and make specific arrangements. In addition, any visitors should be prepared either to camp out of doors or to stay in a motel in Louisa, about ten miles away. And it goes without saying that there will be plenty of work to go around for everybody who drops in.

From WALDEN POOL

May, 1967

SOMETHING TO THINK ABOUT

In less than a month the time will come when a small group of communitarians from different parts of the country, including the author of this article, will converge on a small farm in Virginia. Once there we will begin an attempt to bring together the necessary conditions for a better way of life. Some of these conditions include fairly comfortable housing, growing or raising our own food, and providing a source of income for ourselves. Other conditions involve ways of getting along with each other. Both categories of conditions are highly important, of course, but the second category is more basic than the first because, quite obviously, we won't get very far even with building the physical community unless we learn to work and live together effectively and harmoniously. It's not that we're all that worried about getting along with each other on the farm, but when we consider how much of our lives has been spent developing other supposedly important abilities, we have something to think about. Maybe we should be worried.

We have spent most of our lives dealing with or learning to deal with the world (including our peers) by way of our superiors—first our parents, then our teachers, and finally our professors and employers. It was not our playmates that handed out the ice cream, candy, and ticket money for the movies. It was not our classmates that said "good" when we successfully discriminated between the written words *Dick* and *Jane*. It was not our fellow high school seniors that awarded us our diplomas, scholarships, and acceptances to colleges. It was our bloody superiors.

The important point of all this is that we have not learned how to deal with each other as peers in a situation where people are to be treated as equals.

So we find ourselves underdeveloped not as individuals, but as members of a group. As that day in June comes nearer, our thoughts turn to our uncertainties, our fears, and our inadequacies.

Part Two:

FEET

on the

GROUND

Chapter Two: Year One

LEAVES OF TWIN OAKS

NUMBER 1 July, 1967

GENERAL NEWS

WE ARRIVE

On June 13 the newly-purchased school bus left Washington for Atlanta. It was empty when it left, having had all of its seats removed. It had been painted blue-green and white, in order to comply with a law that prohibits privately owned buses from resembling school buses. On June 16 the bus arrived on the farm, loaded with furniture, appliances, printing presses, household and personal miscellaneous, plus a beehive, a skunk cage with a skunk inside, and two motorcycles. Skillful packing, plus a small trailer behind one of the cars, did the trick. Those of us who had not gone to Atlanta hurried out to the farm to meet the Atlanta group. The farm was dark when we arrived. The house was locked, the electricity disconnected, which meant no running water as well as no lights. The exhausted group located their bedrolls from the midst of their belongings and camped out under the apple trees. And the Community began.

THE FIRST DAY

Though we had to spend the first weekend without electric power, water could be obtained by letting down a bucket into the well. The Coleman two-burner made breakfast possible. Of course it took a couple of hours to get enough of the bus unpacked to find the salt, the frying pan, and enough glasses to go around. We were not overburdened with organization. When one person went into the garden to hoe, five others followed to inquire into the difference between a vegetable and a weed. When another suggested that perhaps unloading the bus was an item of high priority, six people tried to help on that three-man job. There were four trips made into Louisa (twelve miles away), one for groceries, one to try to get the power connected, and two — you won't believe this — two for tomato paste. We have a member who makes spaghetti sauce rather well, but he knows only one recipe, and that one starts with tomato paste. We found the house key and got the furniture into the house. The members sought and found appropriate places to camp out for the night. Parts of the garden were hoed and dusted, and we were tired when the sun went down.

THE FIRST WEEK

Community population is bigger on weekends than it is during the week. The reason for this is that the Walden House people have not been able to sell the house in Washington and therefore must continue to hold jobs in the city in order to keep up the payments. They come to the farm on weekends, and the others stay on the farm fulltime. The first week there were five on the farm and three in the city. There were many good things accomplished in those first days. All the tomatoes and beans got the stakes they had been needing. We acquired four little pigs and built two shelters for them. And the group found time between hoeing tobacco and feeding the pigs to build a small pier into the river. This has proved to be an important improvement, for we soon discovered that our well is not deep enough to provide enough water for showers for such a large "family," and the river has naturally become our bathtub. The river water moves very slowly where it borders our land, which makes bathing pleasant for anyone who can swim. It is over ten feet deep, however, which limits its use for the non-swimmers among us. By the way, although we have some homemade soap which we use at the house, we always use Ivory when we bathe in the river. It floats, you know.

WE BECOME TWIN OAKS

The question of a community name had been a source of warm and frequent discussion for weeks prior to our actual arrival on the farm. We had to have a name immediately, for without one we could not incorporate, or open a proper bank account, or send out a newsletter or start a business, or even be sure of receiving our mail. We did not lack ideas. At one time we had a list of nearly sixty suggestions. We had Latin names, names with great hidden significance, names with no significance at all. We had three-letter names and three-word names. And of course we had all the possible Walden-related names, each with its hopeful adherents. What we lacked was a uniformity of taste. What seemed a perfect name to one member was preposterous to another. We kept putting off the decision.

Finally one member gave out an ultimatum. Either, said he, we decide on a name *today*, or I am going to start calling the place "Walden Farm" tomorrow, and you know the name will stick. We knew he was right, for people were already referring to us as Walden Farm (so natural after Walden House). Thus stirred, the Walden opponents came up with some counter suggestions, and the vote began. We decided to experiment with a voting system that allowed each member to distribute his vote among various names acceptable to him, giving each name that proportion of his total alloted vote that seemed to him to represent his real feelings about their relative value. The system was a bit complicated, but there was something satisfying about being able to express one's split opinions with a split vote.

Just before the vote was taken, some neighbors dropped in to visit; and out of politeness we explained to them what we were doing and asked for suggestions. "Twin Oaks," said the neighbor, glancing at the large twin oak that stands over our well. For politeness, again, we added the name to the list for voting purposes. Fifteen minutes later Twin Oaks came out the winner. There was a general feeling of shock at the result, for Twin Oaks had been no one's favorite. It was merely an acceptable second- or third-choice candidate in case one's favorite did not win. What actually happened is that we were forced to a second-choice name because we couldn't stand each other's first choices. We mused on the startling result of our voting method, and somebody suggested we vote again. Nobody wanted to vote again. We had a name. Let it stand.

Writing three weeks later, Twin Oaks seems a fine name. It pleases those who want a countrified name that would not surprise the neighbors. Those who wanted a significant name have already found symbols to their liking. One member is merely relieved that we did not find it necessary to put "farm" on the end of it. Twin Oaks Community; Twin Oaks Industries; Twin Oaks, Incorporated. It sounds fine.

THE GARDEN

We probably mentioned before that Mr. Jones had given us permission to plant a garden before we took possession of the land. During the first week of actual occupancy our first vegetables began to mature. Beautiful little squashes ripen every day on our vines, and the snap beans are giving us two quarts a day for the freezer. Although most of us have never eaten summer squashes before, we are finding that they are quite edible. And now the cucumbers are ripening, and the beets. We even had new potatoes one evening, but we are leaving most of the potatoes to grow to full size. Considering our lack of experience and the good quality of our vegetables, we are concluding that you don't have to be much of a farmer to grow a nice garden. A little fertilizer, a little hoeing, a little cooperation from the weather, and tiny seeds convert themselves into food.

BUILDING

Whether or not we will be able to build any housing this summer for the coming winter remains a question at this point and is in fact rather doubtful. Cash resources are not plentiful. If we cannot build, it means we cannot really expect our membership to grow very much except in the warmer seasons. The farmhouse has only four rooms and an unfinished attic, and it will hold just so many people. However, we continue our search for cheap ways to build. You will probably think that we are taking the book a bit literally when we tell you that we are experimenting with rammed earth. Actually, we probably thought of rammed earth for the same reason Skinner did: the raw material is available on any farm. Our experiments have not developed very far at this point, but several techniques and mixtures are being tried.

ORGANIZATION

A group of eight interested members needs little in the line of formal organization. We know, however, that we are building toward a much larger group, and that we will need a structure that can encompass both our present situation and future expansion. Relatively few rules have been made. An embryonic Code, containing several of the same provisions we read about in *Walden Two*, is being tried. Our Articles of Incorporation are being written, after which we will be able to apply for tax-exempt status. The bylaws are the next big legal job, covering all the rules about membership and so forth. All of us have, of course, pooled our cash and have it in a bank account in Louisa. No major expenditures are undertaken except with the consent of the entire group.

WILD LIFE

We have been told that 123 acres is a small farm. This is probably true, but in some ways it seems very large to us. None of us has been in the upper woods, for instance, since the day we walked the boundaries with Mr. Jones. The place is too big to visit every corner of it very often. That is probably the reason why the wildlife of the region feel quite at home on our property. We hiked up the hill to the blackberry thicket not long ago to see how the berries were ripening, and we saw a deer standing quietly at the edge of the woods, only a few hundred feet away. We can hardly drive down the road in the evening without having to dodge rabbits, turtles, and raccoons. The woods and fields are full of birds. A bird enthusiast who visited us counted twenty different bird calls in one day. Then there was the skunk. One of our members walked into the woods at night and, hearing an animal nearby, threw a stick into the brush where the noise was coming from to frighten it away. Nobody actually *saw* the skunk, but we were all presently made aware of its presence.

As to wild flowers, they grow in profusion. Big, colorful bunches of fire-orange *something* are scattered throughout the fields and beside the roadways. So far we haven't been visited by any wildflower enthusiast to identify them for us.

We know that, as we grow, the noise of our machines and the sheer number of our members will take away some of the quiet, peaceful feeling of our fields and woods. I think, though, that we will never allow ourselves to get so big or so noisy that we won't be able to find a wild spot on the property where the quail raise their young and the deer come down to drink.

WE BUILD MACHINES

At least two of our members have a long history of collecting junk. Is there a piece of scrap metal beside the road? They will stop and pick it up — it might come in handy. Pieces of string, old paper sacks, egg cartons, odd-shaped pieces of canvas — nothing is to be thrown away. Though the habit in some men might make their wives pull their hair out, on the farm it turns out to be a useful trick. For the first time in our lives, we have the time, the work space, and the initiative to put some of these pieces of scrap together into useful objects. Last weekend we made a table saw and a cement mixer. Total cost for materials—$25 for the two items. The rest was labor, ingenuity, and junk.

WE MAKE MISTAKES

Not every idea of ours turns out quite so well. One day we tried to turn some green apples into apple cider by grinding up the apples and pressing them in the mold and by the method we had been using for rammed earth. The result was half a cup of brown juice that nobody would touch and a neat brick of rammed apple. The pigs ate the rammed apple, but we have decided to make a regular cider press before our next attempt.

THE WATER SITUATION

We told you in the last issue of the Walden House Newsletter that the property had plenty of water. This is true, for three creeks and a river flow through or by the farm. The water table is high and capable of supplying our needs. However, the well, which supplies running water to the house, is not deep enough even for a community of eight. It gives just enough water for cooking and dishes, for flushing the toilet three or four times a day, and for minor clean-up jobs. It is definitely *not* sufficient for bathing, and hooking up the washing machine is unthinkable. At the moment we are getting the laundry done by sending it to Walden House every week with our commuters. But the Walden House people will soon be moving to the farm, which will put double pressure on the water supply.

The fact is that we need a deeper well. We have investigated this and have been told that the cost of a good deep well would probably run about $300. As we watch our cash supplies dwindle and worry about whether our fledg-

ling businesses will be able to support us before the cash gives out completely, we do not feel that we can put out $300 for a well this year. On the other hand, community growth is impossible until we get more water. So we are appealing to our subscribers—those of you who work and make decent salaries and want to help. Will you send us a contribution for the well? Every contribution will be set aside specifically for the well unless otherwise specified.

PETS

A farm is an obvious place for animals of all kinds and pets in particular. Our first pet was P.E.W. (Patrick Everett Wilkerson), a descented skunk that came up from Atlanta. A few days after his arrival here, he began to develop a second scent-maker, and it was thought best to let him go. He is now presumably in our woods along with others of his kind. Then there are the cats that came with the farm, including a black cat named Power and a white one dubbed Backlash. Last week Chickychick joined us. Chickychick is a white chicken of undetermined gender. He (she) started life as an egg in a science project of a little girl named Stephanie. Chickychick didn't end when the science project did, so he continued life in the dining room of Stephanie's parents in Washington, D.C. You may have what opinion you like, but Stephanie's mother's opinion was that chickens and dining rooms are not entirely compatible. So when they heard about Twin Oaks, they piled into their car with their tents and sleeping bags and thoughtfully tucked Chickychick into a box on the back seat. Chickychick is not like other chickens. He has never seen another fowl and is entirely comfortable with humans. He will eat out of your hand if you care to let him. He disdains leftover pancakes but pecks thoughtfully at ice cubes. He particularly likes cooked chicken meat. Sooner or later, Chickychick will presumably either say *Cockadoodledoo* or lay an egg. In either case he (she) is welcome to roam about Twin Oaks at will.

VISITORS

Before we had a name, or any organization at all, before we had so much as a stove or had even connected the electricity, the Community had already had visitors! Experimental communities are a natural object of curiosity, it turns out, and lots of people will drive all the way to central Virginia to see us.

We can accept visitors now, provided only that they be prepared to camp out (sleeping bag is helpful) and that we have some notice of their impending arrival. We ask visitors to contribute money toward the cost of their food and to pitch in with the work if they stay longer than 24 hours.

If you want to visit, write us first, so that we can send you our map. If you get lost, ask for the farm formerly owned by E. E. Jones, near Smith's Mill, and the chances are that someone will be able to direct you. Please let us know you are coming!! We need to know how much food to have on hand. If you are coming by bus or train, we will need a great deal of advance notice and will have to make definite arrangements to pick you up in Louisa. No buses pass closer than twelve miles from the farm.

APPEAL FOR FUNDS

Since the previous part of the newsletter was written and printed, some new developments have occurred that are important. Twin Oaks now has a very promising industry. The industry is the manufacture of rope hammocks. We already have a fairly large order to fill, and we have reason to believe that we will soon have all the orders we can handle.

Also since the previous part of the newsletter was written, we had a well dug, which cost us $1030 and which will require us to spend about $500 for a pump and the necessary pipe. Such expenditures have done much to drain our checking account to an uncomfortable low.

Presently we are working full steam to get the hammock-making industry off the ground. We are remodeling barns, cutting trees for the poles we need to get electricity to the barns, wiring the barns, and weaving hammocks outdoors. We also take care of the tobacco, pick and freeze the vegetables, as well as do the necessary household chores.

Our two problems are time and money. Hammocks sell best in warm weather; for this reason we need to make and sell as many hammocks as possible before the winter arrives. Before the middle of fall we need to have earned enough cash to provide us with the rope, wood, chain, and other materials necessary to keep us in production during the winter so we will have a large backlog of hammocks ready for market next spring. If we had the shops, a little more housing, and a little more equipment, we might be able to accomplish this with the limited funds we still have. We don't have these things, however. The barns will serve as shops only while it is warm, because they are full of cracks and have no insulation and no heating systems. So we need a shop suitable for working during the winter. The housing we now have consists of one farmhouse and two barns. The barns now used for housing, like those being used for shops, will be good for little more than storage this winter.

The proposal to remedy this situation is to build a two-story 40' x 40' building. The first story would be used for shops and the second story for housing. If we could manage this, we would be in good shape. The materials for the building will cost between $2500 and $3000. We don't have that much; but we need at least that much very badly.

To obtain the money we need, we wish to solicit help from our subscribers. Several people have commented that they feel they have a stake in what is going on here and that they wish to help. At this point financial help is the kind of help we need and the kind of help that all of our sympathizers can provide to some extent—some more than others, of course. So this article is beginning to sound like a letter from college to home. It basically says: Please send money. If a dollar is all you can spare, please send it; or better, try to send a dollar a week or a dollar a month. Every penny will help, and every penny will be put to good use in making Twin Oaks a more economically secure community.

NUMBER 2

September, 1967

GENERAL NEWS

By Kathleen

YES, WE'RE STILL HERE

Since our last issue we have received a number of letters indicating that we gave an overgloomy picture of our chances of survival. So perhaps a careful explanation is in order.

For one thing, we don't live as primitively as some of you have interpreted us to imply. We have a house, and it has a kitchen and a bathroom. Meals are cooked on a gas stove and served on tables covered with tablecloths or placemats. Sometimes we even use napkin rings, just for fun. All of us sleep inside a building of some sort, though this means barns for several members. The barns are unheated, but still, we are not literally camping out. (We have mentioned that guests should bring tents, but the reason for this is that we have no extra indoor space for guests.)

As to the water situation, we now have all the hot baths we want, and wash all of our clothes in an automatic clotheswasher. Walden House's old automatic dishwasher will probably be installed soon.

In the vehicle department we have two small cars and the school bus; two tractors and their attachments help us with the farm work.

Our combined library lines the walls of one room, with the overflow stored in one of our barns. Our combined record collection is impressive, both in size and in scope.

We are minimally housed, adequately clothed, and very well fed. We are not in debt. (Old subscribers may remember that the land and equipment was paid for in cash by a personal friend, and that we are not required to make payments on it for the first three years of our community existence.) In spite of the self-appraising remarks that have appeared in this paper that implied we are ignorant, naive, and disorganized, we have thus far compensated for our ignorance by asking our neighbors for advice and taking it;

we are sufficiently organized to have legal status as a non-profit corporation, to have written our bylaws and our property agreements, to have elected officers and appointed managers, and to have achieved a smoothly-running and continuously-evolving labor credit system.

We live mostly out-of-doors, work mostly at jobs of our choice, and associate mostly with the people we like best. (No other way of life can make *that* statement!)

We asked for financial help because we need it in order to grow as a community. We know that many of our readers are sympathetic to our aims and are willing to help. That's why we published a straightforward account of our financial needs in the last issue. We will probably continue to let our readers know about our financial problems, and continue to appreciate the donation and loan checks that come in as a result. You don't have to feel sorry for us, though . . . We have a pretty good life.

WATER

The well in our back yard under the twin oak tree is about forty feet deep and admirably served the needs of Mr. and Mrs. Jones. A community of eleven people and their guests, however, pumped the well dry the first weekend of occupancy, and for two months afterward severe water rationing was necessary. There was water to drink and water to cook with. Usually there was enough to wash dishes. Bathing, clothes washing, toilet flushing, and animal needs all had to depend on creek water, brought up the hill first by bucket, then by the barrel, and finally with the aid of a pump and some hose. As an emergency measure, the creek water system served its purpose. But what we really needed was a deeper well. In the last issue of *Leaves* we mentioned the anticipated cost of this well and that bad luck resulted in its costing more than four times that amount. Nevertheless, the well has now been drilled and is putting out water at the rate of 6½ gallons a minute, which is more than adequate for our present needs. Next problem is a bigger septic tank and drain field. It wouldn't do for a community to try to get by with a septic tank built for two. To avoid flooding this tank, until we can get the money for these items, we are diverting our bath and wash water out into a pasture where it can't do any harm.

FOOD STORAGE DEPARTMENT

The Community now owns two deep freeze units, and both of them are full. In addition to the chickens and other meats that we buy in quantity when they are on special sale, we have put up dozens of quarts of snap beans, blackberries, cauliflower, corn, and four kinds of squashes. Home freezers of the type we have are cheap to buy used, and sometimes kind people even give them away. However, research has shown that the cost of running them during the summer is quite high, and that what we really need to cut

the maintenance cost is a large, walk-in freezer that we can build quite inexpensively. This project has not been started yet, because a great many other activities necessarily take priority. But it is on the list and will probably be undertaken some time this year.

Freezing is less work than canning, but with the freezing space problem what it is, we have decided to can all vegetables that taste as good canned as frozen. That includes tomatoes, applesauce, and pumpkin. Then the winter vegetables, such as turnips, beets, and parsnips, will be kept in cold storage. Our basement shelves are also loaded with our own blackberry jam and three kinds of pickles.

THE TOBACCO CROP

The decision to go ahead and grow tobacco was made early in spring before some of us had any idea what was involved. What *is* involved, it turns out, is a tremendous amount of work. First there is the seed bed, which has to be carefully prepared and planted. Then there is the transplanting of one plant at a time, each with its cup of water. With the hotter weather come cultivating and hoeing. Cultivating is no trick; you just ride the tractor for a while — hoeing is something else again. When the plants get big enough to shade the weeds and inhibit their growth, the hoeing stops and the topping and suckering begin. Harvesting is a strenuous job that must be done in the hottest part of a hot day. Then comes stringing the tobacco up in the tobacco barn, all the way up to the ceiling. That is as far as we have gone, but we understand that there is more to come before we actually sell it.

And in the end the crop grosses something like $500 an acre, our neighbors tell us. Is it worth it? Like many cash farming projects done on a small scale, it is probably fairly obvious that it is not worth it compared to the dollar value of our labor in almost any other endeavor. When you are trying to build a community, however, you don't necessarily always value your labor by the hour unless you have alternatives that also keep your membership within the community premises. Just how good our alternatives are we do not yet know. That is why we cannot say firmly that we will not grow tobacco next year. Agriculture on a small scale is a pretty poorly paying industry. It may turn out to be better than none. Or it may (hopefully) turn out that one of our other ideas will net us a better income, and we can abandon planting things that we don't want to eat.

CATS, CATS

Although we don't actually *feed* the cats that come around our house, we do supplement their diet with an occasional chicken wing or gizzard that nobody ate, and the reinforcement seems to be sufficient to keep them coming. At last count there were seven regulars and two occasional visitors. Chickychick doesn't like them. She runs at them and tries to peck them, but they are not discouraged. The hammock factory (front porch) is a cat sanctuary (for cats do no harm to hammocks other than to distract the workers, but chickens like to roost on them and. . .well. . .).

CATTLE AND PIGS

We have about forty acres of pasture, and half of it is rented out to a neighbor. We decided to put the other half to use to make some petty cash for us, so we bought six head of cattle in midsummer. All six are heifers, and we expect to breed some of them and have some calves next summer. Unlike tobacco, cattle raising requires very little work. Once the fences are up, cattle care consists of checking every now and again to make sure they are still there.

The pigs, on the other hand, want to be fed twice a day, and they like a lot of water on warm days. We will soon have running water in the pig enclosure. They eat the corn husks and stalks from the sweet corn and the watermelon rinds and other sundry garbage, in addition to their grain rations. We don't like pigs much—as people, I mean. Their manners are atrocious. They have no idea of sharing or any of our community aims. They eat like pigs. They smell like pigs. In short, they are suited for nothing but the unconscious manufacture of bacon and ham, which they do admirably well.

THE STRAW

The five acres of wheat that had been planted on the farm when we bought it belonged, according to our sales agreement, to Mr. Jones. But the wheat straw was ours. Accordingly, we hired a baler to come and bale it up, and then it was our job to get it into the barn. The whole group worked on this. The bales were so heavy that the girls could barely lift them onto the wagon. The whole job was finished in three or four hours. So now we are the proud owners of 360 bales of straw. There is a rumor that the highway department will be buying straw next spring for road work; and under that hopeful assumption we continue to store it, for the amount is greater than we can use for our own cattle. One of our members, under pressure of the need for winter quarters and the low balance in our bank account, gave serious thought to building a house of straw. (We call him the first little pig.)

HOUSE OF STICKS

The second little pig got interested in geodesic domes and polyethylene. It was put together with more haste than care, and the finished product, even aside from the fact that it has no door, leaves something to be desired. But it looks marvelously experimental.

PRACTICAL PIG

As we understand the story, the kind of house that keeps the wolf from the door is brick, and we interpret that to mean rammed earth. An experimental building of this material is being planned and will probably be built next spring. For our immediate needs we are putting up a wood frame structure that is to serve as both a hammock workshop and winter sleeping quarters for the members. Its seven bedrooms should serve our present population through the winter without difficulty.

WATERMELONS

We had predicted that our patch would produce 240 melons, and we are now seeing our prediction come true. We have watermelon for dessert, for snacks, and for breakfast; watermelon was carried to the fields for the people harvesting tobacco. A few stores agreed to take some for resale, and our sign proclaiming *Watermelons for Sale* is bringing in our neighbors and some miscellaneous small change for the Community cash box. One of our subscribers has sent a recipe for watermelon sherbet, which helps to put part of the crop away in the freezer. If, after all, we cannot eat and sell all of our melons, we still have four hungry hogs who like them as well as we do.

LABOR CREDITS

For five weeks Twin Oaks managed without any work system of any kind. Everyone did what seemed to him appropriate, and the meals were cooked and the dishes washed, the garden hoed, and numerous miscellaneous small projects carried out. After a time, though, we came to see that we needed more organization in order to get more work accomplished and in order to divide the duller jobs more equally. So we divided the work into categories and appointed managers to be responsible for them. We now have a manager of housekeeping, of gardens, of hammocks, of food processing, and so forth. All together there are over twenty managerships, enough for two or more to be assigned to each member. At the same time we initiated a labor credit system similar to the one formerly used at Walden House. This time we wrote all the jobs down on little cards, along with the number of credits allotted for each, and dealt out the deck. Each member passed his unwanted cards to the right until he had accumulated a full hand — that is, until he had the number of credits he needed to fill his quota. The system worked fine, except that it took a great deal of time, and we kept imagining what it would be like with fifty members, all passing cards. Now the system is undergoing various changes, designed to cut down the administrative time needed to decide who does what, without limiting the feeling of free choice of work. It will probably continue to change for some months until we arrive at something really satisfactory.

WE SHALL HAVE MUSIC

Twin Oaks may have only one toilet, one bathtub, and one tiny house, but it currently owns and uses three hi-fi record players and two tape recorders. This seems to be the one item that no young person is without. One of these record players is in the carpenter shop, where it plays Donovan and the Beatles. Players two and three are both in the house, where they play competing music from the living room and library, respectively. Sometimes it's jazz in the library and gregorian chants from the living room. On the front porch the hammock makers can hear both at once. As to live music, there are three instruments currently enjoyed here. We could try for an ensemble, but we aren't just sure how a clarinet, a guitar, and a recorder sound together.

CHICKYCHICK ASSERTS HER FEMININITY

Chickychick is a she. On September 20 she laid a medium-sized brown egg. We found her examining it curiously in the henhouse that she now shares with twenty-four ducklings. We relieved her of her creation, boiled it with great ceremony, and sent it through the mails to the little girl who first brought Chickychick into the world in her science class.

DUCKS

Chickens, everybody tells us, are not worth the trouble it takes to raise them, considering the low price of chicken meat generally. But ducks, we thought, might be another matter. After all, a duck egg is twice as big as a hen egg, and a duck is half as much trouble. So we sent away for 24-day-old ducklings. They are now about a month old and are beginning to grow feathers. Since Chickychick began to lay eggs, we enclosed her in the same pen with the ducks, and it is interesting to watch them interact. Chickychick is bigger, and she has a tendency to be a bully. She will peck at the ducklings if they get close enough. So the poultry community has settled the matter by dividing their area equally— half for the ducks and half for Chickychick. Within a few months, however, the ducks will be larger than Chickychick; it will be interesting to note what social changes, if any, take place at that point.

THE ORCHARD

Fruit trees take from three to six years after planting to begin to bear, so it takes a bit of faith for us to spend part of our scarce cash resources on baby fruit trees. You may judge the strength of ours by the fact that we put in six plum trees last week and are expecting a shipment of peach, cherry, and pear trees shortly. As to those seven black walnut trees we planted in the northeast corner of the property, we understand that it takes twenty years or more for them to grow to maturity. They are for our grandchildren.

GUESTS

In its first three months, Twin Oaks has "entertained" over fifty visitors. The word "entertained" is not quite accurate; what we did was say hello and tell them where to pitch their tents. After that visitors are pretty much on their own. Meals cost a dollar a day, and visitors are expected to help with the work after they have been here over 24 hours. Most guests, though, can't bear to wait 24 hours before beginning to work. Some go so far as to introduce themselves and then ask what they can do to help. We can usually find something: Last week a visitor dug ten post holes in ground that we had already decided was too hard and rocky for post holes. He got blisters on his hands, too. His fence now keeps the cows out of the newly-planted orchard. The truth is that we do not yet have much of a program for guests. In time we will probably have a guided tour and a public relations manager who answers all questions and explains everything. In the meantime a visitor's reception is likely to be "Glad to meet you; park your car there by the school bus; how would you like to help shell beans?"

LETTERS TO TWIN OAKS

The following are exerpts from letters the Community has received:

From K.T., San Diego, commenting on the "Rights to Use" report (printed in *Walden Pool*, Volume 1, No. 10), which mentioned the possibility of television, hi-fi, and radios in community:

"Actually I do not know exactly what your group is striving for . . . but I assumed . . . [especially judging from your use of the word *Walden*] you were attempting to follow the advice of Thoreau by simplifying your lives, getting rid of the luxuries and gadgets so prevalent in square society, so relied upon for comfort and convenience; that by choosing to live on a farm you were trying to get back to Nature from whom so many of us are unfortunately alienated; that in a scenic rural setting the presence of news bulletins and rock-and-roll music seem to be singularly out of place.

— A Lover of Nature and SILENCE"

Twin Oaks comments:

The use of the word *Walden* by us almost always refers to Dr. Skinner's *Walden Two* rather than to Thoreau. Several of the Community members are admirers of Thoreau, and several are also lovers of silence. But this preference is not one that we can unilaterally impose on the entire Community. Music, too, is part of the good life. Sometimes a bit of grumbling results from an overdose of certain kinds of music, and compromises and tolerance are required on all sides. It is rare that anyone tunes in a news broadcast, however, and as of the date of this writing, the Community's only television set is still packed away in a box.

From N.B., Aiken, South Carolina:

"...I would like to see [and help] Twin Oaks to become as close to Walden Two as possible, but I do not believe in donations, either for the sake of the giver or the receiver. I am enclosing my check for $13.00 for a subscription to *Leaves of Twin Oaks* and for a two-year loan of $10 non-interest to the Twin Oaks Community, Incorporated..."

Twin Oaks comments:

Thank you for the loan. We sympathize with your feelings about our request for donations. However, the fact is that without the loans and donations we received, we could probably not have gotten our community started. When put this way, most of us feel that begging is a lesser evil than not achieving a Walden Two.

DREAMS

See that valley there behind the house? You notice how the land slopes abruptly? There is a little stream down there hidden by those bushes. We're going to dam that up and make that whole valley into a lake. Won't that be pretty? Imagine the ducks on it! What do you think would be better, a pontoon bridge or a suspension bridge? Just for walking, I mean. The cars will go over the dam itself, of course. Now the main building will start up there by that big oak tree and extend around that side of the lake, you see, ending up where that finger of land extends beyond those cedars. That will leave the woods practically in our back yard. Just imagine...

Now this is my favorite part of the woods. See what possibilities there are here, with the river and all. When we have time I'm going to clear out some of this underbrush and leave just the big shade trees, make this into a regular park where we could have picnics or meetings or concerts. We could plant grass, maybe some hardy flowers. It would be so lovely...

Right now, though, if y'all will excuse us, we have to get back to the hammock shop. There's a lot of work to do.

MORE ON THE HAMMOCK INDUSTRY

By Dusty

Since the last issue of the *Leaves*, the situation concerning the hammock industry has crystalized. We have advanced to a point where production is no problem. Our weavers, braiders, harness makers, and wood workers are becoming increasingly efficient and skillful, and the labor expended per hammock has gone down from seven man-hours to four man-hours.

Our problem is marketing our hammocks. Unfortunately it is difficult to sell hammocks to retailers because they fear that they will not be able to sell them until next spring and that the hammocks will until that time merely take up storage space and collect dust. Selling directly to the customer by mail order presents the same problem, also, because of the seasonal nature of our hammocks. Another complication in the hammock situation, although a boon for the Community, is the housing project, which demands a large portion of our labor.

Due to these obstacles and complications, we have slacked off on hammock production to accelerate completion of the domicile. Later, as the housing project nears completion, the hammock production will pick up again. The strategy then will be: *1)* to provide a backlog of several hundred hammocks; *2)* to send a salesman to southern Florida in an effort to sell hammocks to the various souvenir shops there; and *3)* to exhibit our hammocks in outdoor furniture and sporting goods shows throughout the nation. Hopefully taking these steps will lead to a thriving and profitable industry.

One of the ways that you, our subscribers, can help us is to order hammocks from us now. Unless you live in southern Florida or some other place where winters are warm, you won't get much use out of them until spring, of course, but the money we make from any hammocks you order can be used now, and used well. Even if you don't especially want a hammock, don't forget that a friend or relative might want one for his or her next birthday. If you are interested, we've got three sizes of hammocks: a large for $35 (50" x 84" body size, 14' overall length); a medium for $30 (54" x 82" body size, 13' overall length); and a small for $25 (48" x 80" body size, 12' overall length).

Send us a check and we'll send you a hammock; it's that simple.

GENERAL NEWS

By Kathleen

As this is being written, Twin Oaks is four and a half months old. When we arrived, the roses were blooming in cascades all over the plum trees. Outside my window now I can see the red-brown leaves of an oak tree blowing in the wind. The garden is gone; the corn is shocked; the tobacco is hanging in the barn. In the barns, also, live half the membership, still waiting for the completion of the new building before they can sleep in heated quarters. The building progresses: the roof is complete; the slab is nearly all poured; the furnace has been purchased. Next step: the outside walls.

Our membership has risen from the original eight to twelve members, including one small child. Our bank account is very low, and we look forward to the coming winter with a few worries. But generally, morale is high.

HOUSING

The barns grow colder at night, and six members who sleep in them look forward to the completion of the new building, which will be heated and have space enough for us all. The new building is not exactly going to be a luxury hotel. This winter it will consist of little more than a shell. Eventual plans call for seven private rooms and a bath, plus a large central area where indoor shop work of all kinds can be carried on. The beauty of the plan is its flexibility. When we can afford better housing, this one will probably be converted entirely into shops. None of the walls are load-bearing, and this allows them to be easily removed and space enlarged as future convenience may require. We will continue to use the farmhouse for kitchen and dining space. As this is being written, the new building consists only of supporting poles, slabs, and a roof. But it is enough to give us a general idea of what it will be like. If you were visiting Twin Oaks last week, you might have heard conversations like this:

"I'd like this for my bedroom. Look what a marvelous view of the apple trees in bloom in the spring. Can I have this room?"

"That's the bathroom."

"The bathroom! You're going to waste that view of the apple trees in the bathroom!"

"That way everybody gets to see them."

"Oh well, it doesn't matter. When the apple trees are in bloom, who wants to be in their bedroom, anyway?"

. . .or. . .

"Let's have one side of the building for hi-fi listeners and one side for silence lovers."

"But there aren't enough silence lovers to fill one side."

"Well, then, let's have people who go to bed at night on one side and people who stay up all night listening to records on the other side."

"I think the partition materials are going to be fairly soundproof."

. . .or. . .

"The corner rooms are the best. How do we decide who gets the corner rooms? They have a double view."

"No, they don't. This wall is blank. All the rooms have only one window."

'Mmm. In that case the interior rooms might be more desirable, because they'd be warmer. How do we decide who gets the inside rooms?"

FOOTPRINTS FOREVER

There is something about a newly-poured concrete slab that invites youngsters to immortalize themselves by stepping in it. The youngsters here at Twin Oaks consist of Elliott (new member, age 3½) and the various small animals. Elliott ran through the fresh cement once, sank up to his ankles, embarrassedly retraced his steps, and remarked, "Well, I didn't make very many holes." This damage was easily repaired. Not so the marks left by the ducks and cats. Naturally shy, these animals stay clear of the building during the day when workers are present. But at night their curious noses take their feet into the cement, and in the morning we see kitten paws and duck tracks permanently marked on our future bedroom floors.

RAMMED EARTH

Several of our readers have sent us books and materials on rammed earth. While the present building project is being done with other materials, we do plan to use rammed earth some time in the future, probably within the year. With that in mind, we ordered a CINVA-RAM brick-making machine, and it arrived last week. The device is simple enough, being simply a form for pressing earth into a mold and a long-handled lever for applying pressure. According to the manual, the machine is capable of producing 600 bricks in one day. We mean to stockpile a few thousand of them for spring experiments. There are other ways of handling rammed earth besides in brick form, as the books and pamphlets you have sent us tell. We will probably try most of the methods to see which are best for us. We appreciate having all this information at our fingertips, and we will keep you informed how it works out.

EQUAL WORK FOR WOMEN

One of the things that Skinner made a big point of in *Walden Two* was that men and women would, given an environment where it was acceptable, choose work according to their talents and interests, without regard to its long-time association with one sex or the other. Some of us at Twin Oaks think this freedom of choice of work is fairly important, important enough to emphasize even at the expense of considerable efficiency. There are men who sign up for mending and women who help pound nails in the new building. It isn't a social change that is going to occur all at once, though. Generally speaking, the kitchen at Twin Oaks is handled by women, the tractor by men. The girls have repeatedly been offered tractor work, been urged to learn ("But I *tell* you, it's easier to drive than the Volkswagen!"), and the men have been encouraged to try their hand at the cooking (You can *too* cook; you can *read*, can't you?"). But the change is slow. It is easy to justify staying within the conventional limits. ("If I sign up for building, somebody will have to lift the heavy boards for me, and I wouldn't be doing my fair share." or "When I cook, it takes me twice as long as it does a woman, and I only get two credits for it.") Nobody is much disturbed at this. The important thing is that there are no artificial barriers; no one tells us that any job is inappropriate for one sex or the other—there is plenty of work to go around. We choose whatever part of it we like (or least dislike). If it so happens that women choose the kitchen and men the shops, at least we have no complaints about it. The pay is the same.

CLOTHING

In case this issue is being read by anyone who has a mile-high pile of ironing waiting to be done, you may be interested to know that Twin Oaks' ironing is always up to date, and that we spend little more than an hour and a half a week on it. It may surprise you that twelve people have so little ironing, but the reason is fairly simple. Most of the members do not want their clothes ironed. Blue jeans and sweat shirts take remarkably little care. Ironing is done for people who go to school or to town, or for any member who requests it.

Mending is another matter. At least two hours a week are spent on mending. Suddenly it *is* worth our while to darn socks (eight minutes per hole) and patch jeans. We draw the line, however, at patching the elbows of cotton shirts. We tried that one day — it took four hours to patch one shirt that had only cost $3 to begin with and had already been worn for over three years. It was a relaxing job, and the person who did it didn't mind it. But the group knows that for every hour of unnecessary work one member does, the other members do an hour of work to match it. With that in mind, silly mending jobs like shirt elbows are now classed "recreation," and no labor credits are given.

We have so far bought almost no clothing. Exceptions have been winter boots for some members who had none. Ordinary clothes, though, we have in surplus. We have a tendency to wear the things we like best, that are most comfortable, and we wear them until they wear out, which is a long time with mending service available. For that reason, the clothes that we brought are really more than we need. Since we have no fear of their going out of style, we simply save them for future use.

HOW'S THE FOOD?

Twin Oaks spends about $40 a week at the local grocery store. That's three meals a day for twelve people, plus frequent guests, or about $3.50 a week each. We could spend more, or we could live on less. We have chosen a middle ground, calling for meat at least once a day, a generally balanced diet, and satisfied stomachs. We allow ourselves desserts, too, provided they are homemade. In addition to what comes from the store, we have vegetables from the garden (now mostly in the freezer) and an assortment of Community-made jams and pickles. In a few months our own animals will begin to provide us with meat and eggs, as well. In the meantime, we are very careful what we buy. An amazing number of grocery store items are on the "luxury" list — which means we don't buy them at all except on special occasions. The luxury list contains such items as: potato chips, sweets, soft drinks, sour cream, cream cheese, whole milk, bacon, meat over 60 cents a pound, fresh fruit unless very cheap, canned vegetables or fruit, etc.

So do we have a dull diet? Not in the least. The truth is that, given a reasonable variety of ingredients, dull food is a result of poor cooking, not limited funds. We don't have any great cooks among us, but we do have a number of people who can read and some good cookbooks. To date we have been served dozens of dishes based on hamburger, ham, or chicken. We have also discovered that summer squash (our one surplus) can be fixed many different ways. The group comes to the table with good appetites and happy expectations. The cooks are rewarded by seeing their carefully prepared casseroles disappear within ten minutes after leaving the oven.

What? An institution where nobody grumbles about the food? Well, not quite. Rather we are an institution where grumbles are taken seriously. Somebody grumbled about cold lunches, and hot lunches began to appear. Somebody else grumbled that breakfast wasn't breakfast without eggs, and we began to serve eggs.

Another reason we don't spend much time sighing for steaks and sausages is that most of us have come from environments where the food was not very good. Consider that half our membership is fresh from college campuses, where they were either served the same menu every week or else lived off malt-shop fare, or worse yet, cooked for themselves with a hot plate and a dollar a day. Twin Oaks has never descended to that level. So do we have oatmeal for breakfast? Yes. Baloney for lunch? Sometimes. Macaroni for supper? Fairly often. But there are limits past which we will not go; TV dinners are beneath us.

CHICKYCHICK AND THE DUCKS

Chickychick in the duck pen is rather like a house-mother in a girls' school. She makes her presence felt, but she doesn't really accomplish what she intends. What Chickychick intends is to have first priority on all the food, especially the green leaves that the Community members sometimes push through the chicken wire for the poultry's enjoyment. Chickychick would like a moment's peace and quiet while she pecks daintily and thoughtfully at the green leaf. Alas, she never manages more than one bite per leaf. Ducks, ordinarily a docile and peaceful lot, are maddened by the sight of a weed. No risk is too great for the prize. One brave duck goes after the leaf, grabs it in his beak, and tears off across the pen. Chickychick looks indignant. The other twenty-five ducks chase after the one that has the leaf. We give Chickychick another leaf. Another duck makes the wild dash and takes off with the green, eating furiously on the run to save some of his swift-gotten gain before the other ducks overtake him. Chickychick looks annoyed. We give Chickychick a third leaf. A foolhardy duck approaches to take it and PECK! — goes off with several downy feathers missing from his tail. Chickychick pecks thoughtfully at the tail feathers. We feed several hundred green leaves to the ducks, who never can get enough of them. Chickychick tries to establish a claim on each one that comes through the fence, but she is overwhelmed by the numbers. Truthfully she prefers the cracked corn and little bugs. It's the principle of the thing, though.

THE GOLDEN AGE BEGINS
— OR SOMETHING

We can't reasonably be expected to have produced much in the way of an artistic golden age during the first four months of our life as a community, so maybe you won't be too surprised if we tell you that the oils and canvasses are still packed in the boxes they came in, and no one has attempted a Bach chorale.

There is a musical ensemble, though. A group of four meets irregularly and sings hymns in four parts, just for fun. Hymns? Why hymns, the other members ask. Of all the music in the world, why hymns? The quartet mumbles excuses. Hymns are written in very simple harmonies and are easy for an inexperienced group to learn to read the parts, even without a piano to guide. Hymn books are available and free, whereas sheet music costs money, and we don't have any. And so forth. Secretly, though, the Community suspects that the quartet like hymns and will probably continue to sing them, even after they have moved on to greater music. Certainly the others are free to start musical

groups that sing folk songs or jazz if they wish. So far they have not done so, using for an excuse that none of them can carry a tune. So it will have to be hymns until we get some new blood.

COMMUNITY OWNERSHIP

People always want to hear about the problems of communities, and they quite often expect that there will be problems along the lines of communal ownership. Either the people of Twin Oaks are really an extraordinary bunch (not likely; we have met dozens of people who would fit in easily) or else this idea is just off the track. Nobody here ever even thinks about the communal ownership question. It is true that we still have private property at Twin Oaks. Any member who brought something with him that he wants to keep to himself does so simply by not sharing it. Just what this private property consists of, though, hardly anyone here could tell you. One member has a saxaphone. I asked him if he felt it belonged to the Community in the sense that he would let anyone use it. He said he would prefer that the person who wanted to use it be first instructed in its use, so that it wouldn't be damaged, that is all. All tools have been turned over to the group, all appliances, all bedding and towels. From time to time these things will wear out, and yet there has been no complaint from any "owner" or even a (perfectly permissible) request for an exception for any given article. Part of the reason for this is probably that as a small group we are very close to each other enjoy each other, and therefore have a personal sense of sharing with each other. We are not turning over our possessions to a huge institution where they get swallowed up; we are sharing them with our friends. Communities have problems, and we have our share. But community property is not one of them.

LANGUAGE

Language, as we all know, changes with time, and when two languages come together, in one area, a new language emerges from them. Thus from Latin and Anglo Saxon we gradually derived English, and so forth.

At Twin Oaks, we have members from Georgia, Wisconsin, Michigan, Connecticut, South Carolina, Tennessee, and California. Each brings with him his local expressions and accent. The Community listens and chooses. Would you say that the board is just a "tad" off the mark, or just a "smidgen," or possibly a "wee bit"? Would you describe a large quantity of any given substance, from grits to grandchildren, as a "whole potful"? We have a member who does — he also refers to a good-looking girl as a "Scrumptious Babe," and others in the Community are beginning to use the term. Grammar, too, undergoes changes. "Might be able to" is fast disappearing as a grammatical form in Twin Oaks, as the handier "might could" takes its place. A more subtle change appears in one member's language, who uses "isn't" when he is speaking pleasantly, and "ain't" when annoyed.

The local Virginian accent we have not begun to adopt, though it probably won't be long before we say we have had "right much" rain, or are growing "vegetobbles" in our garden.

Speaking of language, some of the old adages that we've heard all our lives are beginning to take on new meaning in our rural environment. Take, for instance, "Eats like a pig." Never would we say that of anyone again. Having watched pigs eat, we admit that we have never seen a human who came close, not even by stretch of metaphor, to such behavior. Then there is "wonderful weather for ducks." We put on our boots and raincoats and tread gingerly through the long grass to feed the animals on a rainy day and what do we see? The ducks are going mad with joy in the wet. "Make hay while the sun shines," too, has its literal meaning — hay-making season is not uniformly sunny, and rain spoils the cut hay. We know all about the one rotten apple in the barrel, too. As to "running around like a chicken with its head cut off," as long as Chickychick keeps laying those nice brown eggs, we will leave that one in the realm of metaphor.

THOSE LITTLE EXTRAS

What if it's your job to drive into Louisa to get gasoline for the tractor, and you see a Coke machine just staring at you on a hot day? Do you grit your teeth and keep in mind that there are cold watermelons waiting for you back on the farm? Or do you buy a Coke and charge it to "gas" on the Community books so that no one knows the difference? Or do you buy the Coke and charge it to "Coke" on the books and wait for someone to say something about it?

What we did about it was institute a weekly cash allowance for each member, so that he can choose whether he wants a Coke or would prefer some other luxury. The magnificent sum of 25 cents per week per member was agreed upon as an experiment. I went around asking the members what they had spent it on since it was instituted, and got the following statistics: several Cokes, a bag of candy, a package of *real* cigarettes, and admission to a high school football game. Some members had never spent a cent of it, explaining that they were saving it for a larger purchase.

You might have enjoyed listening in on the discussion when the allowance system was first instituted. We discussed whether there should or could be any control on exchange of cash within the membership. (For instance, is there any way to prevent one member's lending his quarter to another member at high rates of interest? Or what do we do if some members get together and play poker with their allowance, and one person wins all the cash and uses it to bribe a manager to give him all the easy jobs. . .What if one member saves his quarters and buys a share of ITT with them and gets a secret income. . .) Conclusion: All such occurences are highly unlikely in this group, particularly at these rates. Let's talk about real problems, please.

THE TOBACCO HABIT

If you've ever given any thought to communal finances, you have probably wondered just how a community would go about determining where to draw the line between a necessity, which the community naturally provides for its members, and a luxury, which the member just has to do without until the community becomes wealthy. It isn't at all an easy question, and almost any answer you give to it turns out to be quite arbitrary. Arbitrary or not, Twin Oaks has to answer this question every time a request is made for funds for individual needs or wants of its members. A nice example is the question of cigarette smokers.

All right, so someday we are going to do away with the habit entirely by behavioral engineering. But for the time being we have three members dependent on the weed. Cigarettes are expensive. Is nicotine dependence a medical problem that the Community should take care of? Or is it a luxury that must be bought (along with candy or Cokes) from the member's weekly allowance?

When in doubt, compromise. Our compromise on this subject has evolved into a practice of providing from Community funds enough money for bulk tobacco of the roll-your-own-kind, but tailor-mades are an individual luxury. Too lenient? Probably not. The cost is about a nickle a day per smoker. Too rough? Our smokers don't think so. They do say, though, that the amount of time it takes to roll a cigarette cuts down somewhat on the number they smoke. So far so good — behavioral engineering, we are on our way.

WE GO TO AN AUCTION

There are things that we need that aren't readily available in the local stores. A cider press, for instance, a big stone crock, a dinner bell. In addition, there are things that, though available on the new market, would probably be cheaper used and just as good. Mason jars, for instance, chests of drawers, a hay rake, a wheel barrow. Rural areas don't seem to use the want ads section of the local papers to sell such items. The obvious place to look for them would be at a local farm auction; auctions are advertised nearly every Saturday. We chose a Saturday when we weren't too pressed for time and took off with a trailer hooked to the car, in order to bring home our treasures.

Three hours later we brought home an empty trailer and a new knowledge of auction behavior. Every item that interested us was bid out of our price range by antique hunters. There is nothing, it appears, no matter how badly made, how inartistically conceived, or how marred by time and use, that will not be bought as an antique, provided only that it is more than thirty years old.

We know now that we are not going to find a dinner bell or a cider press on the used market.

The whole thing left us feeling grumpy about wasting our morning, but it gave us an idea. Maybe in a few years we'll have accumulated enough old junk so that we can hold an auction. Those mason jars ought to bring 50 cents each. How much am I bid for this nice antique rope hammock?

GENERAL NEWS

WE MOVE INTO THE NEW BUILDING

"They say," a neighbor of ours informed us the other day, "that if you move into a house before you finish it, it will never be finished." If that turns out to be true, Twin Oaks is doomed to a permanently unfinished building. The first of December we completed the final wall and began moving the beds from the barns. None of the rooms were finished in any sense. All still had wires exposed in the partitions; none had ceilings; some lacked doors. And outside the rooms the cement floor was piled high with lumber and power tools and strewn with sawdust. One part of the floor had not even been poured when the first beds were installed. Still, moving into the new building made sense, for it has a big, wood-burning furnace which, properly stoked, will keep the building comfortably warm most of the night.

There was a certain pleasure in setting up our furniture in the new rooms, for we knew that this move was a more permanent one than the previous ones. (You can't really feel that the dining room is your castle, when you have to get up and out of the way so that people can eat breakfast! Nor did the very private rooms in the barn have that homey feeling, for they were—in addition to being icy cold—clearly a temporary measure.) But the new rooms are another thing; here we are going to stay for some time, probably years. Here we can put up curtains and get out our knick-knacks. Now we have a place to go when we need to be alone, or a place to invite a friend for a private talk.

The rooms are 12' by 12' squares, each with a screened window and a door that opens toward the inside of the building. The floors are concrete, and few of us have any rugs to cover them. Elliott has a room of his own, to be shared with the next child who joins the Community. In the meantime, the upper bunk is empty and can be used for a guest. . .maybe you?

GUESTS BY THE DOZENS

During the winter we don't get as much company as we did during the warmer months. . . At least that is what we thought was going to be true. But it turns out that we are becoming better and better known, and as people find out about our existence, they want to come and look us over. It is a rare week that no visitors are with us.

Usually they come in two's and three's. Last month we had a group of thirty people for supper. The group was a philosophy of education class from the University of Virginia; their professor has a particular interest in utopian endeavors and has assigned *Walden Two* to his classes.

It was fortunate that the last of the concrete had just dried in the new building, since we could not possibly have entertained a group of that size in the farmhouse. Tables were concocted of sawhorses and plasterboard. One of the members spilled food on the plasterboard, so someone will always have spaghetti sauce on his wall, in remembrance of the occasion.

We served spaghetti, which is the only thing we know how to make in huge quantities on a three-burner stove. And they asked questions. What are our child-raising attitudes? How do we differ from the kibbutzim? What is our attitude toward religion? Did we intend to enter local politics? We answered the questions and were having a good time when suddenly the session was over. They had to get back to Charlottesville and Richmond and Culpeper. Several of them promised to return with their children and their tents when the weather gets better. One bought some Christmas Cookie tree decorations, and one subscribed to the *Leaves*. Still another said he might buy a hammock. All in all, it was a successful evening.

We wonder whether sessions like this will get to be commonplace. We consider the number of psychology classes and even high school social science classes within fifty miles of us. Having gotten through our first mass dinner, we are less frightened by the possibility than we were. People are curious; let them come and satisfy their curiosity. Spaghetti is easy to make.

EDUCATION AT TWIN OAKS

Every intentional community wants its own schools. There is so much of community feeling and philosophy that is best taught if the community can control the education of its young. Twin Oaks is no exception in this regard. Our tiny size, however, and our lack of certified teachers kept us from trying to start a school this year. Susan, our only school-age member, went to public school in September. Recently, however, we have discovered that Louisa County has no compulsory education laws. Susan was free to attend or not attend public school. The Community was free to undertake her education if it chose. We pondered the matter for three weeks and made our decision. Susan became an official dropout, and "classes" at Twin Oaks officially began. Classes, of course, consist of tutorial sessions with members of the Community who are informed on the subjects she needs. (She has decided that she wants the full regular high school curriculum.) She is "taking" English composition, Spanish, geometry, and chemistry. Teaching has been put on the labor credit system, and both teacher and student get credits for the classes.

A CHILD IN COMMUNITY

In the book, you will remember, the children were raised apart from the adults, in a community of their own. Some of us like this idea, but it just doesn't work out when there is only one child. Elliott has been with us just two months. He is very much a member and is respected as such. His life is of necessity lived among the adults. The whole thing seems to be working out quite well. He spends his days "helping" with the work, riding in the trailer behind the tractors and chasing ducks. In the evening he asks "Who is signed up to read to me?" and whoever is reads to him or tells him stories for about an hour. After that he either goes to sleep, if he is sleepy, or else runs around in his pajamas until he does get sleepy. He sets his own bedtime; the only thing we insist on is that he get up in the morning with the rest of us. Though he gets less sleep than most children his age, it is evident that he gets as much as he needs, for he is cheerful and bright-eyed throughout the day. Elliott knows which adult members can be teased into telling a story any old time of day (after breakfast, for instance) and which ones will take him riding on the tractor. If a member is grumpy and doesn't feel like being bothered with child-chatter, Elliott goes to find another member who isn't feeling so grumpy. The building site is a wonderful playground in Elliott's opinion. True, certain toys are forbidden him (the drill press and all the power tools, the chisels and the large hand saw), but he may use the hammer and countless nails, the hack saw and numberless pieces of scrap wood. He has recently graduated to the plane and the carpenter's drill. We haven't a doubt that he will chip the blade of the one and break the bit of the other. But then, education always costs money.

It is not easy, in a group of ten adults or so, to maintain any consistency in matters such as what Elliott is allowed to do and what he is not allowed to do — what he can eat between meals, for instance, or whether he may play with the typewriters. We appointed a child manager right away, and he has set us some general guidelines that we try to go by. The following paragraphs are taken from one of the advice sheets that he posted when Elliott first came to live with us:

Ideally the general policy for Elliott should be as close to the general policy for other members as is possible. The simple reason is that we value equality and that we are trying to produce a functioning member with similar non-authoritarian values. We should at least give the ideal a try. If it proves unworkable (that is, if there is something about children that requires different treatment than adults) then we try other things.

Bedtime. 1) First we will try not regulating his sleep other than getting him up in the morning for breakfast. 2) The second problem is in disturbing people who are trying to read or sleep. If you are being disturbed, say "Elliott, I am busy (fill in with what you are busy doing) and I don't want to be disturbed." Then go on with what you are doing

and ignore him. After telling him that you are busy, it would be best if you could suggest something for him to do as an alternative that doesn't disturb anyone. This does not mean sending him to someone else—it means something like drawing or coloring or looking at pictures in a book. If he persistently continues to bother you, continue to ignore him. During this extinction period you will probably be very much bothered. The expectation is that, if continued, Elliott will learn that it is hopeless to bother one after being told that one is busy and will automatically look for other things to do. As to bedtime, you can close your door and hold it there if it comes to that.

Extinction is not painless, but it is in keeping with adult techniques. Punishment is not. There will be the usual repertoir of behaviors to try to get attention from you after you have told him that you are busy or trying to sleep or whatever. Just remember that whatever of these responses you give in to is reinforced.

The Outside so often mistreats children that, without reminding ourselves, we might easily slip from our equalitarian ethic in regard to children. The following are reminders of how we expect to be treated by one another, and thus how our relationship should be with children.

1) No corporal punishment. It invariably leads to hate in some form. *2)* Answer questions honestly, as you would to other adult members. This includes questions of sex, birth, religion, etc. If you don't know, then tell him so and tell him where he can find out. *3)* If annoyed by a child, tell him so in a way you would tell any adult. Don't make up some fake excuse; you have a right to be left alone and not pestered. Likewise, the child has the same right. Regard it. *4)* Do not use children as personal slaves, *e.g.,* 'how about going and telling Rudy that. . .' or any of the other little demands placed on children that one wouldn't think of telling another adult to do. *5)* Don't make promises you don't plan to keep. *6)* Don't create fears. The pigs do *not* eat bad little boys. *7)* If a child lies to you it is a good sign that he fears you. Worry about the fear problem before the lying one. *8)* A simple test of whether one should do anything to restrain a child is 'Is what he is doing in any way really harming anyone else?'

The general rule to apply toward Elliott can be 'Treat him as you would any adult who did the same thing he did.' There are two things to remember, however, that might suggest a different treatment. Elliott comes from a situation involving authoritarian control, mostly through punishment and guilt (if you loved me, you would not do that). Secondly, this is a new environment in which he is not yet secure. Considering these, the following is suggested: *1)* that at least half an hour a day be put on labor credits for an Elliott-time, during which the one signed up does whatever Elliott wants to do, giving him total undivided attention. *2)* If you are doing something during the day that Elliott's presence doesn't disturb very much (*e.g.,* feed pigs), then ask him if he wants to join you.

FOLKLORE FOR COMMUNITIES

Here we are, trying to raise a child in community with community ideals and values, and yet for bedtime stories we are limited to the tales that glorify the very values we are trying to eradicate. We deplore parental neglect and violence, but gleefully tell of Hansel and Gretel, who are left by their parents to die in the woods and finally survive by murdering an old woman. The tale of the Little Red Hen comes a little closer to utopian ethics, for it points up the relation between working and eating. But it lacks something. There must be a better solution to the parasite problem than just saying "Then I'll eat it myself." With that in mind, our child manager rewrote *The Little Red Hen* with a slightly different twist. The crux of the story goes like this. The little red hen, finding that no one will help with planting the garden, gets discouraged, and she doesn't plant it either. Harvest season comes, and all the animals are demanding their accustomed share of the food. Little red hen points out that you can't very well harvest what you didn't plant, and all the animals are sad.

"I have an idea," said the big brown cow. "Let's have a labor credit system."

"Hooray," cried the big white duck. "What's a labor credit system?"

I leave our readers to imagine the rest.

Of course there are traditionalists among us who feel that the stories are worth preserving, violence and all, just as they were told to us when we were children, particularly those of high literary quality. The child manager may do as he likes with *The Little Red Hen*, but some of us draw the line at the Just So Stories. We feel that the *Elephant's Child* should continue to be read in Utopia, even though he *is* spanked by all his dear relatives, ever and ever so hard, and must get his nose pulled out of shape forever at the banks of the great, gray green greasy Limpopo River, all set about with fever trees, regardless of what Darwin has to say on the subject. As to stories with a real community flavor, we will probably have to write our own — hopefully from scratch.

WE CHANGE THE CLOCK

Almost everybody hates to get up in the morning, including utopians. In fact, the absence of bosses and classes and schedules and time clocks may make utopians a bit worse than other people in this matter. We had breakfast scheduled for 8:00, but it was rarely ready before 9:00 because the breakfast cook couldn't get out of bed, either. Work on the building was supposed to start at 9:00, but it didn't get started until 10. The building manager grumbled. We all knew the situation was getting out of hand. One member kept saying we ought to get up earlier. We all knew we couldn't do that. Then someone suggested we set the clock back, just like daylight saving time, and for the same purpose. Most of us thought it wouldn't work—after all, if

we couldn't make ourselves get out of bed at 8:00, having the clock tell us it was 9:00 wasn't going to make any difference, was it? But we tried it. The odd thing is that it worked. We are still a little late getting up, but we are late an hour earlier than we used to be, and therefore use an extra hour of scarce and valuable sunlight for the outdoor work. The skeptics among us are amazed to find that it *is* the clock we go by, and not the feeling of sleepiness.

That puts the Community on Daylight Saving Time, while the surrounding area is on Standard Time. We have to remember that when we have appointments in town.

COMMUNITY HEALTH

The Community health manager was the first managership appointed last July when we first divided up responsibility. The reason it came first was that it was obvious who it would be—our registered nurse, Connie. Health measures have been simple so far. We are a fairly healthy group and have had no family colds or other contagious diseases so far. Our medical expenses have been limited to a couple of doctor's office visits and a prescription or two, plus some minor dental work. One thing we all had to have, decreed the health manager, was a tetanus immunization. Considering the number of things there are to fall over and scratch oneself on, this seemed sensible, and Louisa has a free clinic. In groups of three and four we all went down to the clinic to get our shots. After the fourth group had signed up, the health worker in the clinic relieved her curiosity by asking, "Do you folks have some sort of project out there?" We do, indeed.

CHICKYCHICK AND FRIENDS

For the benefit of those readers who feel that a newsletter isn't a newsletter without mention of Chickychick, that pompous bird is now moulting and not laying eggs. However, there are guinea hens and bantams in the pen with her now, and Twin Oaks generally finds an egg or two each day.

CHRISTMAS AT TWIN OAKS

Three of our members took off for their families' homes this Christmas season, and it did seem as if we who stayed might be lonely over the holidays. As it turned out, though, we had enough company to double our numbers and press our sleeping space. We served two ducks (delicious, by the way) and two chickens and most of the usual accompanying dishes, including cranberry sauce and pumpkin pie.

Our Christmas tree we cut from our own woods. There is no pine suitable, so we settled for a well-formed cedar, 17 feet high. "I've always wanted a really big tree," said George, who brought it back from the woods with the tractor and trailer. Some of us would have been satisfied with a tree we could reach the top of, but George promised to climb the ladder to put on the lights. The tree reached the peak of the roof of the new building, and the lights were plugged into an outlet in the ceiling. We wouldn't have had enough ornaments if it hadn't been for the Christmas Cookie tree ornaments we had been experimenting with as a possible source of income. As it was, we trimmed the tree from top to bottom with psuedo cookies. In case looking at them made our mouths water too much, there was a platter full of the real thing in the kitchen.

CAN I BRING ANYTHING?

From time to time people who are intending to visit us ask if there is anything they can bring us. We usually say no, just to bring themselves and an optimistic outlook. Just lately, though, we have run into a clear-cut need that could be filled easily by visitor friends. Namely, we need rug wool. Two of us are braiding rugs out of old wool coats and skirts, and our own supply of wool is running out. There is hardly a home in America that doesn't have a box or trunk or closet full of useless clothing. If it's wool, we can use it. Other things we are short of, in case you are coming alone in a big car, are rugs, beds, bedding, chairs, and lamps.

FOOLTAX

One of our favorite farm writers is a man named Kains, who, in his book *Five Acres and Independence,* instructs beginners like ourselves on the ins and outs of farming. This sage is continually telling his readers that the biggest expense any novice farmer has in his first year is fooltax, or the cost of his ignorant mistakes. Twin Oaks is paying a considerable amount of fooltax this first year. Since June we have managed the following: losing the sweet potato crop through improper storage (the frost got them); put off Fall plowing until the weather made it muddily impossible (that means we will have to try to plow in the spring, a task local farmers avoid if at all possible); put our Fall vegetables in a spot where the ducks noticed and gobbled up all the young turnip tops; gave little thought to firewood until cold weather actually arrived, at which time most of the wood we could cut is too wet to burn. Result: two weeks of living in a house that was never quite warm enough.

Not all of our agricultural and homemaking procedures have come out badly. Our jams and pickles were very good, and our vegetable garden was a success. And even in those areas where we failed most miserably, we take comfort in the fact that *now* we know what we should have done, and why, and that *next year* things will be different.

THE PIGS

You will recall that we purchased four little pigs this summer. We watched them and fed them, disapproved their manners and declared them unfit for anything except conversion into ham and bacon. That metamorphosis is now nearly complete. We followed our neighbors' example and had the actual butchering and cleaning of the hogs done by local professionals, who took them away in the morning looking like pigs and brought them back in the afternoon looking very much like sides of pork that you might see in a frozen food locker. The meat cutting we did ourselves. By "ourselves" we mean that we pleaded for help from our neighbors, and they dropped their own work and came to help us. They stayed most of the day and instructed in all phases of the work, the men separating the hams from the spareribs, and the women cutting up the sausage meat and rendering the lard.

And now, after six months of meatless breakfasts, we have sausage with our pancakes and eggs. The bacon won't be ready for six or eight weeks yet. It is salted down, along with the hams and shoulders, in the big salt box. The tenderloin is in the freezer, along with miscellaneous roasts. There are no pork chops, it turns out, because to make them requires a power saw that we don't have. We can live without pork chops this year—next year we will have ten hogs to work with.

SILKY

The reason our animal manager is so confident that we will have ten hogs next year is that we have recently purchased a bred sow. She is big and friendly and has a good record for producing large healthy litters. She is, in fact, the mother of the four we raised this summer. The sow's name was Sukey (I'm not sure, but I suspect that all sows in Virginia are named Sukey) but Elliott mispronounced it Silky and we decided the mistake was felicitous. So her name is Silky, after the silk purse, you know.

WINTER WORK

It is interesting to find out that during the winter months the Community requires more skilled workers and has less unskilled labor available to do. Even among our own membership we are pressed to distribute the work equitably and leave free choice for everybody, when the largest part of our workload requires either strength or experience or both. Take wood cutting; we bought a chain saw to fell the dying trees that we mark for firewood. But none of the girls can can handle it. The firewood manager has divided the job into sections, so that the less-muscled can load the wood and bring it up to the house with the tractor and trailer, stack it, and split kindling, while the stronger people divide the (considerable) chain saw work among them. The labor credit value of chain sawing climbs steadily upward, and meals and dishes have become the "easy" work.

The summer was full of low-skill jobs. Anybody can cut corn off the cob, or pick squashes, or sucker tobacco, or plant beans. But not everyone can hammer and saw very well, or use the posthole digger, or repair the faucets.

The obvious answer to the problem is to teach skills to the unskilled, and that is precisely our approach. The building is well marked with the errors of novice carpenters. All the girls have learned to drive the tractors and use most of the power equipment. But it is apparent that we must encourage more and more of this kind of learning. We have modified the labor credit system so that there are credits for learning jobs as well as for teaching them. This applies to all work—from printing newsletters to scrambling eggs. The broader our skills, the better off we all are, especially in winter.

NEW EQUIPMENT

Twin Oaks has purchased a camera and print-maker that should make it possible for us to take in local printing jobs, as well as to improve our own newsletter with photographs. As this issue goes to press, we have used it very little. We hope there will be a cover page on this issue, made by means of the new equipment.

DECISION MAKING

Last July we elected a three-man board (called planners for lack of a better name) with authority to make policy decisions. The board meets once a week or more often to discuss problems as they come up. After each meeting a summary of the material discussed is posted for all the membership to see; and any decisions made at the planners' meeting become effective only after any feedback from the group is received and considered. Probably our readers would be curious to read some of these notices. The following are selections from planners' meeting notes selected for their general interest content and to give an idea of the scope and variety of problems that we presently handle in this way.

DECEMBER 4 — *Junkyard Location*

George has requested that a site be chosen where old cars may be kept out of sight but available for spare parts, perhaps a place inside the woods.

Tobacco, the Work Load, and Morale

We felt that the labor credit system is not quite the appropriate way to handle a job as big and as immediate as tobacco stripping, and that we have probably made a mistake merely adding this job to the system. The better alternative would have been to do it as we did all other phases of the tobacco—together in a huge group, where we can all sit and tell stories or something. The next time we have a comparable job, let's try this group approach.

New Member Booklet

We discussed our inadequate orientation procedures. We feel we need some sort of booklet to send to prospective members or to give to new members. This would contain explanatory material and give the new member a clearer idea of what is expected. It might help avoid goofs and help establish desirable norms.

DECEMBER 12 — *Expense Planning*

Some of us can anticipate our medical and minimum clothing needs, and the Community needs to have this information to help our financial planning. We appointed Scotty to go around and ask everybody whether they have any teeth that have to be filled within the next few months, or glasses that have to be replaced, or boots that have to be bought. Think about your own needs and be prepared for Scotty's questions.

Emergency Draft Credits

From time to time we have emergencies that come and need labor for some job that isn't on the system. Obvious examples that have happened recently are: somebody gets sick and can't fix a meal; someone leaves the Community in the middle of the week; the weather changes and makes some agricultural project more immediately necessary than was thought; some weather condition produces an emergency, floods the basement, threatens to cave in the roof, etc. For such emergencies we propose the following: All of us are on call for such emergencies, at the credit rate of one and a half times the usual rate for such a job. In case the job has no usual rate, it would be credited at 1.5 per hour. The request for draft labor will usually come from the managers, but it will be up to the labor manager to decide whether the emergencies justify draft rates.

DECEMBER 18 — *Time Away from the Community*

We spent the entire session discussing the status of people who leave the Community and then return at a later date. Many alternatives were considered and their advantages and disadvantages discussed. We ended up, however, staying with our present bylaws, which stipulate that people who leave and return must start again as provisional members.

Milk

We decided to buy raw milk from some nearby farmer and try it, with the idea of determining whether we want to buy a cow.

JANUARY 4 — *Breakfast on Time*

We will experiment with a system whereby anybody who is signed up for breakfast and actually has it ready on time —8:00 on the dot—may collect an extra .5 credits for so doing.

Service Credits

We had some discussion on the possibility of giving labor credit for services one member does for another—things that one member finds important but which the whole group doesn't want. The immediate example is Mona's drawing and needing a model to pose for her. We concluded that in principle there is every reason to give credits for such modeling (or whatever) but that we ought to limit this kind of thing because we don't feel that we can afford to add any great burden to our labor load. The limit has been tentatively set at 2 credits per week per member.

JANUARY 9 — *Bitches*

We went through the entire bitch list that Rudy has been

collecting from everybody and discussed each item with an idea of determining whether anything can be done about them, and if so, what. There were all kinds of bitches: big, little, and medium-sized. Here is a summary of what was discussed and hopefully concluded. [*Note:* list has been greatly cut for newsletter purposes. Original list consisted of twenty-two items. What follows is a sample, each representing a complaint by one member.]

1. *Fruit.* The suggestion was that Elliott should have fruit, but the planners felt that we all should. We agreed to recommend to Susan, who is manager of this area, to buy a little fruit each week — not enough to last all week, but enough so that we don't feel like groveling at the sight of a grapefruit.

2. *Kitchen Stove.* Our stove *is* a bitch. What we need is a restaurant-type stove. We agreed to buy a Richmond paper from time to time and start studying ads for such items. We probably will not replace the thing this winter, but there is no question but that we must have something more adequate, with at least six burners and two ovens that work properly, before we try to cook for many more people.

3. *Group Hospitalization.* Our need for this is obvious, since a single bad accident or illness could wreck us. Some of us fear that the price of the insurance would wreck us just as easily and faster. But it doesn't make any sense to come to conclusions without investigating the actual costs. Connie is hereby appointed to take the responsibility for this investigation.

4. *Noisy Building.* There isn't a lot we can do about noise in the new building, since a lot goes on there. The ceilings will of course go up as soon as we can get the bus into Charlottesville for the materials and get them back here, and that will help. In the meantime, we might try *not* shouting to each other through the walls. If we want to talk to someone in his room, knock on his door and gain admittance. This may turn out to be a bigger nuisance than it is worth, but let's give it a try and see how it feels.

NUMBER 5

March, 1968

GENERAL NEWS

WE ARE DISCOVERED BY THE HIPPIES

There is a sense in which Twin Oaks is entirely unique. It is the only community at present that deliberately takes Walden Two as a model. But there are people who consider Twin Oaks part of a national movement — a movement in the direction of small communities. On one side of us (ideologically) are the religious groups, such as the Society of Brothers or the Hutterians. Though our aims are widely divergent, we have in common with these communities our basic communal structure—a common treasury, communally organized work, common dining, etc. And on the other side of us are the hippie communes.

There is little written information on the hippie communes, and we have to rely on word of mouth; but we get the general picture that they, too, have something in common with us. This time the common ground is philosophical. The hippies, like us, believe that life should be full of joy and freedom and restricted as little as possible by conventional trivia. They differ from us in that they entirely reject structure. Their communes have no bylaws, no members in a legal sense, and no clear plans for their own continuance. Then there is the obvious difference in our recreations: there are no drugs permitted at Twin Oaks.

Despite our differences, the hippies are interested in us. A few have already visited, and it is likely that warm weather will bring others. At first we looked on these visits with thinly-veiled dismay, but time and experience are calming our worries. Hippies are, it turns out, only people. They are much like other visitors—a shade less formal than some. They want to know the same things—what are we? What do we do here? And, like other visitors, most of them give some thought to membership, ask themselves how they would fit in. Maybe they decide that they don't want to give up drugs or that communal life isn't important enough to justify raising the entrance fee. If a hippie does join the Community, what then? No problem. When he begins to wash dishes and split wood, we don't think of him as a hippie anymore; he's just a member with long hair.

SEPTIC TANK PROBLEMS

One thing we *do* have in common with the hippie communes is an undersupply of adequate plumbing. The problem is sufficiently serious that we have recently erected an outhouse to take the pressure off our limited facilities. "This is the second outhouse hole I have dug within a year," grunted a visitor who had previously lived at Morning Star. "I'm getting to be an expert." It is probable that Twin Oaks will have more outhouses before it has more septic tanks.

The cost of putting in a really adequate drain field is formidable. We consider the flow of visitors who come through Twin Oaks for a day or so with willing but unskilled hands and ask ourselves whether it might be possible to put that drain field in with a pick and shovel rather than the expensive backhoe. On the one hand it is a terrible waste of energy to set a human doing what a machine can do thirty times faster. On the other hand, it might be a couple of years before we can afford that machine. . .

FIRE

We were sitting in the new building discussing plans for the future when the dinner bell rang. We didn't respond right away, because it really wasn't dinnertime. But it kept ringing in a most erratic way, so we went to investigate. It wasn't dinner; it was fire, spreading rapidly across the dry grass in our back yard and headed straight for the house. We ran, grabbing burlap bags, shovels, and hoses as we went, and began spraying and beating out the flames. Though we have several hoses, only one of them could be made to work because the others were frozen shut. But there were ten of us keeping the fire within bounds with wet burlap bags, until the hose and buckets of water could put it out altogether. We called the local fire department, but they never found the farm.

It took us about fifteen minutes to put the fire out. There was no damage. Probably not even the grass was permanently hurt. It served to provide us a few minutes' excitement and an apt warning, namely, Keep Combustible Materials Away From the Stoves. (The fire was caused by a cardboard box that was too near a stove in a small shack one member was using for magazine storage and quiet reading. Noticing that the box was smoking, he tossed it out of the shack, thinking it would quickly extinguish itself. Instead, the high wind whipped it into flame and caught the dry grass.) Also, we are now careful to thaw all hoses and keep them ready for use. Also, we pay more attention to bells ringing at odd hours.

GREENHOUSE

What we would really like is a giant greenhouse with a furnace, so that we could grow tomatoes and lettuce all winter long, and perhaps a few orange trees on one end. What we are settling for in 1968 is a plywood and plastic structure, 8' by 12', unheated except by the sun. Really a cold frame with standing room, this baby "greenhouse" will be used to start our vegetables, so that we can get early crops of tomatoes, peppers, cauliflower, etc., and also to aid us in growing difficult vegetables, such as celery and head lettuce.

We are taking special care with those vegetables we tried and failed with last year in open ground. Our method is simply to follow instructions in our various garden books and pamphlets. Our aim is to provide Twin Oaks with as complete a variety of vegetables and fruits as we can possibly grow in this climate. We have some advantages this year that we didn't have in 1967—a good head start not least among them. We also can estimate group needs more accurately. We plan seven acres of vegetables for the Community. There is a great deal of work that goes into a garden of this size. We know this, but still are impatient for the ground to soften so that we can begin. In the meantime we are filling the flats with starting soils and planting the tiny seeds. Next year at this time we hope to be still taking the vegetables out of the freezer and cellar instead of buying them at the grocery store.

HAMMOCKS

Spring is also time for making and selling hammocks. Two of our members are planning a trip down the coast for the purpose of placing some of our hammocks in stores. The hammock jigs are set up in our workshop space in the new building, and we are busy measuring rope and weaving harnesses, just like last summer. We have recently discovered a synthetic rope (polypropylene) that seems to make as nice a hammock as the cotton rope we were using, and is lighter to ship across the country. It also has the advantage of being mildew-proof. Some of us don't know which rope we prefer. The cotton is heavier and has a handcrafted look that synthetics don't have. (Both are of course hand-woven by identical methods.) But the polypropylene seems whiter, is lighter, and would have a clear advantage in any climate where mildew is a real problem. (Generally, the cotton rope mildews only in very damp weather, and the reemerging sun kills the spores quickly. We keep our own hammocks outdoors in all weather and are not bothered by the problem.) The hammocks are equally strong, equally comfortable. In case you're ordering one, specify which kind of rope you want.

We are printing a hammock brochure and may enclose it with our next issue (closer to warm weather season for any prospective hammock purchasers among our readers). In the meantime we will just mention the necessary figures: the hammocks come in three sizes, priced $25, $30, and $35. All three are long enough to be comfortable for anyone up to six feet tall. The largest is really luxurious and accommodates humans of any reasonable length. The hammocks are woven from 7/32 rope, held into position by curved oak stretchers. You can order them through the mail, at this point Twin Oaks is still paying shipping charges on all direct mail orders east of the Mississippi. West of the Mississippi add one dollar to help with the shipping.

THE PRINTING BUSINESS

In January we purchased a large camera and platemaker to accompany our Davidson offset printing press. We constructed a small darkroom inside the new building and sent out advertisements to local business people to solicit job printing. We've filled several orders this first month and are beginning to feel quite optimistic that this may become a source of steady income to us. Since our overhead expenses are insignificant, our rates can be quite reasonable. Also, there are no competing printing outfits in our immediate area.

We would of course be glad to handle printing jobs for mail order customers and will send prices on request.

SMOKED HAMS

The hams and bacon have been smoking for a little over two days now. We just test-tasted some small pieces. They taste remarkably like ham and bacon— a trifle salty, perhaps, but delicious.

THE STOVE

The ad said "commercial stove, six burners, grill, oven," and the price was reasonable. We had been watching for just such a stove at just such a price, and we wasted no time getting to town to see it. The stove was being sold by the Louisa Presbyterian Church, who had found it larger than they needed. It is not too large for Twin Oaks. Its large burners cook food far faster than a regular kitchen range does, and it has the advantage of being a good working height. (Most stoves are too high for short people.) Our only difficulty is adjusting ourselves to the cast-iron grill. Cast-iron is quite different from teflon, even apart from the lack of thermostatic control. This morning's pancakes were all either burned or underdone. But we will learn this, as we have learned other minor skills.

LUXURY THROUGH THE MAIL

Two issues ago we talked about our food and listed the items we consider "luxuries," a fairly extensive list. Whether in response to that article or not we do not know, but not long ago we received a box from Koinonia Community containing thirty pounds of pecan nut meats. A nicer gift we could not imagine. It will last us for months. Store-bought sweets may be classed as a "luxury," but the cookies and candies we are making here in the Community now, loaded with chopped pecans, are a luxury most families don't have time to afford. At Twin Oaks baking is done on labor credits, just like dishwashing or building or anything else that contributes to the good life.

WE SHARE THE AIR WAVES

Problem-mongers attention! Twin Oaks is wrestling with a miserable problem that appears to have no really satisfactory immediate solution. The problem is music in public rooms.

Though Twin Oaks members have a great deal in common in many areas, there is great diversity in the matter of musical taste. One member dotes on New Orleans jazz, another on Bulgarian folk dances, a third on hillbilly banjo. One likes Montavanni, another Shostakovich. Add to this those who feel a community ought to put away all electronic devices and make its own music, and those who don't like music at all and sigh for silence. For a while this was all right. We were putting up with each other's music — even learning to enjoy the variety — until we were hit with the group who like New Folk, or Hippie Scene Music. This ranges from Baez and Buffy to the Beatles and the Fugs, taking in Dylan and Donovan on the way. The essential thing about this music, though, to those who love it, is that it be played uninterruptedly at top volume. One works by it, plays by it, makes love by it.

Almost, almost we managed to live with this, too. We had our new building to escape to, for the only record player was in the house. Then someone found a player and installed it in the new building. We had Dylan before breakfast and the Beatles audible even over the whine of the table saw.

We would have hit the ceiling, but there were no ceilings to hit. There are no ceilings to keep out the music, either, which meant that any record played in a private room was necessarily shared by every other private room.

Our approach to all such problems is through Bitch Day. Bitch Day duly arrived, and the problem was aired. But discussing it is not the same thing as solving it. The best we can do with our facilities is to compromise. We made a crude arithmetical compromise (about one-fifth of our membership loves this music; therefore it may be played a certain number of hours, corresponding to about one-fifth of the day, no more than one hour of which may be in the new building), but we make no pretense that this is a solution. It is clearly a curtailment of freedom. Those who love that kind of music are deprived of it during most of the day; those who have grown to hate it must still put up with it for a part of every day.

Most of the solutions that a community must work out to such problems are like this one—compromises that involve all parties giving in a little. In the long run the answers lie in affluence—soundproof quarters, special music rooms, etc. Lacking affluence we do the best we can by simply sharing the air waves the same way we share any other scarce commodity—equally, as far as it goes.

FINANCES — 1967

It's income tax time, and we have been busy at the adding machine finding out exactly what we did with our money last year. We thought you might be interested in some of the figures. As to where the money comes from, the story is very simple. A very small percent came from sales from our little industries, including farming. This is not too surprising, since businesses rarely make a profit their first six months. Almost all of the funds were brought in by the members or later secured by them from personal sources—a total of about $7,000. Over $2,000 came from donations. As to where the money went, since June 16 we have spent:

Food from grocery store	1,300
Food from farm	500
Gasoline and utilities	400
Medical and dental expenses	140
Investment in hammock industry	600
Investment in breed animals	500
Clothing	45
Newsletter and printing	170
Permanent improvements	5,500

In case you're curious, we are taxed as a partnership, which means each member pays income tax as an individual, declaring his share of the profits of the Community businesses as income, whether they are distributed in cash or not. Obviously 1967 brought us no taxable profit, so our income tax problem is merely figuring out how to make the best use of our losses. This is a formidable arithmetic problem, and we yearn for a tax accountant. Are there accountants with utopian dreams? Are there utopians with accounting ability? Neither seems likely, somehow.

TWIN OAKS AND THE LARGER MOVEMENT

By Rudy

Often the question arises as to just how communities such as Twin Oaks fit into the social change movements in the U.S. today. Utopians are often criticized for running off into the wilderness to bury their heads in the sand, while the rest of the world is suffering. Indeed, it may not be immediately apparent that we who have dropped out of society to start over are still in the forefront of the battle for a better world, but that is the point I intend to make in this article.

Just what is radicalism? The radicals or new left today is denoted by many general ideas common to liberals. For example, both groups are pro-civil rights, peace, equal rights for men and women, a classless society, and some sort of equitable distribution system. On top of this list the radical left has placed a great emphasis on the impracticality of accomplishing anything by working with the present establishment or power structure.

The basic tactics used by the radical left involve direct action and grass-roots organizing of the people most affected by a particular injustice. This has led to a realization of the need for a multi-issue approach.

Tactically the multi-issue approach is sound in that the more things you rally around, the more people you will draw into your group who are directly affected by the issues involved and thus are more dedicated. Ideologically this is sound, since most of the issues in question are interdependent. This interdependence has become quite obvious to those in student, draft, peace, civil rights, poverty, labor multi-issue groups such as SDS and the Wobblies.

SDS does seem to have a clear analysis of where the problems are; but when it comes to proposing alternative systems, the only thing one hears is that they are in favor of the people making the decisions that affect their lives. Even this point leaves some room for argument. It is obviously aimed at removing the problem of power and authority so prevalent now, but it leaves a lot to be desired in the area of efficient management of supplying the basic goods and services of a good life. Ideally, one wants the system that not only is the most humane but also is capable of making the best decisions. No one bitches because the decision of how to perform heart surgery is not left up to a vote of the patients. I feel that the same attitude is possible in the area of economic planning, given a community with general agreement on the level of goods and services they desire and the amount of work they are willing to perform. This condition is quite possible in a community of 1000 where membership is voluntary but not haphazard.

The major question to which most organizations for radical social change have no answer is: how do you set up a society that guarantees these basic things we all talk about being in favor of? What is an economic system that insures equitable distribution without mass inefficiency? What system of government has checks against power and corruption but still doesn't sacrifice decision-making by competent people?

These are the sort of questions we consider every day in community, and the answers have to be practical. No time is lost in long-winded theoretical papers that present untestable propositions. Proposals are put to the test immediately. No time is lost waiting for those in power in the U.S. to be convinced that an experiment is worth making.

This represents an alternative approach to social change as presently viewed by radicals. The distinction is between the approach of trying to tear down the present power structure and *then* figuring out what to do and doing it on a large scale, and the approach of building small-scale alternatives now, and simply growing.

There are two general groups following this path of dropping out and starting over: communities such as Twin Oaks, and the hippies. Among the hippies one might separate three groups: those living off the fringe of society, living in cities, panhandling on the streets, eating stale food, and occasionally writing for money from parents. These have dropped out only in the sense that they are not engaged in contributing anything to the society (except indirectly new ideas for advertising and fashion. They, however, have not really dropped out, because they are dependent on their host. The greater their number, the worse off they are.

The second group of hippies is the self-revolution group, interested mostly in bringing about some sort of change in themselves. This includes many mystics and those hunting enlightenment *a la* eastern religion. This group can fall into either of the other two groups, as well as into straight society (*i.e.*, there have been many enlightenment seekers long before hippies).

The third group are the community hippies. One question sometimes raised by inquirers is in what way is Twin Oaks different from the hippie communities. This is rather interesting: anyone who comes to visit Twin Oaks immediately realizes that we *are* different; but just where the difference lies is something else. After talking to visitors who have been to Morning Star and Drop City, we gather that the main difference is that Twin Oaks is organized, whereas hippie communes shun organization of any kind, as though it were a disease in itself. There is of course the obvious difference of our no-drugs-on-premises policy, but that is not so much a basic disagreement as it is a stay-alive policy. The hippie fear of organization is the main difference, and this seems to me analogous to the SDS fear of non-democratic means. In both cases it is obvious to all that the "evils" are performed by organizations, systems, structures, such as the police, the military, the corporate-political structure, the authoritarian educational system, etc., etc. There seems to be among many a hatred or fear of structure *per se*, as if it followed that since one structure is bad, all structures are bad.

But there is evidence that very lack of structure may lend itself to the very same evils. For instance, many hippie visitors have expressed dislike of the labor credit idea, for no other reason than that it is a system, limits freedom for a while, etc. Their alternative is that everyone should "do his own thing." Some visitors have indeed lived where doing your thing was the rule. When questioned further, it turns out that in all cases the cooperative work load was very low, as in the case where there is either voluntary poverty or everyone works in the city and lives in a co-op apartment. Also, more than once I have heard that there was some girl who always did the cooking. "Does she mind?" "No, she just has a thing about cooking." At the bottom of every *easy* Utopia, someone is exploited, and the rationalizations are many.

BEHAVIORAL ENGINEERING
AT TWIN OAKS

By Rudy

Behavioral engineering is essentially the modification of behavior through some predescribed method. Anything anyone does in the presence of another could almost qualify as a behavior modifier. The essential element in behavioral engineering, as in any engineering, is that the technique is describable prior to administration. The process is basically one of recognizing what the behavior to be modified is and then specifying a technique to be used to produce the desired modification.

Behavioral engineering, in the above sense, is used to a large extent in the various institutions of the larger society (we refer to the larger society as the "outside" and the Community as the "inside"). Most of these do not speak of it as planned engineering; it is just the obvious thing to do,

such as holding religious services in huge, awe-inspiring buildings, or showing films of the enemy committing atrocities to soldiers before battle. Probably the one institution of the outside that admits the use of preplanned engineering is the advertising industry. They are at least internally honest when they talk of their techniques simply as techniques to produce the results they are paid to produce.

The advertisement-type of engineering is a good example of the controller-controllee situation analogous to the rat in the Skinner-box. The controller decides what he wants the subject to do and goes about manipulating whatever relevant variable he can get his hands on. The desired results are largely at the discretion of the controller, for the good or bad of the controllee.

The second type of behavioral engineering used on the outside is the psychotherapy type. In this situation the controller (therapist) tries to get the controllee's (patient's) behavior modified from one considered unhealthy to one considered healthy. In this case usually the controllee requests that he be controlled, and it is usually in his best interest.

A third type of behavioral engineering occurs in the situation where an individual or group of people agree on certain behaviors that they would prefer modified in their own repertoir. On the individual level this is called self-control, and on the group level it is what community is all about. Walden Two (and Twin Oaks) is a community designed so as to elicit the behaviors that the members want, such as cooperation, non-aggression, friendliness, and in general those behaviors making for happier people.

Recently I was looking through a book of psychological reprints and ran across an article entitled *The reinforcement of cooperation between children*. Eagerly I read it, only to find out that when two children sit opposite each other at a table and are reinforced for placing their pencils in opposite holes (each had three holes in front of him), they tend to do so. The cooperation is that when one child places his pencil in a hole the other child cooperates by placing his in the opposite hole, and thus both are reinforced. Somewhat annoyed by the triviality of what I had hoped was a more involved experiment, I put the book down and tried to think how this sort of research relates to community.

The one interesting aspect of cooperation is that reinforcement for the individual must be contingent on the joint efforts of the people who are to cooperate. Thus in community if you want cooperation in the everyday tasks, you make the reinforcements of food, shelter, clothing, recreation, health, etc. for each individual contingent on the joint effort of the members of the community. To accomplish this, an economic system is necessary that makes the betterment of the individual contingent on the betterment of the community. At Twin Oaks there are no individual salaries; there is no internal money economy (labor credits are nontransferable), and the level of food, shelter, clothing, etc. is contingent for all members on the prosperity of the overall community. Thus, just like the two children who had to work together to get the reinforcement, each member of the community must cooperate with the others in order to raise his standard of living.

Some people think that if a society doesn't have a competitive system such that each person determines his own reinforcement, then "initiative" will be lost and no one will work. This is obviously not the case. We have not removed the reinforcers; we have merely made them contingent on cooperation rather than on competition. This contingency, teamed with an accounting system that maintains equality of labor (the labor credit system) makes for a society in which the cut-throat tactics of competition and the "every man for himself" attitude are no longer reinforced and thus become extinguished. At Twin Oaks the only way to be selfish is to do something that will make the Community better and thus your own private life better.

Just as the outside makes use of types one and two behavioral engineering, the Community can likewise do so. Only instead of using it for the private gain of some at the expense of others, we will use it for the good of the individuals affected. This might horrify some people who will immediately remember all the negative utopias they had read *(Brave New World; 1984)* and assume that this will easily get out of hand. "Who is to decide whether it is for the good of someone?" and "Power Corrupts" are typical cliches usually quoted at this point. Perhaps in way of answer I can give some examples that will clarify the kinds of control that I am speaking of.

Type one, the controller-controllee situation, is the one most feared, since it includes such examples as dictator-people, master-slave, etc. One example often forgotten is parent-child. This is an example where control of one by another is somewhat accepted. Except for aversive control, most people not only don't mind seeing a controller modify the behavior of a child, but they insist that it be done. Likewise in the Community we insist that it be done. Hopefully there will be an article in a future newsletter on the techniques that we use and how they seem to be doing.

The second type of behavioral engineering, student-teacher, involves the modifying of individuals' behavior through means less total than changing the entire societal structure. This type is usually educational or instructional. Examples range from the simple mechanical skills, such as typing efficiently, to more dramatic programs aimed at making changes in large areas of one's behavior. Examples range from courses in "How to make friends and influence people" to psychotherapy. This type of behavior modification usually involves a teacher who gives feedback as to the correctness of responses while the student practices. One can think of many examples presently in use, but the idea is not at all limited to these. Suppose that someone wishes to learn to speak less aggressively or sarcastically to others, but finds this difficult to do. He and a "teacher" might practice talking in private on various topics that he normally talks on in day-to-day conversations. When an aggressive or sarcastic remark is made, they stop and find a better, more positive remark and then practice using it in various word-

ings. The student might collect a list of these and then practice letting the teacher verbally attack him, and then counter with a positive remark. The next stage could be trying this "in the field." The teacher could accompany the pupil and continue to give him feedback through use of pre-arranged signals, such as scratching his head whenever the student began using aggressive phrases.

Or, for another example, suppose one wishes to learn patience. He might use the technique found effective in programmed textbooks, *i.e.,* work in small steps capable of being handled. He might practice at tasks that involve increasing degrees of patience, never going on to a tougher problem before completely being able to handle the easier ones.

Examples of this sort are relatively easy to dream up. Some may be worth trying; others not. The point is that there is a general framework in community in which to try to produce better people, and as the community becomes more stable economically there will be more time to try these things. Perhaps Frazier was wrong—maybe something *can* be done with us first-generation Walden Two-ers.

FROM A READER

"Only recently have I discovered your existence in Twin Oaks and been introduced to the *Leaves.* With all due appreciation for your other efforts, I find that much to my chagrin you have maligned the personality of the pig *(Leaves,* September, 1967). Appreciating the pig only for its body, you have neglected and attacked the spirit of this animal.

"Unlike other domestic animals that have been bred to serve man in several ways, swine have been developed for the single purpose of meat production. Hence, most commonly the only good pig is a dead one. Such a phylogenetic and ontogenetic curse is of course bound to do something to their personality and undoubtedly leads to the feverishness with which the exploit the small pleasures of their transitory existence. Blame not the pig for his behavior but yourself for the curse that encourages occasional boorishness.

"Folklore has long recognized the pig as a behavioral system analogous to man and has often pointed out behavioral similarities between these two species. Both species are reputed to be intemperate at the trough, elaborate in courtship and marriage, and very intelligent; that is, they rapidly learn what you want them to do and then do just the opposite. At present experimental verification of such reputedly analogous behaviors is lacking, however. Nevertheless, at worse, pigs are simply a disturbing parody of their creators. When appreciated for more than just their bodies, they are a behaviorally interesting animal, of sound character, deserving no lesser status than other species.

"I will follow with interest your program at Twin Oaks. Enclosed please find $3 for twelve issues of the *Leaves.* With hopes that you will not ban pigs from the gates of Utopia, I am . . . . Sincerely yours, Jon Lien

Chapter Three: Year Two

LEAVES OF TWIN OAKS

NUMBER 6

April, 1968

GENERAL NEWS

WE GET OUTSIDE JOBS

During the month of March seven out of ten Twin Oaks members took local jobs in order to help out the Community cashbox. The necessity of doing so was no great shock. Since we began Twin Oaks last June we have known that it would become necessary, for we would surely run out of our savings, and almost as surely be slow to make a profit from our industries. We had thought, indeed, that last September would be the necessary date for job-getting. But in September we began to put up a building, which took until Christmas to complete. Again in January we contemplated working "outside" and decided to hang on, if possible, through the winter without doing so. With the coming of spring the bankbook showed a balance lower than our expected utility bills, and it was clear that there was no way to put it off any longer. We dutifully donned our coats and ties, or stockings and heels, and went job-hunting.

Our luck wasn't bad. A temporary placement service placed two of the women, each for a short period; the University Hospital in Charlottesville was glad to get our nurse and willing for her to work on a part-time and temporary basis. (Connie will work until she outgrows her uniforms. She expects a child in October.) Art classes were glad to get models, though this didn't work out well after all, because of scheduling and transportation problems. As to the men, the Virginia Employment Commission directed them to a man who wants 17,000 acres reseeded in pines—hard work for variable-sized crews.

Though this work is boring in the extreme, the arrangement seemed suitable to Twin Oaks' system, for it is no five-day week. Any of our men are acceptable as workers; any can work as many days or as few as he (or the Community) chooses. This makes it possible to put "commercial tree planting" on the labor credit system and let the men sign up for it, balancing the long hours and gruesome boredom against the advantages and disadvantages of other Community work.

All salaries from all of these jobs go directly, of course, into the Community bank account. Labor credits are given for actual hours' work, plus transportation time. Sometimes this means that a city worker works longer hours than a member who stays on the farm. These inequalities are easily settled by our surplus system, whereby the harder worker earns extra credits toward vacation time, taken at any convenient season, on or off the Community premises.

At first, when only one or two Community members were missing during the day, Community life went on much as usual. But as the outside work crew got larger, Community work suffered a sharp drop in quality. Most noticeable was the drop in the food standard. During one week when all the women were either employed or sick in bed, inexperienced men had to do the best they could with lunches and suppers. Sometimes the "best they could" was simple but good (meat loaf, baked potatoes, canned peas) — sometimes it was awful (fish roe on tortillas).

At this writing the Community has yet to adjust fully to the new schedule. Most difficult is the handling of visitors who come, let us say, on a Wednesday morning expecting to see a small community in full operation, and find only two or three members on the farm plus a couple of other visitors, as confused as themselves.

Certainly the situation is far from ideal. Of the outside workers, only Connie enjoys her work. Once again, as in pre-community days, the weekend becomes a longed-for oasis in a desert of boredom. As we plant pine seedlings or alphabetize checks we keep in mind that the work is necessary and that it is temporary.

P.S. TO THE OUTSIDE JOBS ARTICLE

Three weeks have passed since the above was written, and some interesting things have occurred. The men are becoming quite good cooks, for one thing. And the boys no longer plant pine seedlings. The reason: the job was so undesirable that it was not usually signed up for and had to be assigned by the labor credit manager, thus raising its labor credit value. When the value reached 1.4 credits per hour, other members protested that the money thus brought in was no longer worth the number of credits we had to pay for it. It was no longer feasible for the Community to send the men tree-planting, and the job was taken off the system. In case you find this mystifying, we intend to write more about labor credits in a future issue. In the meantime realize that any job that goes up to 1.4 credits per hour makes other members do more work, made necessary by the fact that the "highly paid" workers can meet their labor quota easily and leave work they would otherwise do to be distributed among others.

CHICKYCHICK

We regret to tell those of you who have learned to think of Chickychick as a member of Twin Oaks that we found her dead in her house last week. She had not been sick, and there was no evidence of any kind to let us know why we lost our only laying hen in her prime. It is not, of course, as an egg-layer that she is most mourned, but as the mascot of our early days. Like us, she came from the city and found the country very much superior. Like us, she had been a loner and had to learn to get along with others. Like us, her existence was not quite economically justifiable, but we thought her worthwhile anyway. Rest in peace, Chickychick.

YOUNG LIFE

Other activities in the chicken house are happier. Two bantam hens are cooperatively sitting on a dozen duck eggs. Psychologists warn us that the resulting ducklings will follow the bantam around as if she were their mother, and that the result will be mating confusion when they reach maturity. But this particular bunch is destined for the freezer before it quite reaches mating age, so we aren't too worried.

Silky delivered nine healthy piglets. One died (again of unknown causes) the next day. We are hoping to raise the remaining eight for our own consumption.

Our first calf was born in March—a male, and also intended for our own meat needs. Our next is expected in July.

We do not yet even approximate growing enough meat for our own table. We continue to buy chickens and hamburger every week at the grocery store. We are aiming at self-sufficiency in this department, but a complete breeding stock big enough to take care of a growing community and its guests requires more capital than we can dedicate to this purpose at one time. So we are doing it little by little. The latest acquisitions are eight goslings and a hive of bees.

HEALTH AND SICKNESS

Was it just last issue that we said we had had no Community diseases, not even a cold? It must have been just after that issue was mailed that our round of colds started. Someone spent a weekend in Washington and came back with a drizzly nose. One member after another got it or something like it, and the cycle did not completely stop until April.

More worrisome than the colds, though, was a mysterious ailment that we were all exposed to for more than a week before it was diagnosed as infectious hepatitis (again contracted in the city). Hepatitis is a bothersome disease for an individual, and a very serious one for a community. For how can we continue to invite visitors, on whom our growth depends in some measure if they would thereby be exposing themselves to a disease that keeps the patient bedridden for a month? As soon as we were sure of the facts (the sick member turned yellow), the Health Manager isolated him in his room and got the rest of us innoculated with Gamma Globulin (which gives partial protection). After that we carried on as usual, watching each day for symptoms in our own systems. Anybody nauseated? Lack of appetite? Diarrhea?

Except for one false alarm that kept one member isolated for four days, we have had no further signs of hepatitis, and we have long since passed the date when a second member might have caught the disease.

Some good things came out of this experience. The sick member got a six-month draft deferment. And the Community learned to be concerned with the spread of infections. Some of us are even in favor of partial isolation for bad colds.

HAMMOCKS

Spring is here, and it is hammock time. Twin Oaks' own hammocks are rarely idle. During the week the members rest in them in between jobs and in the evening; and on the weekends the guests take them over, particularly the children, who bounce and roll in them and drag their unsuspecting dogs into them and otherwise act generally like children in them.

We are pleased to see that the hammock is an excellent toy. It is probably superior to the average swing set in durability, flexibility and general enjoyment—and much better looking. It requires no upkeep and adds rather than detracts from the appearance of the yard. (What other toy can make that statement?)

Hammocks are traditionally for adults, of course, and that tradition still holds good, if you can get the kids out of them long enough.

Which hammock to buy? Most popular is the medium—particularly popular with retailers who are thinking of resale. Even the "small size" hammock is larger than the ordinary canvas kind. The medium gives a better margin of comfort; and the large is rather like a king-size bed: its feeling of extravagant luxury is worth the extra $5.

Cotton and polypropylene hammocks are the same price. The polypropylene is lighter, whiter, and mildew-proof. The cotton is preferred by some people because of its "natural" appearance.

The prices are $25, $30, and $35 respectively, sales tax and parcel post included. Send an extra dollar for shipping if you live west of the Mississippi. Make checks payable to Twin Oaks.

NEW COMMUNITIES

Opinion — By Scott

It is our confident assumption that Twin Oaks is and will continue to be a successful community. Among other things this means that our population will grow steadily, until something must be done about it.

Our present acreage will no doubt be expanded, and our fledgling industries will no doubt become great enterprises. We could perhaps grow indefinitely if we wanted to. But a community of ten million just wouldn't be the same. Even if there are no other limiting factors, there is our desire to remain small and decentralized. And so some day Twin Oaks will have to do something about its over-population.

There will be only one thing to do: our Community must fission and become two communities. This is what the ancient Greek city-states did and what Skinner's fictional community was pictured to be in the process of doing. It might be thought that another alternative would be for Twin Oaks simply to turn away applicants when its optimum size is reached. But of course we are not seeking utopia for ourselves alone, nor for just so many as might possibly be squeezed into one small community. Ours is a revolutionary endeavor, an attempt to remake the whole of society in the way society ought to be. In addition we must remember that communitarians, too, have babies; and are capable of home-growing their own over-populations.

The question, then, is not *if* Twin Oaks is to fission, but *when* and *under what conditions*. Just how big ought a community be, anyway? Aristotle thought that the polis should be small enough so that everyone could know everyone else (if only to avoid his company), but no smaller. He guessed that this would mean a community of perhaps 5000 free adult males. (Aristotle was disinclined to include women, children, and slaves under the heading "everyone"). To me, Aristotle's principle seems a good one, but his guess as to how many persons it entails seems high even when women and children are not discounted. In *Walden Two* Skinner guessed that the optimum size for a community would be somewhat less than 1000. Perhaps the sensible thing for us to do would be to wait and see how large we may grow without becoming strangers to each other, and when that danger looms near, to divide into two communities.

But there are other things besides a theoretical optimum size to consider—at least at present. For one thing, there are the tactics of the Walden Two "revolution." Perhaps we could attract more people to the cause if it were geographically decentralized, for example. If this were thought to be very important it might justify our fissioning before we would otherwise need to. Then too, the mere fact that we could say "and now we are two" might be important for proving to the not-so-stouthearted that we really *are* the coming thing and that maybe they should join us after all.

Of much more importance are two considerations forced on us by the character of the U.S. government. Let us be truthful: democracy or not, the American government today is a tyrannical, oppressive organization that is incapable of fair play, whether at home or abroad. It does whatever it can get away with, which—quite literally—is murder. What few sane men there are in this world have no trouble recognizing American policy in Vietnam to be genocide, pure and simple. Any group capable of the worst imaginable crime is best assumed capable of the lesser ones, too. Like closing down a successful communal experiment at home.

Perhaps the government will never bother with us specifically; but even so, its general invasions of individual freedom will necessitate the founding of new communities outside the country. Even now a major obstacle to the growth of Twin Oaks is the fact that if our sympathizers in

44

colleges were to join us, they would be drafted because of the loss of their student deferments. As I write this there is a student and his wife visiting us who have said they would join the Community except for the draft situation.

And then there is that *other* consideration: as one Community member put it, "We've got to get out of the bull's eye." The government cannot be counted on to prevent a nuclear war. Indeed, it can almost be counted on *to* bring this catastrophe about, sooner or later. It is quite possible that World War III has already begun.

Twin Oaks is 100 miles from Washington, D.C., and it is remotely possible that it might survive a nuclear war, and that other communities within this country might. But if it is difficult for radicals to live in this country now, think how much worse it would probably be then. War always does bad things for human liberty.

It is thus obvious that new communities will have to be founded outside the U.S., and founded as soon as we are able. When will that be, and where?

We don't know for sure. There is no strict timetable or formal plan as yet. However, there is much sentiment for starting the next community in Canada as soon as we have about fifty people here in Virginia. That could very easily be within a couple of years. Canada is attractive because it is easily accessible, has no draft, will accept draft evaders from the U.S., has a stable, half-liberal government, and offers the possibility of free or inexpensive land.

The third community will quite possibly be in South America. (Even the remotest places in the northern hemisphere would be imperiled by an all-out nuclear war.) Many places are even now being investigated.

And what about Twin Oaks? Will it be abandoned? Not until life in this country is intolerable. Persecuted individuals will of course escape to the communities outside the country; but not until the whole community is threatened will the whole community pack up and leave. Hopefully by then there will be many communities in exile to welcome the escaping Twin Oakers.

PERFECTION AND MAKING DO

Opinion — By Scott

The idea that everything ought always to be perfect is a persistent one. We should hope and expect this to be so in the thinking of those who regard themselves as utopians. However, there are times when this idea can be unhealthy. It is unhealthy if it interferes with the attainment of utopia.

How could the notion that all should be perfect interfere with the attainment of universal perfection? It is not so difficult as it may at first seem. Suppose, for example, that in Utopia no one should have to work as much as four hours a day. Still, to achieve that leisure-filled state of existence it may be necessary for the pioneers to work six, eight, or even ten hours a day. If a pioneer insists that, even so, despite all the work to be done, that *he* is only going to work four hours a day *because this is the way things ought*

to be, then he may be dooming the attempt to achieve the situation where a four-hour day is really possible.

Things do not get to be the way they ought to be by merely wishing them so, or merely "deciding" that they shall be so. We are not gods.

Our program must be realistic. We must not suppose that we are capable of all things or that we can afford to do just as we please. We must always remember that our resources —labor, financial, and otherwise—are limited and that severe priorities must be established.

If a member's pet project has to be postponed or abandoned, it is regrettable. But it cannot be helped. If steaks and orange juice cannot be purchased, we must be willing to do without and not let it distress us. If a piece of machinery, however desirable, costs more than the Community can afford, we must do without it and not give up our efforts. A tractor may need to lie idle because we cannot immediately purchase a needed part. A field may need to go unhoed because we have not enough labor. It is of no avail to say that we must have *x* or that we cannot do without *x*. If need be we can do without anything. It is all a question of priorities. We do what we can and we try not to be upset that we can do no more. A dedicated communitarian simply *must* be willing to make do with what we have.

People in the outside world are not willing to do much to see Utopia realized. (Proof: they are not here at Twin Oaks working with us.) So we must be willing to do all the more.

But, after all, it is nothing outrageous we are asking of ourselves. A forty- or fifty-hour work-week is no worse than what most of humanity endures. We eat better than most people do. And we have a much better social situation —even now.

Still, we have not achieved all that we hope to. Things are not "as they ought to be" just yet and it will be some time before they are. We have every reason to expect a gradual improvement in our situation, but we must also expect setbacks and retrenchments from time to time.

One thing we must always remember: perfection cannot be achieved unless we are willing to make do without it in the interim.

A GENERAL STATEMENT ABOUT
OPINION ARTICLES

The *Leaves of Twin Oaks* publishes, from time to time, serious articles written by different members of the Community. These articles always appear under the name of the author: you have seen articles by Dusty, Rudy, and now Scott. It should be understood that such articles represent the opinion of the writer and are not intended to describe any general opinion or policy of Twin Oaks Community as an organization. Twin Oaks has no official political position, no opinion of the United States' or any other government. Even within the Community there is great diversity of opinion on national and international issues. It is not to be supposed, therefore, that we are all leftists, or that we all think Walden Four should be in South America, or even that we are all willing to let the tractor sit in the fields for lack of a spare part. Signed articles are the opinion of the writers thereof. Unsigned articles are mostly by Kathleen and are supposed to be free of controversial material.

As to the Community, we take a clear stand on many subjects, ranging from economics to child care, but our stand on such subjects is always internal. We believe, for instance, in equal opportunity for individuals of all races and both sexes; but we are not prepared to enforce such a standard anywhere except within the confines of our voluntary association.

Obviously the best thing for us to do is to let you hear from many different members through articles in the *Leaves*, so that you may get an idea of the overall attitudes toward issues you may be interested in. But for a political statement of policy from the Community itself you will look in vain. There isn't one.

LETTERS FROM READERS

"This issue was the first I've received. I'm a new subscriber, and I liked it. I didn't know what to expect but I greatly liked this. But why, outside of Rudy, must the apparently sole other contributor be left anonymous? (And who is Rudy, by the way?) I liked the style and attitude; I'd like to know who I'm reading. And I'd like to know, also, who else is there with you. I know there are at least three more (one goes for Dylan; one enjoys silence, etc.) But why this reticence? . . . If you want to tell us things, why not tell us about some of your members? About all of them? How about giving a different profile each issue? What are their names, what do they do, where are they from, what did they leave, and maybe, why are they there now? Let us identify. . ."

— E.F., Brooklyn, New York

Twin Oaks comments:

This suggestion is under consideration. A number of correspondents have expressed a desire to know something about the individuals who live here. If we do decide to do any "profiles," however, they will tell only about the members as they are in the Community. For example, if Dr. Skinner were a member and we chose to do a profile on him, it might read something like this: Fred. Manager of behavioral engineering; manager of correspondence. Then it would go on to tell of his hobbies, his particular interest in community and maybe some of his miscellaneous opinions. And if you really wanted to know something about him, you would read the article subtitled Opinion — By Fred.

"As a public accountant, one constantly beset and bemused by tax returns of all kinds—and furthermore, one who has been working toward evolving the most practicable of Utopias given the structure of our present society and the intrinsic nature of the transcendental man—may I say that your gratuitous insult in the March issue really stuck in my craw. I am referring to:

Are there accountants with utopian dreams? Are there utopians with accounting ability? Neither seems likely somehow.

"Not only is it bloody well likely — it's for real, as I can personally testify to. But what is more important than my tender ego is the implicit assumption that only certain types can go utopian, or that utopianism requires a certain detachment from the grubby and tedious details of taking the measure of one's days, embalming them in crass, lifeless commercial shorthand and interring them forever in some useless black book whose only function is to rat on you to Washington.

"Firstly, accounting, if rightly used, is a creative art whose function in a utopian society can lead to the avoidance of a lot of grief and moreover, point the way to the greatest utilization of time, human effort, and capital toward the realization of your goals. . .

"Secondly, utopianism is the most practical of all pursuits. After all, the major thesis is that there is a best way to live, and the utopian tries to live it. . . Just what is so nutty about that? It's only because of the brainwashing we've been subjected to that states that work must be endured for its own sake and the money it brings, whether that work is distasteful if not downright unbearable—that life must be competitive, guaranteeing perpetual strife and tension—and that joy is an emotion you buy in a bottle, a showroom, or a store but never develop in your self. Only the thoroughly twisted psyches of our society could accept pain and suffering as "practical" and dismiss a call to a better life as "dreaming."

"Why am I lecturing to you who are building your utopia while I sit out here perpetuating society's misery? Because you. . .of all people, talk of utopian *dreams* and say accountants (the public image—unimaginative, no-nonsense, *practical* types) couldn't possibly *dream* the BIG dream. . .

"Are you trying to tell me utopians are dreamers and that practical types need not apply? Haven't you unconsciously fallen for the twaddle you're trying to disengage from? Why don't you switch words and tell it like it is. *Your* dreams are PLANS and *their* dreams are nightmares!! "

— M.A., Brooklyn, New York

Twin Oaks comments:

The above letter is quoted only in part. It went on to give specific practical advice about Twin Oaks' tax returns. So helpful has that writer been, in fact, that we are wondering if we should write faintly insulting articles about other professions—say doctors and dentists. Here goes: we think all doctors and dentists are too money-grubbing to be interested in utopia. Do I have any takers?

GENERAL NEWS

OUR POPULATION EXPLODES

For a year there were ten of us. That isn't quite accurate: we started with eight, and we went as high as twelve members; some people came and some people left, and some did both, within the twelve-month period. But as far as the use of our facilities was concerned, we figured an average of ten people.

Then in June our population doubled. June is a natural month for people to move—school is out then, affecting students, teachers, and parents. It is perfectly natural, then, that more than ten additional members should join Twin Oaks all in one month. Twin Oaks of course welcomed the new members—is not growth one of our main aims? Nevertheless, there was a sense of shock when it happened, a sense of things being out of hand.

For one thing, you no longer know everybody. In place of an environment where everyone is either your close friend or your well-understood opponent, it was suddenly a place filled with strangers' faces, unaccustomed noises, unpredictable opinions. For another, though the population was double, the facilities remained the same.

Take the meals. Last year we filled our plates from a small serving table and all sat around another table to eat supper. This year we line up for ten minutes before we can even get to the food, and when we have filled our plates, we scatter in four or five directions, indoors and out, to eat.

This year you might see someone at suppertime and say to him, "Hey, I haven't seen you all day." That wasn't possible last year.

Then there's the swimming hole. We used the river in 1967, you may recall, for necessary bathing because our water supply was insufficient. In 1968 we still use the river for necessary bathing, but this time because the number of members makes it difficult to find the bathroom free. Another difference in the swimming is that the river is rarely unoccupied now; almost at any hour you can count on company if you want to swim.

There are a lot of advantages to a bigger group. You have more choice of companions, for instance. There are members who are always quiet and pleasant, and one seeks them out when one wants peace. And there are others willing to discuss a disgruntlement, in case one is in *that* kind of a mood. The group is big enough now to have several people who enjoy singing, a few who are interested in learning to dance, a number who play or attempt to play various instruments.

Among the newcomers are needed skills, too. One is an excellent cook; another likes to repair cars; one is a dairy specialist; another a typist with a typing speed in the 80's. (No, no doctor yet, but we haven't given up hope.)

There are disadvantages, too, to the sudden growth of Twin Oaks. It is clear that there is not really space enough for us to live as comfortably as we want, not nearly enough for the workshops we need. Not enough money for the equipment, tools, and materials that would make our lives smoother. In addition, the sudden influx was a psychological shock. Newcomers questioned things that old people had taken for granted. Newcomers had brilliant inspirations that the old people considered and discarded months previously. Every important item of Walden Two and the Code had to be defended anew. The first month wasn't easy.

Some of us think that community growth in the future will be easier if we make it a point not to allow so large an influx of members in any one short period of time. The integration of new members should surely be easier if we took them two or three at a time instead of by the dozen.

But, confusion and annoyance notwithstanding, we seem to to recovering from the shock, and integration has already begun. Friendships have formed between "old" and "new" members, and the line between them is already becoming fuzzy.

WE PREPARE FOR WINTER

Last year we planted a garden, harvested and processed it, and still ran out of our own food well before December, 1967. This year we resolved to make better estimates. Our farm manager planted twelve long rows of beans, an acre of corn, and corresponding quantities of other vegetables that do well in our area. The first part of July saw the beginning of the pressure to get these things frozen and canned for winter, and now in August we are still at it.

The snap beans came in first. We canned over 700 quarts of snap beans, in addition to some that we sun-dried, and in addition to the dry beans that ripen on the vine. That we stopped when we did is not due to any shortage of beans; we do not know how many more quarts we could have processed if we had picked all that the garden produced for us. But we began to count the number of days in a year and figure out just how many beans any one little community can eat, anyway; and our food processing manager reluctantly called a halt to the bean canning and gave his attention to the corn.

Corn comes in all at once, and an acre is a lot, in case you wondered. It has to be stripped from the cob, because we have no room in our freezers for frozen corn-on-the-cob. This time we canned only 350 quarts. We could have eaten more than that, perhaps, but the corn ripens too fast and our labor could get just so much of it put away. Our biggest impediment is freezer space. We have four freezers, all jammed full, and we are forced to can most of what we want to preserve. What we need is a big, walk-in freezer; but our financial affairs have not permitted its construction to date. We are trying to get a root cellar dug before fall. We need it already, to store our potatoes in.

Tomatoes are coming in now, and the apples have begun to ripen. Also, there are the cucumbers and okra and squashes. Next month the watermelons will be ripe. It will be well into October before this work will be done.

CONSTRUCTION PROJECTS

A building to house our increased population this winter has not yet begun, primarily because of the tremendous labor demands that the food processing and farming have made on the group. But smaller construction projects have been partly accomplished. The attic to the small farmhouse, for instance, now has a floor so that it can be occupied this winter as a bedroom. (It is not suitable for summer habitation because it is too hot.) The farmhouse, as a matter of fact, is quite different from what it was the first year. The room that formerly served as a living room is now an auxiliary kitchen, where canning and freezing are carried on and in which it is planned to do all the dishwashing as soon as we get the appropriate plumbing done. The office, which once did double duty as a bedroom, now does double duty as a dining room, instead. The kitchen, too, has been changed. At this time last year we had a table in the kitchen where the overflow from the dining room ate. Some time ago that table was converted to serving only. But when the group suddenly became larger, we built a serving counter, cafeteria style, to expedite things. In the plans, but not yet complete, are flour and sugar bins and other built-ins.

THE WEATHER

Spring was late, but summer has more than made up for it. It is *hot* in central Virginia. The heat comes in spells of four or five days, then cools somewhat with a light rain or a breeze, then starts over with the heat again. Although the Community owns several air conditioners, we have elected not to use them, because the cost of running them is prohibitive. The new building, though quite comfortable at night, is unpleasantly warm during the day. The farmhouse, though better insulated, has a huge stove going most of the day for meal preparation and canning. That leaves two places on the farm where one can keep cool. One is the group of hammocks underneath the apple trees; the other is the river. The latter is by far the fastest way of cooling off and is preferred by most of the group. The river varies from day to day, depending on the rainfall. Sometimes it is shallow enough that you can stand up on the bottom; other times it is high enough to make nonswimmers cling to innertubes. It is always wet and cool, however, an instant relief from the heat. We congratulate ourselves, once more, on our choice of this farm, which was greatly influenced by its possession of this river frontage.

A BABY IN COMMUNITY

Old subscribers will remember Elliott, the four-year-old who was with us in 1967. Elliott went away at the beginning of this year to live once more with his mother, and we were without children until June. Now once again there are children on the premises, with all their attendant joys and problems. Theron, aged 7, has not yet had any special community care. He plays by himself and with the older young people. One member plays chess with him, another is teaching him to swim. Theron's satisfaction with Twin Oaks stems largely from his new freedom. He tells his mother with some regularity that she is no longer his boss. He is a member just like everybody else, and he will sleep through breakfast if he pleases. His mother, being a sensible person (people who join Twin Oaks tend to be sensible people) takes this independence in good part, not ceasing to watch her son and encourage him to eat some vegetables now and then, but leaving him largely to feel out his privileges and responsibilities in community.

Zandra, aged 13 months, is less aware of the revolutionary nature of community. What interests her about Twin Oaks is that it is remarkably full of fun things to do — for instance, climb into the tub of the dogs' drinking water and splash, throw the newly snapped beans around in all directions, climb up and down the front porch steps, chase kittens, bury her fingers in the grown cats' fur, and generally explore her environment. Twin Oaks' first step toward community childraising was to put Zandra's care on the labor credit system in two-hour blocks, starting at 8:00 a.m. and ending at 10:30 p.m. Although any member may sign up for child care, only about eight members have elected to do so. Those who care for her give her an interesting variety of experience. One reads to her for an hour or so at a time (*The Hobbit*, if you're interested), claiming that according to an experiment he read about, being read to between the ages of one and two increases reading ability at a later age. Some members think this is a waste of time, but no one has been able to discern that it does Zandra any harm or that she objects to it in any way. So the reading goes on. Some members consistently sign up for the hours when Zandra gets her bottle and drifts off to sleep; others avoid this hour and take her during the period when their chief duty is following her around and preventing her from doing herself any damage in her explorations. Zandra's biological parents take a large share of her care and keep a watchful eye on her generally. Our general approach to childraising theory so far has been to accustom Zandra to multiple parents gradually but firmly and otherwise keep her free from frustration. Since she has been with us only two months, we cannot take full credit for her sunny charm; she was a happy baby when she arrived and she is a happy baby now. We are aware that this is an easy age, and that there may be more difficult things ahead.

Our next baby will be born at Twin Oaks. We announced in our last issue that Connie expects a baby the first part of October. Connie will have the baby in the nearby Louisa

Hospital and is arranging with her doctor to follow the Lamaze Pavlovian natural childbirth methods.

When the baby comes home, we would like to have an aircrib for it. The aircrib, an invention of Dr. Skinners', is a temperature-controlled glassed-in unit that takes the place of crib and playpen, and which protects young babies from diseases and excess noise. The aircrib makes a great deal of sense for Twin Oaks, because of the temperature control problem we have—a large building and a wood-coal furnace. There is no possibility of doing anything about our heating system this year; but an aircrib, with its temperature control system, could protect the new baby from colds and general discomfort, the necessity for excess clothing and heavy blankets, etc. The aircrib costs over $200 new, which is a difficult amount for Twin Oaks to part with. It is possible that we could make one, but even our time is in heavy demand. It has occurred to us that one of our readers may possibly know where we could obtain one that has been used. We are aware that they are not common, but then, who knows what our particular readership may have stuck away in the attic?

WE GIVE LECTURES

Augmenting our income slightly these days is a new business for Twin Oaks—namely, visiting interested groups and giving talks about the Community. This is fun to do, and there is always the possibility of finding here or there a really interested person who may want to join or contribute in some other way. The main difficulty Twin Oaks' visiting lecturers have had is with the length of their speeches. One member found that she could talk about Twin Oaks for two and a half hours straight without the slightest difficulty. This is a fairly useless talent when your audience wants you to restrain yourself to forty minutes and leave time for a question period besides. So we are cutting our speeches, keeping in mind that most audiences want a few basic facts told in an amusing fashion and will not be disappointed if they are left in the dark as to the exact workings of the labor credit system or the precise means by which a member may requisition a pair of shoes.

AUTOMOBILE PROBLEMS

One of the advantages of a new community when it starts out is that each member brings with him items of good quality that have a lot of good left in them, which means that the Community doesn't have to go right out and buy hundreds and hundreds of necessary items. Take personal clothing, for example. Twin Oaks has bought almost no clothing for its members, who manage to get along on what they brought with them. Then there are the dishes and pots and bed linens and hand tools. True, sheets wear out and dishes break, and their replacement has to be accomplished little by little. Still, the head start from every member's personal closets will take us a long way.

Then there are the automobiles. There is a dismal fact well known to all automobile owners and much moaned by all poor ones, and that is that automobiles break down. Twin Oaks' members brought with them a Volkswagen, a Saab, a Falcon, a Dart, a Pontiac, and a Rambler. In addition, the Corporation itself owns the school bus-truck and another old Volkswagen. In the space of one year that we have been on the land, most of these have broken down. We have replaced engines in the Dart, the school bus, and the Volkswagen (cannibalizing the other VW to do it). The Falcon managed to get its owner to the Community but gave up its last breath a week after it got here. The Saab we had to tow 75 miles home after it threw a rod in the middle of the night last winter. In addition to engine problems, three of the vehicles have had repeated brake trouble.

Twin Oaks has several members who have a mechanical bent, but none who are professional mechanics. They try to do as much of the mechanical work as possible here on the farm, in spite of our lack of proper equipment, and to take the cars to a garage only when necessary. We generally keep three cars running, really a bare minimum for a community of over twenty people, especially when one of the cars is used daily to take "outside" workers back and forth to their city jobs. Our rate of automobile breakdown is increasing, and it is clear that we are going to have to allocate more money to keep our vehicles on the road.

MILK FOR THE COMMUNITY

The Milk Cow has been a Twin Oaks theme since even before the Community was founded. Back when we were just having meetings, feeling out each other's opinions and making up our bylaws, we ran into a problem about the milk cow. The problem was simply that some of us thought we ought to buy one right away and some of us thought we should go without one. The pro-cow people argued that the price of a cow is easily made up for within its first year by the savings in milk alone, let alone butter and other goodies, and let alone the sale of the calves she produces, that milk is a wholesome food and would put us on the road to self-sufficiency. The anti-cow people argued that milk is a luxury for adults, that we can drink iced tea and Kool-Aid and supplement with powdered milk for cooking, that milking a cow is a pain in the neck, that the labor that goes into butter-making is a ridiculous waste of time, and that it is pointless to try to be self-sufficient. The argument was a hot and bitter one, and at the time it seemed easiest for all concerned just not to argue about it any more (and therefore not buy a cow, either). So we drank iced tea and Kool-Aid and supplemented our diet with powdered milk, and the pro-cow people waited, until one day they discovered that the purchase price of a milk-cow could be justified by the amount we were spending on powdered milk alone. This new argument held some attention and nearly defeated the opposition, except for one new fact. During the period when the argument had been set aside to spare personal feeling, we had run low on money, and there was no longer anything to buy a cow with. So the milk cow argument was dropped a while longer.

Then one member got a tax refund check (technically under our rules her own money and not the Community's) and offered to buy a cow with it. The group considered this but, in deference to the opposition, agreed that we would first shop around in the neighborhood and try to buy some milk from one of our neighbors who kept a cow, to find out if we would be able to drink raw milk (for, said the anti-cow people, raw milk is quite funny tasting, and it makes you sick if you're not used to it). We shopped around and asked our neighbors, but their cows were all dry at the time.

The pro-cow people began to talk cow again, and to discuss what breed we wanted (we vacillated between a Guernsey and an Ayershire) when we were visited by a professional dairy man (Max) who owned several cows, and who announced that he wanted to join the Community! Obviously the thing to do was not to go out and buy a cow, but to wait until this new member could join us bringing with him not only his cow and two heifers, but his skill in handling them, and his daughter, who reputedly could milk ten cows before going to school in the morning. This was January, and the family could not join us until June, but we agreed to wait. Whenever a pro-cow person would sigh about ice cream or whipped cream, or somebody would moan for a glass of real milk, we would say "Wait until June. It won't be long now."

June came, and so did Max and his family and Honeydew, the cow, and the two heifers. Just now, though, Max told us, Honeydew is dry. She's due to freshen July 15. We cried a little but petted Honeydew and told her she was a nice cow and waited.

Honeydew gave birth to Holly on July 11, and a week later we had fresh milk and cream (reserving some for Holly also). We would like to tell you that at this point all our milk problems were solved and that everyone was happy, but this is not quite the case. The fact is that Honeydew is only one cow; and though she is an excellent milker, one cow cannot supply twenty-five people, including a bottle baby, with as much milk as they want. Sometimes indeed, we mix the whole milk with powdered milk in order to make it go farther. The morning's milking is always completely gone before the evening's milking is brought from the barn. The milk tastes exactly like milk, and nobody got in the least sick from it. The only problem is quantity. Fortunately, the other two heifers are due to freshen in September and December, respectively, which will give us a more than adequate supply, including enough for ice cream and those other things we used to dream about.

THE OPEN DOOR CLOSES A LITTLE

We have often mentioned that we welcome visitors at Twin Oaks. Sometimes people question us about this policy, asking how we can maintain this practice. Other communi-

ties, we are told, have had to restrict visiting for various reasons. For the first ten months of our community existence, we didn't feel that any restrictions were necessary. We kept our economic head above water by charging a small amount for meals and asking the guests to participate in the work. Guests' questions stimulated us and actually helped us clarify our ideals and goals.

In April, however, it began to be evident that a limit had to be set. More and more of our time was being devoted to showing people around and discussing the utopian view, defending our position as instruments of social change, arguing with the Summerhillians (who think we are too behavioristic) and with the behaviorists (who think we are too Summerhillian), and so forth. It is fun, but there are only a few of us, and enough is enough.

The question is how and where to cut down on the visitors. A complete ban is out of the question. Among our visitors, after all, are our future members, and we never know who they are until they declare themselves. Besides, the people who come here are almost always intelligent and interesting, and we don't want to cut ourselves off from them.

It is hard to divide our guests into categories for purposes of discrimination, but we have had to do it; and what we come up with is this: we enjoy most those visitors who stay with us for several days; we are most often misunderstood by people who come for just a day or an afternoon. If we have to eliminate anybody, then, let us make it on the basis of time.

To put it succinctly, we would prefer that persons who want to visit us *not* drop by on Sunday afternoon planning to return home that night. Come and stay with us for several days; work with us; eat with us; talk with us. But for your Sunday afternoon drive in the country, don't take in Twin Oaks.

SCHOOL STARTS

There are five school-age young people at Twin Oaks this fall, and four of them are attending public school. The choice (between being educated in the Community and going to public school) was left to the young people themselves and somewhat to their parents. Major among the reasons for choosing public school is the matter of accreditation. The Community is young and insecure. Its scant year of existence does not inspire sufficient confidence that it will still exist and provide a full and satisfying life for the next fifty years. So it is natural for parents to be wary of having their children drop out of the accredited system. There is the matter of the diploma, or of being accepted in the proper grade in case he should leave the Community and go elsewhere, etc.

None of which changes the fact that one of Twin Oaks prime interests is the education of its young. So we turn our attention to the one student who has elected to be educated on the premises, Susan, grade 10.

There are two schools of thought among Twin Oaks members as to the proper approach to education. One point of view is that Twin Oaks has to offer to its children at least the equivalent of what public school offers, and on top of that can present whatever is interesting or worth learning. The other view is that the material taught in the public schools is mostly irrelevant to living, and that the children should be taught whatever they choose to learn, whether it results in a balanced program or not. Susan presents no problem to either of these theories. She was left entirely free to choose her own curriculum, and she chose subjects that she might have studied in high school. She is taking English composition, Spanish conversation, history of the Renaissance, chemistry, plane geometry, and secretarial skills (including typing, shorthand, and bookkeeping).

It is too early to evaluate Twin Oaks' education. Only two days of classes have taken place at this writing. We can only say what we plan. Classes are scheduled from 9:00 a.m. until noon, five days a week. (Saturday through Wednesday, so that some of our public-school attenders can sit in on Twin Oaks classes on weekends if they want to.) The classes are contingent on an acceptable student-teacher relationship. That is, if either party feels that the class is not worthwhile, it will be dropped and something else substituted in its place. Susan is not required to take classes at all, but incentive is provided by the giving of labor credits for classwork (if you don't want to study, you can always wash dishes). Classes are generally held in the house trailer living room, but there are exceptions. The first Spanish-conversation class this fall was held in the swimming hole, standing waist deep in water. (It was a very hot day, and that particular class requires no textbooks or paper work.) The advantages of the private tutoring approach to education are of course obvious. All of Susan's classes are prepared precisely for her. There is no question of waiting for the slow ones or rushing ahead to meet a deadline or preparing for tests or meeting a grade standard. The subjects offered are limited only by the knowledge of the adult members available to teach, and sometimes not even by that. For example, no one here knows shorthand, but we thought it a desirable thing to learn, so teacher and pupil are tackling the subject together.

In the meantime the public school headaches begin. Is it all right for a Walden Two person to go out for football? How about cheerleading? If so, does a member get credits for driving the participants to the games? Do the kids have to take the school bus or will the Community drive them to school?, etc., etc., etc.

WE CELEBRATE OUR ANNIVERSARY

Though we don't pay much attention to most holidays, it seemed appropriate that we should do something special to commemorate the 16th of June, when we completed our first full year on the farm. We had very little idea how to celebrate it. Parades and speeches just didn't seem appropriate.

What we finally hit upon was calling a holiday from ⌐ but the most necessary labor credits and having special things to eat. We asked every "old" member, "What foods have you missed here at Twin Oaks that you would like to have served on our anniversary?" The requests were varied, but there was a heavy emphasis on breakfast. Orange juice and sausage were in demand. One member wanted "Cap'n Crunch for breakfast, lunch, and supper." Another hungered for potato chips and onion dip. Everybody wanted real milk. We planned our menu as best we could around this miscellaneous assortment, adding strawberry shortcake to make the day complete.

Other than eating, we didn't do much that was very special. Some went right ahead and worked on hammocks or farming. Some got together and sang folk songs. A small folk dance session was held. The day passed quietly, and we went to bed with strawberries on our breath.

WHAT ABOUT THE PEOPLE?

Several letters have requested information about Twin Oaks members. So I have been searching for little ways to get the members to reveal their personalities through the *Leaves.*

"Tell me one thing you like about the Community," I said to Skip, "and one thing you don't like."

"What for?" asked Skip.

"For the *Leaves,*" I said. "It makes interesting reading. The people out there want to hear from the membership."

"Do you want something profound, or something funny?" asked Skip.

"Either," I said. "Anything at all, as long as it's printable."

"Well, let me think about it." said Skip.

And "let me think about it" was just what almost every other member said when asked the same thing. I let them think, and then I collected the following remarks:

Skip—

One thing I like is the fact that Twin Oaks has been able to attract people from various walks of life, of various ages and skills, engineer, dairy breeder, psychologist, secretary, revolutionary, mechanic, philosopher; that we are not, as you might expect, a uniform group of young radicals.

One thing I don't like is that we haven't made any organized effort to solve interpersonal problems.

George—

What do I like? Well, the food is pretty good. Also this one-day laundry service is something. I bring over my clothes in the morning, and they are delivered back to my room the same day.

What I can't stand is that nobody around here will take a project and see it through to the end.

Bud—

The best thing is the close relationship between what we produce and what we consume.

What I don't care for is the pedantic equalitarianism.

Susan—

The best thing around here is the swimming hole.

The worst thing is the long, hot walk to and from the swimming hole.

Tamar—

The wonderful thing is that everyone accepts you as soon as you get here.

The bad thing is the heat—especially hoeing in the heat.

Kinch—

What I like is working together with other people and being in a group.

I can't think of anything I dislike.

Terry—

I like the variability of schedule—different work from day to day.

I don't like the fact that there isn't enough space for private hobbies.

Donna—

I like the fact that my work here promotes my own goals more than it did on the outside and that I have some choice of whom I work with.

But it is hard to find a place to be alone or to have a private conversation or to study, and I am a great deal bothered by the lack of plumbing facilities.

Max—

I like the fact that Chareen (daughter) can have a pre-planned schedule of work along with the adults, rather than being at the beck and call of her parents.

One thing I don't like is the failure of communication between members, when it is so necessary, living so close together.

Theron—

I like being able to stay up as late as I want. Also, I like the majority of the food.

I don't like breakfast being served so early, so I have to get up early if I want any.

Connie—

I like the farm life — just living in the country.

However, I would like to see the house stay cleaner.

Chareen—

What I like is that there is always somebody around. I can always find someone to talk to. So if my mother and father aren't there, I don't get lonesome.

I don't like the outhouse much. It doesn't smell good.

Carnell—

It's nice that I don't have to take care of Zandra all the time and that I don't have to cook all the time.

But there could be more cooperation from other members in keeping the house clean.

Kathleen—

Life here is stimulating. I may at times be annoyed, distressed, or wretched; but I am never bored.

On the other hand, there is very little peace. We have taken on a project of such dimensions that there is always something to worry about, always a problem needing a solution, always several problems that have no solutions. It takes nerves of steel, and I haven't got them.

Rudy—

This is the nearest to Walden Two of any place I know about.

But it isn't near enough.

NUMBER 8

December, 1968

GENERAL NEWS

TWIN OAKS SCHOOLING CONTINUES

We told you last time about our decision to educate one high-schooler on the premises as a beginning of our community education program. We are now three months into this program and feel ready to make some evaluations.

We have to admit that Twin Oaks schooling at this point does not have the smooth continuity that public school does. Susan was progressing at a good rate through a geometry text, for example, when her geometry teacher, threatened by the draft, took off for Canada. Now someone else must take up the geometry lessons, and there is bound to be a difference in the approach. We are not at all sure, though, that this enforced variety doesn't have its good points.

Susan has elected to slow down her progress in other subjects in order to take up a brief course (together with other interested members) in speed reading. She is free to do the same at any time with any subject that interests her and that she can find someone to direct her in. It could be basket-weaving or symbolic logic or learning to play the autoharp.

So far Susan has stuck with the subjects she started with (a fairly long list of academic subjects ranging from chemistry to shorthand) and is making good progress in all of them. There is no testing, of course, no grading, and no specific required rate of progress, not even compulsory attendance. Susan comments:

"I am finding myself interested in more and more things. I keep running into things I want to study about. It's really a lot of fun to just learn."

FOOD FROM THE FARM

More and more of our diet comes now from our own farm and our own labor. In addition to the milk products, our own ducks, pork, and beef are served; all of our vegetables (except lettuce and celery, which we haven't been successful with yet) come from our garden. Even our evening snacks quite often consist of home-grown popcorn in home-churned butter.

True, we can't raise rice or macaroni, but we are learning to eat more potatoes and less of other starches. True, also, that our sugar has to come from the Safeway. But honey and homemade sorghum fill part of our sweet tooth. Our grocery list tends more and more to consist of just those things we cannot grow in Virginia—bananas, coffee, chocolate, spices—and those things we cannot grow at all— parafin, detergents, toothpaste.

LECTURING AGAIN

We got a call last month from Lafayette College, up in Pennsylvania, asking if we would send a speaker for their Psychology Club. We said we would be delighted and sent a representative November 19, who reports as follows:

"It was great fun. I spoke or answered questions for about five different groups, I think. They asked everything under the sun. Some of the questions were sympathetic, some challenging, a few hostile. Some of the questions got pretty far out—like what we would do under a given circumstance in the dim future. I believe someone wanted to know what we would do if the Community had a couple, and the woman had a child, and the father left the Community and wanted to take the child, but he wasn't the legal parent, and the mother didn't care who got the child? Would we try for custody? To tell you the truth, I didn't have the faintest idea, and I was glad when one of the professors got me off the hook by asking what we would do if some Martians invaded Twin Oaks. That broke up the question session. Generally speaking, the students were very alert and intelligent. The faculty I met were a very superior bunch—very warm and immensely alive. I'm not charging any labor credits for the faculty lunch, nor for the psychology class where I answered questions for an hour and a half without stopping, nor for the final coffee hour. Most of the credits I'm requesting are for the bus trip. I want full credits for that. These speeches at colleges are probably good for us. We earn a little money, and have a good time doing it. I don't know if we make any converts or not. . ."

BRAND NEW MEMBER

Connie gave birth to Lisa Kay on October 5 in the local Louisa Hospital. Lisa has dark hair, eyes of indefinite color, and generally looks and acts like a baby.

Nobody on our mailing list, apparently, knew about any used aircribs, so we made our own. The materials for the aircrib cost nearly $100, but its construction compares well with commercial models currently available. It is made of plexiglas and plywood.

We are not prepared to say just yet how important we think the aircrib is or how well we like it. Lisa has thus far spent most of her time outside it, being fed and held and generally adored.

WORK SATISFACTION

"Do you feel," asked a visitor not long ago, "that the things you do from day to day have more meaning than what you might be doing on the 'outside'?" It doesn't take much thinking to answer that question. Emphatically yes. Even if it's only washing dishes or picking beans, we are putting in our time and effort toward making this Community work, and the meaningfulness transcends the exact kind of work we do. However, the question reminds some of us of the work we sometimes do on the "outside," and perhaps this deserves a comment all by itself. One of us went to the city to do some office work recently. She worked for a temporary employment service that sent her on three assignments during one week.

The first assignment was for an organization that was changing its offices from one building to another. Our member was hired for two days to address envelopes to embassy personnel to inform them of the change of address.

The second assignment took her to a research firm that needed an extra typist to get out a proposal to NASA. The firm was bidding on a job that consisted of studying in just what ways further studies in water conservation might contribute to a fuller understanding of urban ghetto problems.

The third job was handling an overflow of correspondence from a busy executive of an organization that organizes and associates other organizations that try to aid the handicapped. The executive's letters went about like this: "Dear Fred, I just wanted to let you know how much I thought of Joe Tipping, who spoke at our Albany meeting last Wednesday. He really was convincing in his effort to get the Convention to Dallas in 1971. I hope you will make this letter public. . ."

A week of this made dishwashing seem even more significant than usual.

GLITTER

Aren't our young people drawn away from the Community by the glitter of the outside world?, people want to know.

Well, they are occasionally drawn away. They like variety, and lately some of them have taken to visiting a coffee house in Charlottesville once a week. We were curious what went on in a coffee house. "Well," they tell us, "as soon as we go in, somebody says, 'Oh, there's the girls from Twin Oaks', and we spend the rest of the evening proseletizing."

There's glitter all right, but it isn't in the outside world.

CHILD CARE

The care of Zandra continues smoothly and with very little difficulty. Zandra is allowed to do very much as she pleases, being watched only to see that she does not destroy property or hurt herself. The group is little by little learning to use the simple principles of positive reinforcement when caring for her. Of particular note is our effort to teach her habits of tidiness and care of property (qualities which are conspicuously lacking in ourselves and which we recognize the importance of in communal living). No one urges Zandra to pick up after herself or scolds her for not doing so, but every time she puts a block away in a box or lays a book back on a shelf, the group is quick to praise her. It is quite noticeable that this "putting things away" behavior is much more pronounced now than it was.

Zandra's first word, in case anybody is curious, was *Hi*, which she says alternately with a Southern and with a Yankee accent. This strikes us as being a particularly appropriate first word for a community child, who sees and greets so many different people in one day. Other discernible words so far are *hot, bye, dog, ball, oh look*, and *baby*.

CONSTRUCTION

The only construction projects we undertook this year were the new root cellar and some improvements in the existing building. The root cellar unfortunately did not get finished in time to save our root crops from spoilage, and we are eating up our potatoes, apples, and sweet potatoes as fast as we can in order not to waste them. The root cellar will probably be finished this coming spring and will serve us next winter.

The building is getting a thick layer of insulation in its ceiling, which should make the building much more comfortable this winter than last. (Last year we were not able to sit and read in the building without getting chilled.) And at last we are getting ceilings on our rooms. These do cut sound to some extent, giving us just a trifle more privacy. You may remember that this building was originally planned and is still intended to serve eventually as workshop space, with better-designed living quarters being built as funds become available. In the meantime the workshop serves as living and sleeping space, and we make it as comfortable as we can with our rugs, furniture, and personal belongings. Most of us sleep in this large (50' x 50') building, which has seven bedrooms, a furnace room, a large workshop, and a living room area that also serves as a library.

MILK COW SAGA – CONTINUED

We now have three registered Guernsey cows in full milk production. They give us more milk than we can possibly drink, plus a great deal of cream. These days common fare at Twin Oaks includes sweet cream, sour cream, cottage cheese, yoghurt, and home-churned butter. The sour cream and yoghurt were started with bacterial strains from their commercial counterparts and taste very much like the products we have been accustomed to. The butter is quite different from margarine, of course. The number of people who prefer margarine to butter is decreasing rapidly. The butter is really very good. When we put whipped cream on our strawberries, we put it on by the ladleful. But cream need not be whipped at all to be very good. Home-made apple pie covered with sweet cream is something most of us had never tasted in our lives before and is extraordinarily delicious.

Still, there is too much milk. So we have purchased some newborn calves to profitably use the surplus. They do the milking themselves, which saves us some work. (One of the cows has been turned over to the calves. Two we milk for our own use.) These calves will later be fattened on pasture and later be sold as beef. This is the beginning of our beef program, which in a few years should contribute substantially to the Community's financial well-being.

HOMER MORRIS FUND

Twin Oaks' greatest need is for home industries that will take the place of the "outside jobs" routine that currently brings in the greater part of our cash income. Since Twin Oaks has a good deal of pasture land, plus a member who is competent to handle such a business, we decided to go into raising cattle for beef as one of our first steps toward self-sufficiency. Buying the original cattle takes capital, of course. This capital was provided for us by the Homer Morris Fund. This fund was set up some years ago specifically to provide loan monies for intentional communities that might not be able to borrow from conventional sources. Repayment of the loan will take place over a three-year period, and the money for the repayment is intended to come entirely from the proceeds of the cattle business as it progresses. Naturally, it will take all we can do just to pay back the loan and accumulate a herd the first three years. But after that, the project should earn the Community a steady income that will provide for part of its support.

LABOR CREDITS – Theory and Practice

In designing a society there is a standard of living set that determines the amount of labor that members are willing to put into the building and maintaining of the physical plant. In a society emphasizing equality as well as efficiency, we have a problem of designing a system that gets the labor distributed in both an efficient and an equalitarian way.

At one end of the scale is a suggestion that we simply let everyone "do what he sees needs to be done" with no overall organization or plan. At Twin Oaks we have come to classify this as the "anti-structure hippie approach." Not only hippies have this approach; there are utopian idealists who propose that in utopia the people are so naturally good that everything gets done and no one is exploited. Twin Oaks tried this approach for about a month. At first there was much enthusiasm (it was our first month of existence), and everyone was busy doing something. After a couple of weeks, however, we began to notice that some jobs were avoided by most members, thus leaving them to those people who felt that "somebody's got to do it, so I'd better, or it won't get done." This was the first sign of difficulty — someone was exploited because he didn't like to complain. The job was dishwashing. Having come from the outside society, it was easy for us not to notice that the work began to polarize, the men getting up from the table and leaving the women with the housework, meals, dishes. A second subtle problem arose: the problem of wanting to sit down and rest but feeling guilty if the others were busy working. In order to make it obvious that everybody was doing his share, we practically had to do every job at the same time and then rest at the same time. Some jobs are built so that this teamwork is excellent. However, other jobs are efficiently handled by one or two people.

The idea of "do your own thing," as applied to labor in an equalitarian society, seemed to us lacking in both equality and efficiency, and did not prove to be a successful system for labor distribution.

Probably the most common system for equal distribution is rotation. Rotation is a crude method of getting equality—crude because it does more assigning of jobs than is necessary. For example, let us suppose that there are two people who are to divide the jobs of meals and dishes. The rotation system assigns Person A with dishes one time and Person B with meals; next time they swap jobs. What if A would rather do dishes and B would rather do meals? Then rotation makes both people miserable half the time. It *does* solve the problem of the strong and weak personalities. That is, often when two people try to decide who is to do what, one of them will say that it doesn't matter either way to him, when actually it does matter and he is just trying to be nice. If they were more honest and less nice, they could evolve a modified rotation in which only those jobs that both people didn't want were rotated. Even this leaves much to be desired. For instance, one's choice of desirable jobs changes from time to time. Also this system provides no way of determining the differences in job desirability.

The next stage of development of ideas toward an economics of equality is a sign-up system. The jobs are listed and people sign up for the ones they want. If two people sign up for the same one, a coin is flipped to decide the winner. Those jobs left unsigned-up-for are assigned randomly to those who lost the coin flip. Again, this system makes no allowances for differences in job desirability. It is equal in the sense that everyone has an equal chance of getting an undesirable job and in that sense it works out that in the long run everyone ends up feeling overloaded at some time or another.

What is needed is some adjustment based on desirability of the jobs, whereby the people doing the undesirable work have to do less overall work and the people doing the easy work do more of it. What is wanted is for everyone to feel that he is not envious of anyone else's work. This is what is meant by "psychological equality." It is not that everyone does the same thing, but rather that everyone feels that, of all the job choices and combinations, the one that he has to do is the most desirable to him—or at least that no one else has a more desirable combination.

This is where the concept of the "labor credit" comes in. A labor credit value is assigned to each job. Every person has to sign up for an equal number of total labor credits. The labor credits are adjusted such that the desirable jobs have a low value and the undesirable jobs have a high value. This means that if you sign up for undesirable jobs, you don't have to sign up for as many of them as you would if you signed up for desirable jobs only. For instance, one hour of septic tank cleaning might be worth two hours of typing the newsletter.

The way we determine the desirability of jobs is by whether or not people sign up for them. If more people sign up for one job than are needed, then it is assumed that the job is desirable and the labor credit value is lowered 10 per cent. If a job is not signed up for or if not enough people sign up for it, then someone who needs the credits (someone who lost a coin flip) is assigned to that job and the value goes up 10 per cent.

That solves the equality problem. But what about efficiency? How can any work get done well if the people working on it change from week to week, from day to day, and even from hour to hour? The answers to the efficiency question lie in various small regulations and adjustments in the basic system.

First of all, the major part of Twin Oaks' labor lies in areas that most people can readily master—cooking, housework, child care, farming, construction, and clerical work. Most of these things present little problem. Two or three supervised sessions, and a new member is ready to supervise newer people. We have had no difficulty just letting anyone sign up for anything he feels competent to do or wants to learn.

In areas that really do require some training (printing, teaching, typing, skilled construction), we allow managers to request skilled labor only—that is, to restrict the signup to those who can prove they are capable of doing the work. However, even here we insist that the jobs be open to those who want to learn. The apprenticeship rule (you must explain your work to anyone who wants to learn it) is implemented by giving credits to learners as well as teachers of any skill.

Sometimes, indeed, labor is wasted by apprenticeship. A person might spend several hours learning bookkeeping or printing and then decide he doesn't like it well enough to sign up for the work. But in the long run this openness is important to our equality principle, and any loss of efficiency is considered more than compensated for by that fact.

RAMMED EARTH

Remember the machine we bought that was to make 600 rammed earth blocks in one day? Dear Reader, let us again remind ourselves never to believe advertisements. The fellow who figured out that particular statistic must have had in mind the following conditions: that the earth was already dug out of the ground, already strained through a screen, and already mixed with cement in the proper proportions. These things being accomplished, the machine conceivably could be made to produce 600 bricks. But the ramming operation represents such a small part of the total labor involved in rammed earth brickmaking that one can actually produce only a fraction of that output. The time-consuming work is the digging, sifting, and mixing.

Twin Oaks does not have that kind of labor available. There are too many alternative possible ways of using our time, too many other ways to build a house. So we sold the rammed earth machine this spring.

We have not entirely given up the idea of rammed earth construction. There is still the wall-at-a-time method to be experimented with. None of the present membership, however, happens to be enthusiastic about the project; and so "rammed earth" remains in the files, along with dozens of other things we might get to some day, waiting for the right member to dig it out, dust it off, and make it work.

HAMMOCK TRIPS

Twin Oaks makes, as we have said before, a beautiful rope hammock. Production of the hammock has long ago ceased to be a problem. They take between four and six hours to produce, depending on the degree of experience of the worker and the size of the hammock. The raw material costs nearly $10 per hammock. The retailer takes 40 per cent, which leaves Twin Oaks earning about $1.50 per hour on its labor, allowing a little margin for selling costs. That doesn't sound like very much, but it is considerably better than any other way we currently have of bringing in cash income. And of course we sell an occasional hammock direct to the customer (such as through the mails or to visitors), on which we make a better profit. The fact is that *if* we could sell as many hammocks as we could produce, even at the wholesale rate, we could bring all of our outside workers back to the farm, and everybody would be a whole lot happier.

So we look at the possibilities. Is there a market for the hammocks? It seems clear that there is a market, for the product is beautiful and useful, it is not available in any but a very few stores (our competitors do not have extensive operations, either). The hammock is suitable for sale in large department stores of the better class, and in small "craft" shops in big cities, as well as on the seacoasts generally, and near other resort areas. Furthermore, it wouldn't take more than one or two decent contracts to put us in a position of full employment on the farm, which in its turn

would make other nice things available — like making it easier for us to absorb new members without warning them that they may have to take an outside job. All in all it is obvious that we must get out and make contacts with stores and place our hammocks in them where the public can get at them.

And therein lies the problem, for Twin Oaks members are congenitally incapable of selling anything. There is something about selling that terrifies us. It is obvious that this is and always has been our problem—no salesman.

Over Thanksgiving, though, one member steeled himself for possible rejection and took a hammock around to stores in his home town, where he was visiting his parents. "I'm no salesman," he says. "I say, 'Look, here's a hammock. We make them. Do you want to buy it?' and they do." He came back with orders from three stores. His success inspired him. Having successfully bearded the buyers in their dens and returned without being eaten, he thinks he can make himself do the same in other cities.

Which is where you come in. If you live in the sort of city where there are stores that might appropriately carry our hammocks, and if you have a spare bed for our travelling salesman, would you let us know? Motel costs are out of the question, but we know we have friends all over the country. Several of you have already offered, which is why this occurred to us. We can't say what the itinerary will be. The East coast is the most likely. But we would like to know where we can stay in any part of the country.

AUTO EXPENSES

Does anybody out there in Readerland know for sure how much it really costs per mile to run an automobile? Lately we have been having an economy drive, and we've been talking a lot about the cost of trips to Charlottesville, Richmond, and Louisa. We can figure the gas without difficulty. But wear and tear is beyond us. We haven't been here long enough to make any generalizations from our own bookkeeping. We know that many firms allow 8 cents to 12 cents a mile to their employees, but we don't know if these figures represent real costs or are padded. In the meantime, we have guessed it at 7 cents a mile for the purposes of rationing and budgeting within the Community. Are we over or under? Does anybody know?

ALLOWANCES

Remember the 25-cent allowance per week we instituted last year? Last January 1st we raised it to $1 a week (made possible by a marked donation from a friend). Since the Community provides all the basic necessities, we thought it might be interesting to report to readers what the members tend to spend their allowances on. So we took a small survey.

Biggest item by far is transportation to and from places that members want to visit. After that come materials for hobbies and crafts, notably yarn. Then come fancy foods, mostly "junk" food like soft drinks, candy, and potato chips. Other miscellaneous items are: long-distance telephone calls, subscriptions to special-interest magazines, small items of clothing, materials with which to make Christmas presents for relatives outside the Community.

THE BULLETIN BOARD

There is a bulletin board on the wall of Twin Oaks' kitchen, where anybody may place a notice of any kind. The board is cleared every twenty-four hours, so that there is always something fresh on it. Offerings range from planners' meeting notes to limericks, from newspaper articles about the Community to gripes about somebody not cleaning out the bathtub. Following are some examples of things that have appeared on the bulletin board sometime during the last several weeks.

Tonight. Everyone Invited. Community Recreation Excursion to See a Flick. Dr. Zhivago. We leave here at 9:30 Twin Oaks Time. At the Local Capitalist Drive-In. Bring Allowance. $1.

Guitar Class tonight for anyone who can already play chords.

Announcing the Great Easter Cup Hunt. Not an Easter Egg Hunt, but similar. See how many coffee cups you can find around the Community. The cupboard is almost bare.

For Land's sake, your sake, and the Community's sake, are you drinking all the milk you can? It is a crying shame to have to throw it out to the hogs.

Learn the painless way. Play reading group. Plays to be nominated by members according to their interests. Members choose parts. Read and discuss together. If you are interested, see Skip or Terry.

During the next few weeks one after another of the current provisional members will qualify for full membership (their three months will be up). So I will be going around asking the membership individually how you feel about each of them. This is not a vote. It is not even a poll. No results will be announced. It is merely an attempt to find out how the individual members feel about each incoming member, in order to give us a good basis on which to make decisions.

The questions to ask yourself are: *1)* Can I personally stand him or her? That is, can I live comfortably in the Community with that person as a member? *2)* Do I think he or she is an asset to the Community or a liability, or some of each; and if some of each, which way do you think the balance goes?

Announcing. A Statute of limitations on claiming labor credits. You can't claim anything older than four weeks. If you remember that you baled hay last August and forgot to claim credits for it, or went to church in February and haven't put in for your credits, tough luck. Report all work within four weeks or lose the credits. The reasons for this are probably obvious.

(From instructions for child care):
If you are capable of singing well enough to stay in key, then by all means sing to Zandra. She has shown an interest in music, and even tries to sing when others do. It is important for her to have good models for music at a time when she is interested.

Have you brushed your teeth today?
— Health Manager

Does anyone know where the hair-cutting scissors are?

Anybody wanting to flip (a coin) with Tamar and me for the big red rug please sign here.   — Susan
(Carnell and Walt flipped. Carnell won the rug.)

NUMBER 9

GENERAL NEWS

THE COW PLAN DEVELOPS

The "Homer Morris Plan," as we call it (named after the fund that loaned us the money) involves, as a going business, ten cows and a constant stream of calves. As each calf reaches veal stage, it is taken to market and is replaced by another day-old calf from a nearby dairy. Our difficulty

in getting started is that it is not always easy to buy cows and calves in the proportions one wants just when one wants them. There was a period when we had five calves and only two cows (we had to feed the extra calf on powdered milk) and a much worse period when we had more cows and calves (we had to put a great deal of extra labor into milking and processing in order to use the extra milk). Our full complement of cows contains registered specimens of every major dairy breed—Holstein, Ayrshire, Guernsey, Brown Swiss, and Jersey.

Ivory, the Brown Swiss, has only two functioning teats (the other two were destroyed some time ago by a disease) but milks as much from the remaining two teats as many cows do on all four.

We milk two cows for our own consumption. The other eight are the dairy-beef business. There is a certain amount of labor each morning and evening, bringing the cows to the calves' stalls, and then letting them out again. Then there is giving scours pills to the calves, which involves inserting your arm up to your elbow in the calves' mouths. Most of the time, though, the cattle just graze and put on weight and give birth to more calves, which is how they make money for us.

VISITORS IN BUNCHES

We had to call a halt to one-day visits last summer. It seemed to us that people who visited for one day got no feeling for what we are doing, and didn't even really get acquainted with the members. Quite often they would go away with the impression that we were an unfriendly group. Naturally, we who actually live here have our activities and did not always want to interrupt them in order to answer visitors' questions. So it seemed to us that longer visits were in order, or else no visit at all.

Like most of our policies, though, this one was subject to experimental modification. What experiment showed was that there are groups of people, especially college classes, who simply cannot come down here for three days at a time but who are nevertheless terribly disappointed to be informed that they would not be welcome for a single day.

So we reevaluated our policy. Was there not some way in which we could accommodate these groups without ending up with the feeling that both sides were wasting their time? It happened that a group (seven) from William and Mary College wanted to visit at a period of acute labor shortage here at Twin Oaks. Naturally it occurred to us that we might compromise by putting the visitors to work. Our usual policy for visitors is to allow them twenty-four hours on the premises before they are requested to help out. If we changed this rule for groups of visitors, could we not organize them and get them to do really useful work?

We could and did. The seven from William and Mary sawed up a whole wagonload of wood and stacked it neatly by the house, built ceilings for two of the private rooms, dusted shelves in the library, and added to the continually growing braided rug. When they left, having spent only one day and one night here, they were already friends with the members who had worked with them. They felt at ease. Everybody had the feeling that the visit had been worthwhile. We even felt that we could do the same with other groups.

Other groups were not slow in coming. That same week ten architecture students put up the rest of the ceilings, sawed up more firewood, and braided more rug. Still another group collated the last newsletter and built feed troughs for the calves. As spring advanced and the garden began to claim attention, we found that we could put in a large garden almost without any labor at all from the membership. Dozens of fruit trees and berry bushes have been put in by visitor labor, and almost all of the garden. For the next group we are reserving the job of washing windows—like in the book, you know.

REPORT FROM THE FARM MANAGER

Farming at Twin Oaks this year consists primarily of trying to raise enough hay to feed our growing herd of cattle through next winter. At present we have clover and orchard grass, which appear to be doing fine. We also have approximately seven acres of wheat, which will be used for cattle feed, straw, and some will be made into flour for communal consumption.

As soon as the Community and the weather come to some sort of agreement over the amount of rain we should get and still be able to plow and disk, then Sudex Grass and more clover will be planted to supplement our hay crop. This agreement will hopefully be reached this week; or at least we seem to be making more progress than they are in Paris.

Equipment is also one of our major problems. Although we are doing rather well with what we have, old equipment (and even new) seem to need costly repairs when trying to plow or disk hilly and/or rocky soil. But fortunately only a small percentage of our land falls into those categories.

Stay tuned for the results of the Twin Oaks/Weather agreements in our very next issue. . .which hopefully won't be as long in coming as this one.

FRUIT TREES

Twin Oaks planted $80 worth of baby fruit trees and berry bushes this spring. Those that we planted in 1967 did not do well, primarily because of buying inferior plants and partly because of last summer's draught. This year we are remedying both problems (buying better stock and hand-watering when necessary). Our survival rate on the new plantings is well, about 90 per cent. We have put in peaches, pears, cherries, grapes, raspberries, blackberries, apricots, and various nut trees, as well as some miscellaneous items like bush cherries and currants. Again, fruit trees planting is an act of faith. We will harvest no fruit for at least another year (a few berries), and will have to wait several years for the nut trees to bear.

EDUCATION— We Stop and Start Over

Last issue we reported that we had one high-schooler taking classes at Twin Oaks. The classes were going well, and Susan and her teachers felt complacent about progress. Then Susan decided to quit and get a job in town.

Other members tried to discourage her, reminding her that at her age she could earn very little and that no one seriously expected her to take her turn at "outside work," however much we considered her in every other respect an adult. But Susan was fascinated with the idea, and we gave in. Howard Johnsons hired her as a waitress trainee, and she eagerly learned to please the customers and balance the steak sauce on a tray.

For a week it was fun. The second week she discovered that the manager had exaggerated the amount she could expect in tips. The third week she began to notice that she never had any time to do anything but go to work and sleep. The fourth week she quit. The Community quietly approved, and we started to reinstate the classes.

But we ran into a theoretical barrier. There was disagreement about our educational system, disagreement serious enough to be carried to the board of planners for decision.

The controversy amounted to this: the education manager contended that all formal learning in which a person manifests an interest is desirable, regardless of the subject matter, because our Community wants its members to be informed, interesting people who have been exposed to a variety of subjects. This long-range goal is worth the short-range pain of reading and studying, but on the surface it does not seem so to the student. Therefore, the Community should help the student accomplish these goals by giving labor credits for attending classes. We are, by giving study credits, just sharing with the individual student the short-range pain of extra work in order to effect the long-range goals of intelligent membership. It's a Community gain, and it should be done with Community labor. What this meant in practice was that we ought to give labor credits for taking courses in such things as history, geometry, chemistry, and foreign languages, or even art or music.

The opposition contended: "I'm afraid I can't agree that educational endeavor is intrinsically better for you than recreation or taking a nap. Indeed, it may often be just the opposite. What really is the use of knowing ancient British history, anyway? I can't for the life of me think of any reasonable excuse—except that one might be interested in it. I mean *really* interested in it, enough to at least attend a class in it without being bribed.

Am I interested in learning Chinese? Yes, but not enough to dig it out for myself. Enough to attend a free and interesting class in Chinese? Perhaps. Enough to attend at the rate of $10 per hour—*They* pay me? You bet! It could even be Swahili, at that rate.

There is no educational endeavor that is worth paying everything for, and none that is not worth being paid everything for. But if the particular bit of education is not worth spending your own free time on, then it is just not worth it at all, in any real sense. To be bribed is to be forced. You do not need to be forced to do anything genuinely worth doing. If Susan would rather gossip about the boys than learn chemistry, then why shouldn't she? And if the Community would rather she learned chemistry, then we should take every opportunity to point out what is in it for her.

And if we are unsuccessful, it just may be because there isn't anything in it for her."

The opposition point of view was backed by the board of planners, and the educational system had to be revised. It was agreed on all sides that any class desired by anyone could be scheduled in order to make it possible for people to get together, whether it was a credit class or not. It was also agreed that teachers would in all cases get credits. It remained merely to ask people what subjects they wanted to learn badly enough to do it in their free time, over and above the fifty-hour workweek.

One noncredit course has from the beginning survived the spare-time test. That one deserves special attention. It was requested by Susan and described as *Biology—but not from books*—"walking in the woods and talking about the plants and animals and what they do. I just want to know all the stuff that Sara knows." Sara agreed to share the contents of her head. She dubbed the class *Nature* and discovered to her surprise that she had more than one student. Other members and even guests wanted to take tramps in the woods with someone who knows a wild strawberry from a poison ivy plant. This is, of course, the sort of thing one ought to do with ten-year-olds. But the fact is that most of us didn't do it when we were ten years old, and we are still interested.

In the accredited department are classes that are doing well, also. (One advantage to the new system is that the paucity of accredited matter made it possible for the Community to afford to open the classes to all members, not just young people.) Classes offered for labor credits must qualify by being directly and obviously useful to the Community; How to Run a Printing Press, for example, is an accredited course. Fortunately, the concept was broadened to include psychology and a course called Utopia. Both classes are given for the same fundamental reason: It is desirable for all of our membership to have thought through the reasons for starting a community like Twin Oaks and the theoretical bases on which it was formed. The psychology class stresses fundamental theories of classical and operant conditioning, and the Utopia class takes in the social theory of Walden Two.

"Utopia" is simply a discussion group. We read various "utopian" works, beginning with Plato and going through all the interesting writers, including accounts of actual communities, with constant reference to Walden Two and Twin Oaks. Virtually every important subject comes up through this reading. We are not, of course, studying Plato. (Anyone who wants to study Plato may do so, but not for labor credits.) We are studying Twin Oaks' institutions and Walden Two ideals, with an eye to understanding and improving them.

By the same token, the attention we are giving to Pavlov has more than academic interest. "Do you understand classical conditioning?" asked Rudy's review quiz after the second class. "Then you should be able to: 1) remove a child's fear of the dark; 2) remember things at the appropriate time; 3) eliminate stage fright; 4) cure stuttering; 5)

cure impotency or frigidity; 6) cure bedwetting; 7) eliminate your fears of certain objects or situations; 8) break or
make habits that seem involuntary; 9) reduce pain that is
related to tense muscles such as in childbirth; 10) control
whether you like or dislike such things as books, certain
music, certain people, certain topics of conversation, certain
types of art, types of work or recreation...

"Next week: Operant Conditioning, or How to Rule the
World."

A psychology teacher might recognize that this list is
simply a list of examples of possible applications of classical
conditioning. Probably he has mentioned such things in his
classes and given examples taken from case histories. At
Twin Oaks, with a class of four students, we stopped Rudy
right there and spent the next two hours going over the list
in painful detail, picking out the "bell" and the "meat juice"
and the "saliva" in each example. Nobody doodled or day-
dreamed or got sleepy in class. (Three people illustrated
classical conditioning by smoking heavily during the discussion of smoking.) The reason for the intense interest was
not merely good presentation. Certainly it was not novelty;
we have all brushed with Pavlov before — but this was the
first time that we had ever considered doing anything useful
with it.

It was like what you think psychology is going to be like
when you are in your teens and haven't been exposed to
any classes yet—the adolescent dream of gaining practical
knowledge about how to change people through psychology.

Eventually, of course, we stepped from discussing theory
to performing experiments. We built a large box with a
lever, an M&M dispenser, and several peepholes, and
watched our puppies demonstrate the principles of fixed
and variable ratio reinforcement. Of course there are difficulties. For every successful session there are two when the
apparatus breaks down or the dog just isn't hungry. But the
results are good enough for learning purposes. Even learning
that apparati break down or that food doesn't reinforce a
dog right after lunch is useful information, if you think
about it a little. The most obvious result of our experiments
so far has been that psychological terminology is becoming
part of Community vocabulary. Such remarks as "Well,
don't put her on a variable reinforcement schedule, for
God's sake," are now commonplace.

Among the noncredit courses, academics at first fared
badly. But as visitor labor made the work quota lower, the
noncredit classes were once more requested. What seems to
be true is that it is not really whether one gets credit for a
class that is important, but whether it is scheduled so that
other work does not interfere with it. Classes in history,
foreign language, and mathematics have all been requested
and begun. It is too early to say how long they will survive.

LETTERS FROM READERS

From Walter Millsap

(The reference is to the Llano Colony)

"We tried labor credits but the best workers would

neglect to claim credit, and the ones that we never should
have accepted managed to claim more credits than they
were entitled to. We may try it again..."

Twin Oaks comments:

We are familiar with this problem. It does take a bit of
time to get good workers to learn to go through the annoyance of signup and credit reporting. And there are always
some people who claim more credits than they reasonably
should. But neither problem at Twin Oaks has been sufficiently serious to call for a major reevaluation of the system.
Of course we make a great deal contingent on the completion of a proper number of labor credits, so no one is likely
to forget them very often—any more than a good factory
worker on the Outside would forget to collect his paycheck.
Every credit a member has in the "bank" is an hour's worth
of vacation he can take at a later date.

As to the occasional lazy member who tends to cheat on
his reports, we would have to be a much bigger group than
we are for this to work for him very well. It is fairly obvious
when someone isn't doing anywhere near his share, and the
labor credit reports are in an open file for anyone to check
on. If someone should claim a conspicuous bunch of credits
he wasn't entitled to, it would be noticed and disallowed.

Mainly, though, we all understand the underlying ration-
ale of the labor credit system, and cheating is uncommon.
If I don't do my work, someone else will have to do it for
me; if I do this very often, I just won't be doing my share;
and anyone who doesn't do his share is a schmuck.

TWIN OAKS LEADERSHIP

Opinion — By Kathleen

We are often amused by visitors who say, in effect, "Take
me to your leader." Some of them are looking for Frazier;
others for a financial backer; but most expect to find a
single person who provides the emotional and ideological
force behind Twin Oaks. "Tell me about your history,"
they say. "Who started the group?"

Our history is prosaic enough. It is told in full in the
Yearbook (which will surely be published soon!), so I won't
go into it now. But it does not, no matter how completely
understood, answer the question most people are after,
namely WHO (one person) is responsible for Twin Oaks?

There is no single leader here. Not one of us is even
capable of handling such a role. Visitors can, of course,
generally find someone to satisfy their theories, but this
proves nothing. Speaking from the inside, with a fairly full
knowledge of how decisions are really made and who makes
them, I can state pretty confidently that the visitors are
mistaken.

So who needs a leader? It is generally assumed that they
are necessary; and there are good reasons for the assumption, particularly in a group as highly organized as Twin
Oaks. Somebody needs to allocate labor, to develop indus-

tries, to see to the crops and farming; someone must plan the child-rearing and educational practices; someone needs to represent the Community to the Outside, to solicit good will, new members, and support. All of these tasks are called (and indeed are) leadership. But there is no reason whatever that they should all fall to the same person.

It may be protested at this point that all of the above-named tasks are indeed just tasks, and that dividing up such work represents merely a division of labor and not necessarily at all a division of leadership. What a leader does is see to it that the industries, the farming, the child-rearing, and the Community public relations all tend to the same end; he decides what that end will be; and he has enough personal magnetism to persuade others to go along with him.

In a sense it is true that one person has influenced the group enormously. That person is of course Dr. Skinner—or more accurately his fictional counterpart, Frazier. To him we are indebted for the ease with which we have established governmental procedures, a Code, the planner-manager system, and the labor credit system. Without him it would have been difficult, indeed, to bring together and hold together (and continue to recruit) people with a fairly consistent idea of what they mean by a good society, without having a powerful leader.

There was another indispensable man, also. The person who made money available with which to buy this farm and erect the first building could not reasonably have been done without. But neither Frazier nor our financial benefactor exercise current leadership in the usual sense. What is more, neither does anybody else.

Somebody has to make decision. Shall we raise corn next year? How much labor can we afford to spare for building an experimental dome? How many automobiles shall we license? To what extent should a biological mother care for a newborn? Can we put any money into recreational activities this year? Is it desirable to raise individual cash allowances? How fast can we effectively absorb new members? Should visitors be encouraged? Shall we openly solicit funds? And so forth. Of course someone has to decide. These decisions are made by the board of planners, unless it's clearly a managerial decision.

Aha! Now we're getting somewhere. Who are the planners?

There are three of them. But they rotate out of office, one being replaced every six months. There are currently six people in the Community who have been in that position at one time or another. You won't find the answer there. We have had planners who weren't leaders; furthermore, we have had leaders who weren't planners. Being a planner means that the group requests you to make decisions on matters they don't care to mess with, because they're busy pursuing their private lives. It isn't any particular honor—just a job. It doesn't give you a great deal of power, either. Hemmed in on one side by a constitution that guarantees members their basic freedoms, and having on the other side no army to enforce unpalatable laws, even if you did make one, you have little choice but to govern

with "positive reinforcement." Our planners are appointed, not elected; but regardless of this, they must govern with the consent of the governed; there just isn't any other way to do it.

Leadership at Twin Oaks is done cooperatively. One can manage the beef raising business; another can construct a building. The ideas and plans of both are checked for conflicts by the board of planners, and then they are on their own.

But who holds the group together? Surely we are not just a group of people who live together. Someone gives us a sense of unity.

The group is held together by personal friendships in a complex pattern that is continually changing. (A sociologist would have a good time drawing sociograms at Twin Oaks. They would never be the same two months in a row.) Sometimes there seems to be a central figure; but everyone goes away on vacation from time to time, and it is noticeable that during the absence of the central figure, the group functions quite well, readjusts its social patterns slightly, and continues its pursuit of the good life.

Well, all right, says another critic (this time one who knows us better and can therefore criticize better), you have successfully demonstrated that you are leaderless. Now can you successfully demonstrate that you are really surviving without one? It is precisely your lack of leadership that is deplorable. Not one of you knows how to get out and get the money that you need, and there is grant money just lying around waiting to be taken, if you learn how to go about getting it. You've been there nearly two years, and not one industry is yet flourishing, even to the point of supporting the group. As to the planners, the name is a travesty. What planning do you ever do? You have no long-range plans, either for architecture or for industry.

These accusations are perfectly true. But they are rather pointless, for what they say is that we are not as able as some people theoretically could be. The implications are that we should either a) go and find someone who is really qualified as a leader and ask him to set us straight; or b) we should not have had the gall to start a community.

For reasons that may and may not be clear to our readership, neither of these alternatives holds the slightest interest for us. Competent leadership ability, when and if it arrives in the Community, either in the form of a new member or of a further development of an old member, will be recognized and used. As to the question of whether we had, with our limited personal resources, a right to start a community, we generally hold to the opinion that people who don't start communities (or join them) are slightly immoral. So much for that.

The third critic is a speculative sort, and he wants to know what would happen if one of these magnetic-type personalities appeared on the Twin Oaks scene. Would the group be taken over? Would cooperative leadership dissolve? The answers are necessarily speculative also. We have already met the self-appointed leader types, the ones who require obedience or respect in order to be happy — they can't live happily at Twin Oaks. Respect is accorded only to proven personal merit (and then not in large doses), and obedience is unheard of. Their usual techniques ("Come on, everybody, let's all go out and do such and such.") are met with replies of "Don't feel like it," and "Not now." (Twin Oaks can probably not take credit for this piece of cultural engineering; 1969's young people just come like that.) The "Do what I want and I'll let you be part of my group" technique wouldn't be likely to work here, either, for we are all already part of a group or groups and are not lonely.

In short, the kind of leadership that would really work at Twin Oaks is exactly the kind we most like to see—someone who has specific skills and know-how in areas that we don't, and who puts his knowledge at the group's disposal. That kind of leadership built our present building and got us started in hammocks and in dairy cows. It is highly unlikely that we would ever get a specialist in our kind of government, so that kind of leadership will be exercised by amateurs until we ourselves become specialists at it. Since we are all developing at the same time and over the same problems, the likelihood is that we will always have a group, not an individual, who is best able to handle administrative affairs.

In fact, we predict the year-by-year decrease, not increase, in the importance of individual personality in leadership. What is the function of a leader? asks Frazier, in *Walden Two*. Is it not to piece out a faulty government? The answer to the whole question in *Walden Two* was that their government had no need of being pieced out. Twin Oaks may be some years in arriving at that stage, but even now we sense that the hero figure is a myth we intend to do without.

MEMBERS COMMENT

We went around this month and asked different members to answer for the *Leaves* the question, "What have you learned since you came to Twin Oaks?" Here are some of the answers. . .

Tamar—

Everything practical that I know. I never cooked before I came here. I already knew how to wash dishes and sweep, but I never handled laundry before. Then all that writing the checks for the Community bills and balancing the checkbook, and posting in the account books. And running the offset press, and milking a cow.

Besides that, I have learned that you have to work at it if you want to live happily with other people. Before I came here I thought that the reason I sometimes had trouble with my parents was because they were sometimes difficult people. And I figured that once I grew up and got married, living with another person would be very easy—because of course I'd marry someone I loved. Now I've found out that it takes more than love for people to get along together. And you're going to have difficulties, no matter who or how many are in the group. . .it's just plain hard to live with people.

Scott—

I am continually impressed (and sometimes depressed) by just how amazingly difficult it really is to set up a successful community. I thought I knew the difficulties before I came. But I didn't know the half of them. No wonder so many communities are always being born and always dying shortly thereafter. Because what we are after is such a reasonable society, it seems like it ought to be easy to get there; but it will be the phenomenon of the age if anyone ever does. At Twin Oaks we are learning many valuable lessons about how to achieve utopia, and I remain convinced that we are at present the group most likely to succeed.

Sara—

I learned that it isn't anywhere near as hard to set up a community as I thought it would be. I used to think you had to have a whole lot of money and a huge group of people. But you don't. I predicted we would flop within six months, but we've been going nearly two years.

Christine—

I learned that you can't blithely reach over a cow's head to chain her. If you do, you'll get thrown to the other side of the pen. I've learned to milk a cow, and that cows have wonderful, interesting personalities: Lucy is greedy; Ivory is a big bully, but smart—if I call her from the door, she'll come running. . .

Rudy—

A clearer idea of my faults, such as procrastination and tending to compromise or give up when confronted with hassle. I sometimes have depressions based on "we ought to be further; let's do something." And then I try to think of grand schemes like new industries, grants, more buildings by a cheap way, a change in the labor credit system, etc. I talk about it to someone, feel better, do nothing.

How to operate an offset press and camera. How to build a building (but I still have the problem of wanting to finish too fast or cheap and do shoddy work). That I can't teach public school and probably can't handle any situation where I'm in a position of authority.

I have learned to play guitar in public, sing occasionally to some people if I really want them to hear a song I wrote. That I can't keep a beat long enough to accompany others. How to blue a note on the harmonica.

That I can hold an Outside job about a month before I get sick of it. That my hair is curly. That there is some country music I really like.

A whole pile of general info about a farm, what a plow is, etc.

That the Community will probably be built by college students or people with past community experience. Families don't work. "Responsible" people are too frustrated by working with others.

Kathleen—

I have a new vocabulary. I now know the difference between a pig, a hog, a shoat, a gilt, a boar, and a sow. I have learned bookkeeping and a little about income tax.

Twin Oaks is people. . .

. . .but it is also a place. . .

. . .where we grow things, build things, manufacture hammocks,

inform the curious, relax, taste the fruits of our work. . .

. . .and enjoy. . .

. . .being together.

The most interesting recent thing I am discovering is that I can control some of my own behaviors by means of techniques right out of a textbook. Positive reinforcement and extinction and all those things that work on rats also work on me, and I can be both controller and controllee.

Also, I have learned to be completely comfortable with and take for granted the friendship of over a dozen people. Before I came here I never had more than one or two friends at a time. I don't mean everyone in the Community is a close friend of mine, or even that everybody likes me. But everyone here has a pretty realistic view of me and likes or dislikes me pretty much in proportion to my virtues and faults. There aren't any pretenses to speak of, and very little fear.

Clem—

This colum is all about greatly things I have learned since arriving at Twin Oaks and also other trivial poop which having no meany to anyone, will be included. I first herd of Twin Oaks from a kindly man of my past. The kindly man spoke at me that Twin Oaks was indeed a community of great worthiness. Upon hearing this I rode to Twin Oaks were I was grated by smiley people of all sizes. After disengaging me from the smiley people I questioned about living here and wood I be a better person for it. They interfered I would. Having dwelled in another community in my past, I was more or least acquitted with community ideas. (The above is all trivial poop which should have been skipped, along with the rest of this.) Explaining impressions and feelies you get after being at Twin Oaks for a piece is a very hardy thing to do. It seems people are much happier here than nowhere. You have more tries to be happy in. Even while working worthily away you can bath in the happy thought that right before your very eyes you are helping to decay something important and goodly. Also you learn more about living with people around you, which is in itself a great boom to one's naked happiness. Everyone here is considered equal, which you remembered people thought wisely when Able Lincoln pondered at it at Gettysburg. But now some people are more equal than others. But enough of this political garble. To learn about a utopian community you have to visit are live in one. One does exit.

Susan—

Virtually everything I know. Italian history, shorthand, most of my typing, cooking, housework, planting and hoeing, driving a tractor, driving a car. How to use positive reinforcement to handle a small child, and what happens when you try to answer aggression with aggression.

Just before I came here I discovered that I really don't have to do much of anything I don't want to do—or at least that hardly anybody has any **authority** to speak of if you want to push them far enough. Basically, I can get away with doing whatever I want. But at Twin Oaks I am beginning to believe that in the long run I don't really want to try to get away with everything, because I've seen other people here act like that, and seen how it affects the whole

group; and I think people who act completely selfishly are shits. I don't want to think of myself that way.

HOW ARE WE DOING?

A Comparison of Twin Oaks with
Certain Aspects of Walden Two

DRESSING FOR DINNER

"Many people are surprised that we dress up," Mrs. Myerson said. "But we have our reasons. . . Perhaps we don't want to think ourselves queer. . . We have plenty of time for everything. We like a break between the active part of the day and the quieter social hours at dinner and in the evening. A bath and a change are an important point in the day's schedule. They are psychologically refreshing."
— *Walden Two*

Twin Oaks: We always smile at this one. It is very difficult indeed for us to imagine a life so leisured that we would want to spend time dressing twice in one day, just for the psychological refreshment. The actual practice at Twin Oaks currently is divided neatly into two groups: those who dress to please and attract other members, and those who merely cover their bodies to protect them from the weather. It must be remembered that many members are still going through a period of rebellion against clothing regulations and merely want to be left alone. We have not been here long enough to have established any clear directions in dress except that we are interested in comfort, economy, and attractiveness, in that order. Most of us wear jeans in winter, shorts in summer, with a variety of shirts and sweaters. The girls sometimes wear dresses for the fun of it. Nylon stockings, girdles, ties, and other such uncomfortable garments are worn only on "outside jobs" or to church or other places where protective coloration is desirable.

COMMUNITY LECTURE HALLS

"You mean to say," said Castle slowly and with a challenging stare, "that all of your members interested in, say, a discussion of world peace could be put in one of these small rooms?" "In one corner!" said Frazier, fairly crowing at his success in disconcerting us. "What about an interest in the affairs of the Community?" I said. "In the other corner," said Frazier.
— *Walden Two*

Twin Oaks: Even in a group as small as ours (sixteen), this prediction is coming true. It is very difficult, indeed, for any subject to be brought up for discussion that would actively interest more than two or three of us. And that certainly includes both national politics and internal community affairs. Nobody here exerts any pressure on anybody else to take an interest in matters that don't directly concern him. Planners' meetings, open to the membership if they choose to attend, rarely have more than one or two extra attendees, and these generally do not visit more than once or twice.

THE STAGGERED SCHEDULE

"An amazing piece of cultural engineering—the staggered schedule. The effect is almost unbelievable. We need less equipment of all sorts. . . But perhaps the most valuable result. . .is psychological. We're utterly free of that institutional atmosphere which is inevitable when everyone is doing the same thing at the same time. Our days have a roundness, a flexibility, a diversity, a flow."

— *Walden Two*

Twin Oaks: This is true even now. Our work is arranged in two-hour shifts, and a member may be on duty from 9 to 11 in the morning, and then not again until 3 to 5 in the afternoon, and then again after supper. Or his schedule (largely chosen by himself) could bunch up all his work hours in one part of the day and leave the afternoon and evening free. It is quite usual to find members working, and other members standing around near them talking to them with a perfectly clear conscience. Everybody knows that everyone else has done or will do his share. This makes possible such things as afternoon naps for people who like them, or nice walks in the woods on pretty days (even with the Twin Oaks work schedule, which is a long way from the four-hour day).

INCENTIVE IN A COOPERATIVE ECONOMY

"Secondly," said Frazier, with a satisfied smile. . ."we have the extra motivation that comes when a man is working for himself instead of for a profit-taking boss. That's true incentive wages, and the effect is prodigious. Waste is avoided, workmanship is better, deliberate slowdowns unheard of."

— *Walden Two*

Twin Oaks: So far we don't notice this effect. Whether the Community itself has become to some extent "the system" and the individual members tend to think of the labor credits simply as a means of placating the system sufficiently to buy their continued membership, or whether conscientious workmanship is a behavior that has to be carefully taught we are not sure. But the facts are that most of us are about as good workmen as we were before we came here, the absence of a profit-taking boss notwithstanding.

LABOR FOR VISITORS

"While you're in that mood," he said, "I should tell you that you'll be permitted to contribute labor credits while you're here, too. We ask only two per day, since you're not acquiring a legal interest in the Community or clothing yourselves at our expense."

— *Walden Two*

Twin Oaks: Our guests are also permitted to contribute labor credits. We ask only four a day, since it is difficult for us to find more than that for you to do. Furthermore, we charge you for your food, also, since the value of guest labor, though great, is not convertible into cash to buy food with; and the amount of guest labor available, though considerable, is not enough to compensate for the extra farming and canning involved.

SPECIAL COMMUNITY FOODS

"We helped ourselves to scrambled eggs and bacon, and a cooked cereal of mixed grains — a special product of Walden Two which proved to be delicious."

— *Walden Two*

Twin Oaks: For our part, Twin Oaks invented a cold cereal. That is, popcorn with sugar and cream. It tastes very much like any of the popped corn cereals on the market, and it's a great deal cheaper, but nobody liked it. We have the same sort of difficulty with peanut soup or roast groundhog. Most of the members taste the unusual dish, pronounce it edible, and leave half of it on their plates. It would seem that edibility has more to do with custom than flavor.

SEGREGATED DRESSING ROOMS

"I should explain," said Frazier in great haste, "that there are two series of rooms, one for each sex."

— *Walden Two*

Twin Oaks: We should explain that building two sets of dressing rooms just for the purpose of preserving physical modesty strikes us as absurd. It is extremely doubtful that Twin Oaks will ever designate even its toilets as *Ladies* and *Gents.*

UNFORESEEN PROBLEMS

"But what would you do if it occurred?" Castle insisted. "We should deal with it somehow. I don't know. You might as well ask what we should do if leprosy broke out. We'd think of something. We aren't helpless."

— *Walden Two*

Twin Oaks: We are continually having to tell people this same obvious thing. What would we do if one of our members were seriously ill (considering our financial insecurity)? Or if the local Minutemen decided to wipe us out? Or if the authorities decided to enforce compulsory public school attendance? We do not know exactly, but we could find something to do. We are not helpless.

Chapter Four: Year Three

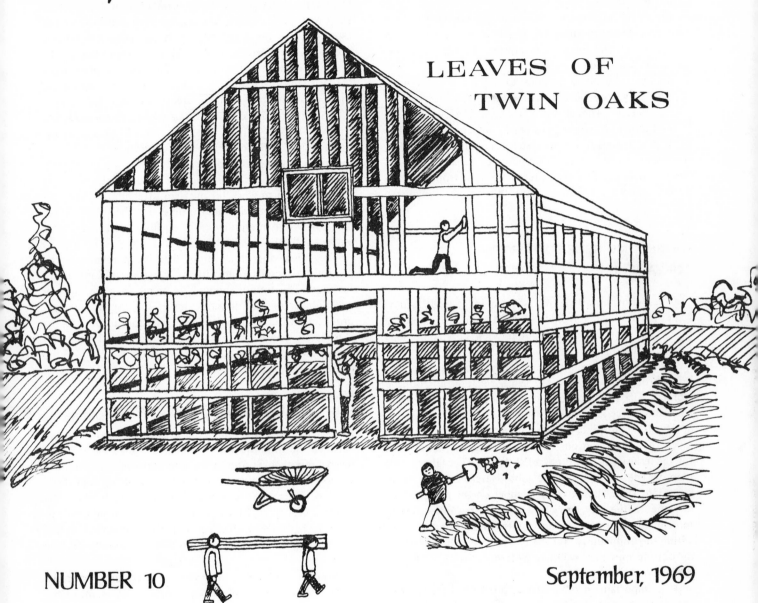

LEAVES OF TWIN OAKS

NUMBER 10

September, 1969

GENERAL NEWS

NEW BUILDING

We did not build any new construction in 1968, and we are crowded now. We began work on a new dormitory building this summer. The slab and supporting poles are in, and the roof is over half finished. The construction of this building is very similar to the last one we built, except that this one will be two-storied. We will not be able to finish the second story this year; we will run out of money before we get that far. But before really cold weather gets here we plan to have several additional bedrooms and another public room available on the ground floor.

NEW SEWERS

Two years ago we described to our readers the makeshift arrangements we had made in order to make do with the septic tank facilities that were here on the premises when we arrived. Last month the local health authorities declared that they were not only insufficient but actually illegal. (We had diverted our wash and bath water out onto open ground and left the septic tank and drain field for just the toilet.) We were given thirty days to remedy the situation. They drew up the plan, for which there is no charge, and we called the contractor. The plan called for two huge septic tanks, three distribution boxes, and 1000 feet of drain field. The contractor was impressed. He had seldom put in anything so extensive in this area. "Big enough for a motel," he said. The cost was $1,600. "Big enough for forty people," said the contractor. "Twenty," said the health department.

The thirty days are up now, and the system has been entirely installed and paid for. Within a short time another bathroom will be installed in another building, and the outhouse closed down entirely.

We are particularly anxious to get rid of outhouses, because they may be a source (with flies as carriers) of enteric diseases. Though there has been no serious disease in the Community, there have been a large number of cases of flu and various fevers of mysterious origin, suspected by the doctor to be related to thyphoid or hepatitis diseases. Sanitation is the first requisite of freedom from these illnesses, and we are glad to have this big, expensive step behind us.

WE BECOME SELF-SUPPORTING. . .
FOR A WHILE

(The following article was written in June. It is now somewhat out of date, since we once again are depending on outside jobs for income; but it does show some hope for the future.)

Twin Oaks is having a small but important economic breakthrough. As of May 15, 1969, we took all "outside workers" off their "outside jobs" and put all of our available labor force into making hammocks.

This is a "small" breakthrough, because we do not make much of a profit on our hammocks. The best we can say for the industry is that it pays slightly more per labor credit than we net on the outside jobs. Nevertheless, it is an important step. Having every member on the farm instead of gone to the city every day makes a big difference in morale. It also means a much better distribution of labor within the Community (for the two or three who have been on outside jobs may well like to farm, or cook, or milk a cow on occasion.)

It is important in other ways, too. If we have reached the point of being able to sell every hammock our present population can reasonably produce (and it looks as if we have indeed reached that point, at least in the summer months), then we have arrived at a clear cash value for labor, and that opens up other interesting possibilities.

THE RECREATION FUND

Suppose, for example, that the Community would like to own a luxury—an item that no amount of rationalizing can make us take out of our ordinary budget. We might want a riding horse, or a canoe, or a movie projector. The case of the movie projector came up recently when we read of an opportunity to buy a reconditioned 16mm sound projector at quite a reasonable price.

A projector is a good thing to have. It brings movies within our means, and even supplies us with the possibility of seeing all sorts of noncommercial films free.

Now if we can sell as many hammocks as we can produce, then we can earn money for special projects merely by exerting ourselves to make hammocks over and above what we usually demand of ourselves. For a special project, especially one which promises as much pleasure as a movie projector, we might be willing to work above our quota. Those who want the projector most would perhaps work harder than others. And all such time would be *donated* to the recreation fund—no labor credits received.

We thought this one over for a while and couldn't find anything wrong with it. The projector will belong to the Community. (We would not even consider using the same means to buy private property.) The labor will be entirely voluntary, and no catastrophe will follow if the members do not choose to work for the item, after all. It is true that some will work harder than others, but the situation will not violate our interpretation of equality (that no member envies another).

This does not at all mean that the purchase of the projector or similar items is not a legitimate Community function. The time will hopefully come when we can buy any number of such luxuries out of the regular treasury, produced by Community labor and paid for in labor credits. It is merely that we are fairly poor right now, and recreation items have low priority. Extra work on the part of the members can change the priorities.

PROBLEMS

Living entirely off the hammock industry also has its drawbacks. For one thing, there is a considerable delay between the time the orders come in and the time when we receive our checks. And in the meantime we must not only support ourselves but also put out hundreds or even thousands of dollars for rope and other materials to make the hammocks with. It isn't easy to find sources from which to borrow that money. We are taking it from our building fund, which puts rather a crimp in the summer's building plans.

Another problem is that hammock making is factory work. Twin Oaks is a pleasant enough factory—some of the work being done out of doors, all of it in short shifts of one's own choosing. But weaving a hammock is not what you would call intellectually stimulating work, and we get bored with it. The same can be said of caring for the cattle or cooking the meals, but those jobs are of limited duration. Hammocks, it seems, can go on forever.

SOLUTIONS

Besides short hours and good working conditions, we have instituted the practice of doing two things at a time, in order to make hammock making less dull. Sometimes one member will read to the workers. We have occasionally made tapes of reading material to be played during the weaving hours. The most successful device for alleviating the boredom of hammock making is simply to make them in groups of three or more people. In such circumstances, conversation is likely to make the work time seem shorter.

The ultimate answer to the problem, though, is to diversify our industries. We are already taking steps to do this. A considerable amount of effort has been expended into the making and advertising of a film-rewinder. If this opens up as a Twin Oaks business, we will talk more about it in a future issue.

When winter comes and hammock orders drop off, we will have to have money to live on; and it is probable that "outside jobs" will go back on the labor credit system. But we have at least reached the point where we can plan on having the whole Community home during the summer.

THE FLOOD

We discovered the water when the outside workers drove out of the driveway and turned into the road to go to work in the morning. We went perhaps 100 yards and were stopped by a lake extending right over the road. "Looks like we go the other route," we said. "Boy, what a rainstorm that was!" And we turned around. This time we didn't even have to drive fifty feet before seeing the other lake covering our other exit. We drove back up the driveway and changed back into our jeans. It was obvious that we would not be driving to Charlottesville that day. For the first time in its existence Twin Oaks was isolated.

We celebrated the isolation and the flood by going swimming in the middle of the road, though it was a cold day. There was nothing for us to worry about: all of our buildings, vehicles, and livestock are situated on high ground. True, we had a hay crop under water, but the weather has been so wet all summer that there was already extreme doubt as to our ability to harvest the crop. (Reason: the machinery would get stuck in the mud.) We had fences to fix, and we undoubtedly lost some topsoil, but that was the extent of it. Our swimming dock survived the flood (though it was knocked lopsided by a log coming downstream). Even the hammock and the towels that we keep down by the river seemed nothing worse than dirty after being under water for two days.

Not everyone was so lucky. You will all have read about the deaths in Nelson County. Louisa County lost no human lives, but one of our close neighbors lost nine cows (worth about $200 each) by drowning. For the benefit of those readers who have visited Twin Oaks, we should say that Smith's Mill was under water up to the second story, and that the bridge by the mill was completely invisible under water. There was no indication where the river's boundaries had originally been. All of the lower pastures were a gigantic swamp. If we had only had a boat, we could really have enjoyed rowing among the trees; but the boat, which had been tied to the dock, was under water somewhere, and we had no way of finding it.

Two days later the waters were back to normal, and we could walk around and inspect the farm. The road damage was almost as impressive as the water had been. Great hunks of what had been good paved roads were gouged out,

making Highway 697 impassable, and 640 very difficult driving. The State of Virginia has its repair trucks on the road every day, grading and laying gravel to make travel at least possible in the interim before large-scale road repair can be undertaken.

MOVIES IN THE LIVING ROOM

Since we bought the movie projector we have seen probably fifteen short films on various subjects. Several of them had to do with psychology; we watched pigeons, rats, and dogs being trained to peck discs, press levers, and jump over barriers, respectively. There was a film on the Hutterians and one on the Amish, two on the atom, and three on wild life conservation. Some of this material is more interesting than other, but we never know which films are going to be worth seeing until they start showing, so attendance at movie-showings has been generally high.

We will start getting "real movies" as soon as our recreation fund can permit renting them. Right now we are limited to films we can get free from libraries and various institutions, such as the Atomic Energy Commission and the Canadian Embassy. If any of our readers know of particularly interesting films or suitable sources, we would like to hear from you about them.

WE NEED A LAWYER

If there is among our readers a lawyer with sympathy for Twin Oaks' general aims who would be willing to do a small amount of research and write us a letter from time to time, we want to hear from you. We really need this service. Of course we are not expecting anyone to take a great deal of time or trouble on our behalf. But sometimes we have questions that would take only a few minutes for an attorney to answer (or point the way to the answer). For example, we need to know where we can find information about the extent and type of authority vested in the Health Department, and precisely what are the avenues of appeal in the event any such organization should try to close us down or otherwise give us an order that we could not obey. We have access to a law library but little idea of how to use it. An attorney could simply write us a letter telling us how to look up the information we need.

REPORT FROM PSYCHOLOGY CLASS

After we spent a few classes talking about responses and operants, and a few more classes playing with our puppies in the big box with the M&M dispenser, we felt we really ought to try out the simpler techniques on real Community problems. Each member of the class was to choose an area of behavior in which change would be desirable and bend his energies toward making the changes. We were at liberty to choose a behavior of the group, of a single individual, including ourselves, or of any of the animals. The field was vast. Most of us made our choices on the grounds of being within our range of skill. Some of us just chose whatever interested us at the moment.

The first thing we had to do before setting about changing anything was to establish a "base line" against which to compare the behavior after the techniques had been set into motion. In other words, we had to spend a week or two just counting. One member counted the number of cigarettes he smoked per day. Another counted the number and kinds of typing errors she made. One very young member counted the times she found herself sucking her thumb. Another counted the times one of our collie dogs jumped on her. A few projects collapsed midweek because they were not amenable to accurate counting, or because that member thought up a more interesting project. We took our accounts back to psychology class and helped each other set up appropriate graphs to picture the counted behavior. The graphs do not all look alike.

Next step: change. The thumb sucker was persuaded to put herself on a schedule of no thumb-sucking for the first fifteen minutes after going to bed, thus trying to break down the stimulus-response pattern of bed = thumbsuck. After the initial fifteen minutes, if she is still awake, she may suck her thumb all she likes. The cigarette smoker went on a similar schedule. Once per hour on the hour he asks his roommate for a cigarette, and his roommate will give him one, provided that he has not in the meantime smoked the cigarette that is hanging around his neck on a string. (There go those literal-minded Walden Two-ers again. Around the neck, indeed!) In case he has given in to temptation and smoked the everpresent cigarette between hours, he is not awarded his hourly smoke but must wait until the *next* hour (on the hour). The theory here is similar to that of thumb-sucking. On this schedule the actual nicotine addiction is fully taken care of, but the emotional dependence on cigarettes is broken. Thus, except occasionally by chance, the hour-on-the-hour smoke does not fall during the period when the smoker would usually crave tobacco — after a meal, or when very nervous.

The success of the psychology class does not rest entirely on the success of these experiments. If they do indeed make permanent changes in behavior, we will probably be pretty impressed and stimulated to tackle more or bigger problems. If they do not (I decided I didn't really *want* to stop sucking my thumb, etc.), we will tackle simpler problems and keep on going.

MUTUAL CRITICISM

The idea came out of Utopia class. We were discussing Oneida Community (a highly successful religious community that existed over a hundred years ago) and their methods of social control. The technique they employed was called "mutual criticism" and consisted of a formal gathering to discuss the shortcomings of individual members of the community. Members of Oneida Community would submit their names and request criticism. The other members of the community would have a week to think about what they were going to say, and then the group would gather. The person to be criticized sat silently through the meeting, and the other members expressed their opinions of him. Then next week it would be someone else's turn.

The more we talked about it, the better we liked the idea. Though Twin Oaks has done some brief experiments in other kinds of confrontation, nothing we have heard of fits the Twin Oaks temperament and Twin Oaks problems quite so well as the Oneida suggestion. For one thing, it amounted to a community-wide admission that one of our aims is to change our behavior, and that we are interested in exploring techniques that have that effect. For another, it relieved the frustration caused by the anti-gossip rule. (If you want your opinion of somebody's behavior heard, not only by that person but by the whole group, here is your opportunity.)

We all agreed that we didn't want Criticism to turn into a general forum of discontent, nor did we feel that vicious attacks or contemptuous remarks had any place in the sessions. And we wanted to protect the individual being criticized from getting too uncomfortably tense. So we made a few simple ground rules. Criticisms were to be expressed courteously and in a helpful manner; the subject could cut off any criticism at any time if he didn't feel he could take it; no member may volunteer any name for criticism except his own; no visitors allowed at the sessions except at the express invitation of the subject; no spectators except children; the subject can speak to the extent of asking for amplification of a point.

To date we have had six sessions. There was no lack of volunteers. The waiting list is still long. As the sessions progress, we are losing our fears of their getting out of hand or of their destroying the protection of the anti-gossip rule. Though someone will occasionally make an unjust accusation, the fact that it is made in the presence of the person accused, as well as in the presence of several other people, some of whom know all the facts of the case, puts a clear and reasonable restraint on such accusations and prevents them from being dangerous even when they are made. But most of the criticism is not made up of accusations at all. It tends to be concentrated on the gross personality defects of the subject and on their effect on other members. And it has to date been very gently worded. Where a member might have said "You bore me because you talk too much" (which expresses little except hostility and does not even tell the subject how to change his behavior), instead he says "When we were having a general discussion at lunch the other day, you brought up irrelevant conversation about your family and some people you used to know, which didn't interest me much." (This tells the subject exactly what behavior is referred to and makes it possible for him to change the behavior if he wants to.)

Probably the best comment on the sessions comes from the subjects themselves. I asked each of them to comment in a sentence or two how he felt about his own session. They are printed here, without names, each paragraph representing a different person.

Session 1 —

"What an ego trip. I discovered that I'm pretty good at hiding my faults. I thought it was a valuable experience, because it brought the group together, and it was a very warm feeling. This has been true of some of the other sessions, too, where more negative things were said."

Session 2 —

"It wasn't as bad as I expected. People said things that might have been rough on me, but they said it so nicely that I didn't feel resentful. I just felt 'I'd better watch that; I didn't realize it annoyed people so much.' And I did find out new things."

Session 3 —

"I think it's a very valuable experiment. In the first place, it gives people a chance to say things they could never say otherwise without feeling schmuckish. And the person has volunteered to be criticized, so he is prepared and can take it without being so hurt as he otherwise might be. In my own case not much was said except that I ought to join the Community. I guess that session was the main thing that made me decide to join. . ."

Session 4 —

"The main thing I got out of the session was that everybody criticized the same thing — my public bitching, even when it was justified. I had really thought that some people were mature enough to appreciate public criticism when it was needed, and I didn't realize that dislike of it was so universal. The other thing I got was that some people had some positive things to say that I hadn't expected."

Session 5 —

"It felt good to know that that many people would gather to talk to me about my problems. That they cared enough. And I learned quite a bit, both about myself and about my relationship to the Community, some of which I didn't have any idea of before. And I learned quite a bit about some of the other people, too."

Session 6 —

"The atmosphere was powerfully positive. I felt not attacked but loved. Other people's sessions have been just as interesting to me as my own, though, and have affected me just as much. I find that whenever I go to a session, I have a very affectionate feeling for the person being criticized. He has, by volunteering, declared that he knows he isn't perfect, and that he cares what we think of him. That always makes me like him, whether I did before or not. . ."

NOTICE

We probably need to make a general and repeated announcement about our membership and guest policies. Generally speaking, our membership is open to anyone, provided that the Community is able to take new members, and provided that we feel the applicant will be an asset to the Community. It is also perfectly possible to visit the Community for several weeks or months, and all such guests either pay $1.50 a day or else actually join the Community and pay their $200 entrance fee, whichever makes more sense for their particular case. (It is perfectly all right to "join" for a limited time.)

We cannot accept people under 18 years of age without the written consent of at least one parent.

All members and long-term guests do their share of the labor credits, which varies a great deal but is sometimes as high as fifty hours a week.

During the summer months we are often crowded, and visitors must sometimes sleep in the barns unless they bring their own tent.

We do need advance notice of visitors' arrival, and we prefer individuals over groups, long stays over short ones.

A TYPICAL DAY IN CLEM'S
LIFE AT TWIN OAKS

Many people query what's it like to live in an all communal place like Twin Oaks. So to satisfy someone, I will give a description of a normal day.

8:15 — Woke up and put on my pajamas. Although I was quite dreary when I arose, I skipped off to the bathroom and gargled joyfully while secretly brushing my teeth.

8:30 — Took off my P.J.'s and put on my short pants and checked out the day. (Nice day.)

8:45 — Chewed down a hearty breakfast of wholersome breakfast feed.

9:00 — Lurked about the office inconspicuously for a normal amount of minutes, thinking of all the really worthwhile things I could do today.

9:30 — Decided to go work on our new building.

9:35 — On top of the building fearfully hanging on, while putting on the roof.

9:45 — Received a few encouraging words from Scott, in a shaky voice. He was beside me.

9:50 — Looked way, way down and saw Rudy smiling, and realized he wouldn't be smiling if I was about to fall.

9:51 — Bravely put on the roof, casting all fear aside.

12:00 — In the office answering some suggestive mail about duck breeding.

12:45 — Sneaked into the kitchen to wait for hand-outs.

12:47 — Walked outside; commented on what a sunny day it was, to all that would listen.

12:50 — Walked boldly into kitchen in search of food.

12:51 — Walked meekly outside and greeted everyone thoroughly. Joked about the horn of famine silently.

1:00 — Rushed into the kitchen, to find I was last in line to eat.

1:10 — Found a chair to place myself and crudely ate my chocolate milk and green bean casserole.

1:20 — Went to my room and rested my stomach.

2:00 — Went to the river and played bravely in the water, with many other happy, safety-minded Twin Oakers.

3:40 — Left the river and gayly returned to the Community to attend a "earn while you learn" class.

4:00 — Talked about Utopia, happily but with seriousness. Also made comments on the law of gravity in regards to our apple trees.

5:00 — Made a hammock.

6:00 — Sat around the living room exchanging friendly words with everyone that had some to exchange.

7:00 — Ran to the kitchen, only to find I was last in line to eat.

7:10 — Sat down and smiled warmly at all the food I had. Finally ate it.

7:30 — Went to the river, played in the water, and fought mosquitos (non-violently, of course).

8:30 — Returned to the Community and played my guitar until everyone left the room.

8:45 — Marveled at my ability to drive away the masses.

9:00 — Rounded up all the people that left and promised not to play any more.

9:15 — Sat in the office and discussed the mating habits of bumble bees with some very intelligent guests.

11:00 — Took a shower and all the other things people do when preparing for bed, as I thought that surely cleanliness is next to Skinnerness.

11:40 — Went to bed and dreamed of all the worthwhile things I would do tomorrow.

LEISURE TIME

This month's roving reporter asked the members the question: "What do you do with your leisure time?" Here are the answers:

Kenneth: I read, and sleep, and practice the guitar.

Rudy: I mostly play the guitar, and talk to people, and read, and sleep.

Euripides: I talk to people, and read, and play my guitar.

Jimgo: I sleep and read and cover my ears so I won't have to listen to all those goddamned guitars. I also sit around and watch the trees grow.

Christine: I play guitar for pleasure whenever I feel like it; I practice a lot. . . Long walks in the woods alone, or swimming upstream. I read a lot more, even some serious reading, such as psych and utopian novels, but mostly pleasure reading.

Clem: My abundance of leisure time is spent in many different ways, so I won't bother to mention them. The ones I wouldn't mention are too interesting, and the ones I would mention are too uninteresting. But I have been told to say I play guitar, swim, read, lurk inconspicuously, and write trash like this. Now you're probably thinking "That isn't much fun." How true, but in the future when more time, money, and members allow, I hope to play the guitar more, swim more, read more, lurk more inconspicuously, and write more trash. I may also start a rock group, but as of now Luke is the only rock I have.

WHEN I WRITE MY UTOPIAN NOVEL
Commentary — By Kathleen

One of these days I am going to write a Utopian Novel. The utopian novel has been one of my reading pleasures for a long time, and I think I know how to go about it. There is a pattern to them—each author varies the pattern a little; still, the form is clear.

POINT OF VIEW

First, there's point of view. All utopian novels, so far as I know, are told from the point of view of a visitor. The reasons for this are obvious. Only a visitor sees the culture from the outside, so that the differences between the utopian and the cultural norms of the author's day are brought sharply into focus. A visitor would naturally describe the grounds and facilities and would comment upon the personal appearance of the members. If I tried to write a utopian novel from the point of view of a member, I would be sacrificing a great deal of literary ease. I'll stick to the convention. But my visitor won't be like any visitor that has ever descended upon any fictional colony of the past. For my visitor will not be a skeptic. From More to Huxley, all utopian novel writers I know about have used the device of a skeptical visitor being gradually persuaded of the goodness of the ideal life by contact with the members of the ideal society. I have the utmost respect for these writers, but I know very well that none of them ever lived in a utopian community. If they had, they would know more about visitors than that. Skeptical? Probably the most outstanding characteristic of people who visit communities is naivette. Among my more painful duties as a member of Twin Oaks has been answering the questions of a stream of visitors—questions that reveal a romanticism far surpassing that which motivated us to form the Community. The typical visitor believes *1)* that communities need very little money, because they raise their own food (tractor maintenance, fertilizer, and lime in 1968 cost Twin Oaks over $700); *2)* that the major problem a community would have is interpersonal relations (the major problem a community has is lack of money. Dealing with matters of personal relations is a luxury that a community can afford when it has solved its essential economic problem. Indeed, hundreds of problems that seem personal would disappear entirely if appropriate facilities were available.); *3)* that communities must meet as a group to make group decisions (group decisions take far too long for this method to be seriously entertained by any group that has to make a living. We delegate decision making to a small group primarily to save the rest of us a lot of time and trouble).

SETTING

I am always made uneasy by the settings of utopian novels—they are so very utopian (and so very novel). One is buried in the heart of a mountain, the only entrance being a secret passage through the heart of a waterfall; another had the good fortune to inherit the ancient buildings of a Spanish marquis—and the members modestly enjoy themselves amidst splendors meant for an aristocratic family. When I write my utopian novel, I am going to set it in ordinary farm land. No avenues of ancient oaks will lead our visitor into the delights of an old monastery. He will simply follow a good highway map and drive up in his Volkswagen in plain daylight past a mailbox that says *Utopia* (or something). It will be considerably less impressive than the local State Penitentiary.

RECRUITMENT

Another thing I'm going to reverse is the long, slow seduction of the visitor by the community, trying (at first with difficulty, but finally successfully) to convince him that the community can offer him the best life possible. Most utopian novels end with the visitor going away from the community on some absurd rationalization or other. Skinner threw out that convention as it deserves. But I'm going to go one step further. It is obvious to me that any utopia as good as the ones the fiction writers dream up would be besieged with applicants for admission. So I'm going to have my visitor spend the entire book trying to get admission to the group, and have the community trying to discourage him.

"Look," they'll say to him, when he finally locates the Membership Committee, "Do you realize that your house on the Connecticut shore and your new Porsche and your family heirloom silverware will become community property, and that the community will probably sell all of them?" And he'll say, "I don't care. I want to join."

Then they'll warn him, "But you must know that here in community your children won't have to take orders from you. In fact, you aren't even likely to be permitted to supervise their training." And he'll say, "The less I have to say

about those kids, the better off we'll both be. God knows I've done a lousy job so far."

By this time the Membership Committee will be weakening, but they'll have one last shot. "Well, I hope you know that after you're a member, you can't just take off any time you want to; you'll have to wait until your vacations are approved by the labor manager."

"Look," my visitor will say, "you people don't seem to get the point. I don't want to take off. I want to *live here.*" After that the Membership Committee will confess themselves licked and start dragging out the provisional membership contracts.

REALISTIC TOUCH

And finally, I think I'd make my utopia just a shade less utopian than the others I've read. It seems to me that the best society we can possibly come up with will necessarily have aspects that need to be faced with patience and humor. There will be times when bureaucracy gets out of hand, and times when responsibilities are sought by those who should not have them. Any society that accepts adult members will constantly have to deal with value clashes, and some fine experiments may be wiped out by a particular group that manages to legislate against them on quite sincere but mistaken principles. A whole nestful of fledgling communitarians may be infected overnight with symptoms of self-consciousness (or race prejudice, or hysterical giggling) just because a new member brings in a child from the Outside who challenges the norm. Life is not going to be smooth and perfect, not even in Utopia. Even a visitor will notice this. My visitor will notice and forgive. If he started out naive, there is no reason he should stay that way. His stay in Utopia will mark his progress from Wide-Eyed Glorious Expectations to Clear-Eyed Realistic Appraisal. He will decide to join the community, of course, but not because it is perfect. A lifestyle doesn't have to be perfect to attract adherents. It just has to be satisfying. My visitor will be fundamentally capable of being satisfied, and my utopia will not stand in his way. That's about as much as I ever expect from society.

Maybe I'm just not a utopian novel writer.

TRIVIAL POOP

The *Leaves of Twin Oaks* is Twin Oaks' contact with the Outside. It is a sort of company organ, letting our friends know what is happening at Twin Oaks, and telling the world at large that we exist. But other kinds of publications may be worthwhile, too. At some point we are going to want an internal newspaper, letting the members of the Community know what is going on in areas of the Community with which they are not very familiar. With that in mind, we have started a weekly news sheet for internal consumption. It is called the *Trivial Poop*. A single copy is typed and posted on the bulletin board. Though it was originally intended to assist communication, it soon became evident that the group is not really of a size to need that function; and the paper quickly became a comic sheet, published for the reading pleasure of the members.

Most of the *Trivial Poop* is pretty obscure to outsiders. In-group humor dominates the sheet, and we have seen guests perusing it with puzzled looks and no laughter. Some of the humor, indeed, is so obscure that even the members don't understand it. (A cartoon strip called *Stokely* and *Fang Comics* leaves most of us giggling uneasily and wondering what we're laughing at.) Still, there are parts of the paper that can be understood by anybody, and we thought you might be interested. So here are some exerpts:

May 23

TIP—Danny says the tree house is about half-finished.

Prayer Needed—Two walnut trees are very sick. Please mention them in your prayers.

Obituary—One pear tree died and is survived by four healthy young pear trees. Six blackberry plants never made it. After a long illness our hot-water heater has passed on.

May 30

Mixed Poop—Kat, after her first week back at the farm, says, "I'd rather make a hammock than type papers for those capitalists that helped to support us during the last couple of months." She seems to like being back among us godly people of her shape. Guest labor has been a great help in keeping the quota down during the last week. More guests will be arriving at the land of milk and green beans soon.

Filmwinder Manager—Our first filmwinder is half finished, and we are waiting on parts to finish it. Seems it needs some nice legs. I'm told that making filmwinders could develop into a five-dollar-an-hour business.

Construction Manager—This is the big week for our new building to get its foundation. (Maybe.) Next week we may put a roof on the root cellar. The attic will be insulated this week. The first stall on the right in the second barn will be cleaned out and used for a guest room. (It isn't too modern, but it does have somewhat of a religious air about it.) The hay loft in the second barn will also be cleaned out to accommodate some of our guests. The furnace room will be cleaned out, receive a door, and be called a private room.

Maintenance Manager—It seems that everything that needs maintaining is either being maintained, can't be maintained, or just isn't worth maintaining.

Recreation Manager—Two-thirds of the number of hours work we needed to purchase the film projector have been completed. And with all the money we're going to make off of filmwinders we might even be able to rent a film. (So come on, gang.) Goodies for fishing have been purchased for the use of every man, woman, and Danny who want to fish around a bit.

Obituary—A pecan tree was killed instantly when it was accidentally hit by a tractor. A baby pig was born dead. It is survived by eight baby pigs, a mother, and a father that doesn't give a damn.

June 5

Farm Manager—We baled our first crop of hay for the year. We got seventy-one bales, which isn't too good. Next week we should be baling again and get about twice as much as we did this week. Which means twice as much fun.

Recreation Manager—Two rubber rafts were purchased for playing with while taking baths. (This is to encourage bathing.) Our film projector (which we haven't been working too hard for) will be here this week.

Kat—Strawberries were few, tiny, and sour. We were too late in deciding the spinach wasn't poisonous; it went to seed. The corn is committing suicide. And I will not be garden manager next year.

Sport Section—Danny was seen doing a front flip off of a tractorless wagon as it disappeared over the hill. Both Coach (Jim) and Danny have decided this sport is too dangerous and will not compete next week.

June 18

Construction Manager—Scott predicts last nail to be pounded in new building on Halloween, just before Great Pumpkin rises. $1,850 has been spent on new building so far.

Educational Hocus-Pocus—Walt and Christine were hypnotized this week, although they didn't go into a deep trance. They report they felt very relaxed afterwards. More experiments will be tried later. An attempt was made to hypnotize Kat, but it was unsuccessful.

June 26

A Little Humor (very little)—Scott claims he overheard a conversation between Rudy and another member, while they were working on the new building. The member was nailing some boards together for the rafters and he was throwing away about every other nail. Rudy saw this and asked, "Why are you only using about half the nails and throwing the others away?" The member haughtily replied, "Some of them have the points on the wrong end." But Rudy explained that those nails were for the other side of the building.

July 3

Hammock Manager—He was riding down 605 on his bike at 100 mph when he started losing control. On both sides of the road were ditches, so he quickly took out his recorder, a pencil and some paper, and began to write his last song; but all he wrote was *"I don't want a pickle; I just wanna ride on my bicycle;"* then he hit the ditch. Now, had he been making hammocks, which we need so badly, this would never have happened. As it is, he may never walk again. Make hammocks for fun; we have never lost a member while he was making a hammock.

House Manager—The kitchen floor is being washed away due to the daily floods, which we call mopping.

July 10

Construction Manager—Work on the new building moves on with a great lack of vigor; but what we do have finished, the daily monsoon rains keep clean.

July 24

Farm Manager—The farm is being washed away. Perhaps it would be wise for the construction manager to start figuring out how to make an ark. I already know what a cubit is.

NUMBER 11   January, 1970

GENERAL NEWS

THE BUILDING PROGRESSES

The season has advanced to the point that we wish the new building were completed. We are crowded, two and sometimes three to a room, in the building we erected in 1967. Seeing the new building so close to completion and yet not close enough to inhabit is frustrating. For one thing, it is really a large building. The empty second floor (until we grow to much larger membership) could possibly be used for dancing or any number of other activities. And it would be a great pleasure to get the typewriter into an office that was not also the music room.

All the basic structure is completed. The electricity is installed. The building is all enclosed, and we have begun the interior walls. The bottleneck at the moment is insulation under the roof and installing hot air ducts. We hope to have this done within three weeks and begin to move in.

THE PUMP GOES OUT

It is always very satisfying to make solid material progress, such as the erection of a new building or the addition of sewage systems. We felt pretty good, in 1967, when we drilled a 200-foot well and installed an electric pump that gave us all the water we could use. We had a feeling that a permanent improvement had been made, an important step had been taken and gotten out of the way.

So it was heartbreaking when the pump ceased working. For a while it looked as if we might lose the whole well and have to drill another, for the pump was stuck down 200 feet below the surface and would not be lifted by pulling on the steel cable that attached to it. The cable, in fact, snapped in half when we tugged at it with a winch. Was the pump loaded down with dirt and sand? Would we have to drill right through the old pump to get to our well? We began to pull very gently on the plastic pipe that also attached to the pump. Nothing held it together but the plastic threading on the couplings. But it held. We pulled

200 feet of plastic pipe out of the well, and the pump came up at the end of it.

The pump was not salvageable. Gritty sand has eaten its workings beyond repair. $300 bought us another pump just like it, which we worked until late evening putting into place.

What is to guarantee that the sand will not corrode and destroy this pump as it did the other? We have sunk the new pump at a different level, and it is pumping much less sand than before. We have high hopes.

WITHOUT WATER

In the meantime, we went for two days without water. The old well, which might have provided us with drinking water by the hand-drawn bucket, had been recently filled with dirt, by order of the health department, for it lies too close to our new sewage drain field. The only available water is in the creeks. To the nearest creek, therefore, we went, with buckets and clean garbage cans, and brought back enough water to wash dishes with. None of us wanted to drink the creek water. For two days there was no Kool-Aid. Community thirst demolished the milk supply as soon as it came in from the barn. A few determined people boiled the creek water and brushed their teeth with it. The rest of us put up with mossy teeth. The toilet did not function; laundry came to a halt. The dishes all had to be washed by hand and rinsed in the creek water. It was only two days, but two days without washing properly are demoralizing. We all cheered when the new pump sent water into the kitchen once more. The dishwasher, washing machine, and bathtub were speedily put to use, and life was back to normal.

NEW? EQUIPMENT

We regularly receive bulletins announcing government surplus items for sale, and from time to time we put in a bid. We have visions of picking up a good truck for $100, or a hundred years' supply of woolen socks for 50 cents; but so far we haven't had any such luck as that.

Last month we saw an announcement of some kitchen equipment that appealed to us, and we decided to bid seriously on it. The lot included a commercial-type dishwasher, three large coffee urns, a glass washer, a large deep-fry unit, a commercial meat saw (electric), and a malted milk maker. The new value of the lot was marked at $3,800, but the things were not new: several need repair — the saw has no blade, the glass washer no brushes.

We bid $150 and won. This is something like 4 per cent of the new value. We went to pick up our prize and are fairly impressed by the general high quality of the equipment we bought. With very little repair most of it will be very useful—some day.

And therein lies the irony of the situation. Almost all of the equipment is too large for our current use. We don't have enough dishes to use anything so large, nor enough French fries even to bother plugging in the fryer. So the lot sits impressively in our garage, waiting—like the rest of us—for a bigger kitchen.

WE DEFLATE THE CREDIT

Though our credit system is worked out with the idea of keeping the *average* labor credit worth one hour of work, in practice this has not occurred. In theory, for every job that goes up in value, another goes down. But what happens is that large areas of work enter and leave the system all the time, and the result is almost always an imbalance, which eventually creates an inflated credit. Periodically we have to check the total number of credits issued per week against the total number of hours represented. Last month we did this and came up with the astonishing figure of 1.2. That meant that the work quota, which was riding at about 52 credits a week, actually represented only 41.6 hours of work. Like any inflation, this one hurt the people who had credits "in the bank," being saved for vacation. So we deflated the credit. The hardest part of deflation is explaining it. There was some grumbling. It was nice, indeed, to see the work quota go down around the 40 mark again, but who would sign up for breakfast dishes at 1.4 for a two-hour job? And construction is down to .7 per hour. (That means two hours' credit for three hours' work.)

The job currently rating the highest (1.4 per hour) is fence and gate mending. The lowest-rating item on the system (meaning the most popular) has been visitor-greeting, which is at times down to .5 per hour. Outside jobs, which were bid as high as 3.0 per hour (we even had a member bid "a google to a google power") have been "frozen" at 1.2, since all members are required to take their turn at it, anyway.

PIGS AGAIN

In 1967 we raised a few pigs and ate them, not bothering to calculate the price of pork so obtained. In 1968 we had our own sow and raised some more, ate a few, and sold the rest in a depressed market that showed us clearly that we could have bought the pork more cheaply at the A&P. Since it didn't pay us to keep pigs enclosed and feed them grain, the 1969 plan was simply to let the brood animals eat the available slops and a little grain and to sell the piglets as soon as they could be weaned. But the market was low again when weaning time came around; and besides, the pigs were small enough to escape the electric fence enclosure and forage for themselves among the weeds and falling apples.

There were protests. Some people felt that five pet dogs, eleven cats, and two goats sufficiently crowded our immediate grounds without adding fifteen wandering shoats to the collection. Having finished off the apples lying on the ground, the pigs tried rooting for the ones that hadn't come up yet, and that didn't help the condition of the grass a whole lot. "Wait until the price goes up," said the animal manager. In July they finished off that part of the garden that hadn't been already finished off by the rains. In September they went in search of bigger watermelons, and investigated the patch of neighbor Jones. Good neighbors being more important than good prices, we took the piggies to market the next day.

It is easy enough to sell a pig, once you get him to market. Catching him and putting him into the truck is harder. You have to herd them gently into an enclosure where you can catch them. Once they start to run, nothing in the world will stop them. There is nothing on a pig to grab hold of, and they pay no more attention to a stick or a stone than to a pat on the head. If you stand directly in their way, they simply knock you down (and we have the bruises to prove it).

Maybe next year we'll raise soy beans, instead. They don't taste as good, but they stay where you put them.

AND GOATS

The idea of buying the goats was that they would keep the grass short, like the herd of sheep in *Walden Two*. We would tether them in the yard, moving them from day to day, and they would provide a pleasant and picturesque super-efficiency lawn mower. Accordingly, we bought two kids, a nanny and a billy, and made pets of them. As pets they are excellent, being charming and friendly and not even very messy. As lawn mowers they have one drawback—they don't like grass. They will eat everything else: shrubs and rose bushes have been sampled; they go for hay and clover; they have a mania for roof cement. But the grass is as long as ever.

TWIN OAKS AND RUNAWAYS

The phone rings, and we answer it. A voice says, "I'm desperate. My folks have set the cops on me. I need a place to stay. I love the idea of community living. Can I come and stay with you?"

We feel very sorry for these young people (and for their parents, for that matter), but we have to say no to runaways. Twin Oaks is after goals more important than the immediate relief of individual suffering, and in order to come anywhere near those goals, we must survive as a community. Surviving really does require adherence to the laws of the land, and the law looks unfavorably upon harboring runaways.

Just the same, we have from time to time had some teenage people living here without their parents. We require a written consent from at least one parent, so the only way a teenager can stay with us at all is to talk his parents into letting him. This is a difficult decision for a parent, for Twin Oaks considers anybody over 13 an adult and does not restrict his conduct in any way except by the same community restrictions that affect all the adult members (lack of money, necessity of working, etc). Most parents are quarreling with their young people over precisely that issue, and to allow them to live at Twin Oaks is almost to surrender to the demand for freedom. Sometimes, though, a parent will see Twin Oaks as the best of a number of undesirable alternatives. While it is true that the son or daughter will be sleeping in a barn, going to bed at any hour he chooses, and organizing his social life as he sees fit, still there *is* structure at Twin Oaks. He does a full share of the work, and probably participates in classes or other group activities. And there are no drugs. So every once in a while, our numbers are augmented by a 16-year-old or two.

Not every 16-year-old can be happy here. Our 40- to 50-hour weekly work load is enough to make some of them reconsider their home situation. But the young person who can cope with the work load generally finds life here attractive. Part of the reason for this is the new freedom of action. More important seems to be the fact that they cease being "teenagers" and a race set apart as soon as they get here. Twin Oaks treats them exactly as if they were capable of behaving as adults, and they usually rise to the role very quickly.

SELF-MANAGEMENT

That's a pretty impressive title, but it has reference to a fairly simple process. What it amounts to is some interesting recordkeeping and some experimenting with certain methods (such as self-rewards and self-penalties) to change one's habits.

Matt Israel visited us this last summer and showed us the system. Matt keeps a notebook over an inch thick, full of graphs that tell the day-by-day story of his behavior. He has a graph on his weight, one on the amount of sleep he gets, another on physical exercise. In another section of his book he plans his day, then records how he actually spent the day. He records his dating and social behaviors, his emotions, moods, and everything else you can think of.

Our first reaction was one of amusement and awe, mixed with a bit of puzzlement. What does anybody want such complete records for? To Matt, who is a behavioral scientist,

the graphs are of scientific value. He spends about half an hour daily on his recording. And the gains: Matt claims the graphs have helped him to stop drinking, reduce his weight, exercise daily, get up on time, brush his teeth after meals, use dental floss, answer mail promptly, write personal letters, and organize his life generally.

Matt uses a four-step system for changing behavior that was developed by Ogden Lindsley, Professor of Special Education of the University of Kansas. The four steps are:

1. Pinpoint the behavior. Describe it specifically enough so that you can count each instance of it when it occurs.

2) Record its rate. Record the number of times it occurs per day, per hour, or per minute. One's goal is either to accelerate the behavior (make it happen more frequently) or to decelerate it.

3) Change something. For example, set up a reminder-sign, or administer a self-reward or a self-penalty. Matt has found it effective, in his own case, to charge himself $1 for each misbehavior, and has sent some of his penalty money as a contribution to Twin Oaks.

4) Try, try again. If the first change you try doesn't accelerate or decelerate the behavior to the desired rate, try something else. Data shows that you are bound to succeed if you try up to three times.

Matt went back to Boston, and we thought about self-management for a while. Then one by one we began to get interested in the idea. Rudy was first. He made a graph on "Sat all the way through an unpleasant hassle without walking out" and one on "Felt I wasted a day," another on how many drinking glasses he uses per day, and how many of those he returns to the kitchen and washes.

Kat watched Rudy's graphs grow daily more interesting and got caught up in the idea. She keeps about thirty-five graphs of behaviors that interest her—one on keeping her room livably neat, one on gossip control, one on "felt happy and comfortable in what I was wearing today," one on "felt optimistic about the Community."

And now other members are beginning to ask for graph paper. "I want to keep track of the number of times I feel irritated each day," says one. "I want to know how much my mood varies with the weather," says another.

Are we, too, contributing to the literature of science? We doubt it. But in its modest way, our self-management is an experiment. We ought to find out a number of things from it, not least among which might be just how long the graphing fad will last.

POPULATION GROWTH

Twin Oaks' population goes up and down, varying with the season and with other circumstances and problems. The summer of 1968 saw us at twenty-two members, but we were back at thirteen again the beginning of this winter. The smallness of our group has not concerned us too much until now, for we have in any case not had the space or facilities to accommodate a large group. However, with our new dormitory building nearly complete, we felt that we were ready to accept a larger membership. We did two things to this end: we began to advertise widely, and we dropped the barrier of the entrance fee. True to our expectations, our membership has enlarged at a brisk pace. Integration of the new members has this time proved smooth and pleasant, and we look forward to accepting even more members in the next few weeks.

CLEM COMMENTS on the POPULATION

Several times ago it was known throughout the Community that a new member was needed. After considering thought on this memberless subject, we decided why knot need many new members. So we did. Some said why not advertise; others sad why not put adds in papers. Others said nice things and some said nothing, which isn't worthy of mention. Being the kindly people that we are, we dropped our $200 membership fee to a minor some of $20. As the weeks pass, many people across the nation read our ads and decided that Twin Oaks was indeed the place for them. They came in ones and twos and buses and many walked. They filled up our rooms overnight (but were moved out in the morning). People were busy tossing coins to see who would share their rooms with the new members. People spoke of the growth, while others wondered what sort of growth it was and if it could be cured. Now it is well known among all the new members that if we don't finish our new building soon, we will certainly lose our growth.

THE FOUR-HOUR DAY AND ART

The sudden influx of members caught the labor people unprepared, and for three or four weeks in a row Twin Oaks enjoyed a work quota very close to the four-hour day. In seriousness, we cannot afford this. We are still in a stage of community growth that requires us to put in more labor in order to be certain that we will survive and grow. But while the hammock manager was gearing his production back up to the larger group, we did have a long break in the work.

We have been re-reading *Walden Two* for our Utopia class, and it came to our attention that the four-hour day is supposed to bring about a golden age of art. We examined our life — had these four weeks of rest raised our artistic level? If not, why not? Some members said that the leisure had indeed already begun to bear fruit. Was it not true that Fox was practicing his cornet every day? And what about Lonnie's poems? And Clem's apocryphal Pooh Bear story? Just the same, we concluded that it takes more than leisure to produce creative work. It takes a bit of stimulation. The Utopia class provided the stimulation, and the following days were filled with live music and literary endeavor. Three recorders, a flute, a cornet, and five or six guitars almost put the record player out of business, and drove several people almost out of their minds. We had to make special

regulations about proper places to practice on loud musical instruments.

We have to admit that none of this effort has produced anything very spectacular, unless you count the pleasure of learning to play an instrument and the fun of playing together in harmony. The only publishable piece of "literature" comes from Karl, who was inspired by psychology class and decided to be creative in the field of advertising.

GOVERNMENT
Opinion — By Kat

The one facet of Walden Two that disturbs more people than any other is its government. Walden Two was set up with a system of planners and managers, appointed in a circular manner that left very little to the choice of the membership as a whole. Decisions were made on this level and implemented, seemingly without consulting the majority about their wishes.

This system sounds a good deal like dictatorships the world has been familiar with for thousands of years, and its threats are obvious. While anyone will admit that a benevolent dictator can do a great deal to promote the happiness and prosperity of his people, there is the ever-present danger of a not-so-benevolent dictator, or even of the kindly ruler with mistaken ideas about people's happiness. And with any system involving a large number of people, it is always the case that ruling must be done, in the long run, not by the monarch himself, but by his underlings, whose moral qualities vary with the individual but who have traditionally served chiefly the function of self-aggrandizement.

The argument in favor of a democratic system always boils down to this: that it is the best we have come up with to date. No advocate of democracy is so blind as not to see its faults. Still, for all of its clumsiness and defects, it seems to Americans that people living under democracy probably have a better control of their leaders, and therefore a better guarantee of a good life, than people living under autocratic systems.

Whatever the merits of this argument, there are things that it does not take into account. What I mean to establish in this article is that democracy is not at all practical for small group management, and that a sort of dictatorship is. What I specifically want to talk about is the kind of structure that we have at Twin Oaks and why I believe it is the best one we could have, or at least better than anything else we've heard of. To do that, I need to examine various forms of democracy.

CONSENSUS

First, I want to look at what is often referred to as "consensus procedure." Under consensus the entire group meets and discusses matters of importance. They discuss them until they agree on them. I have been told by people I respect that this can "work" in groups that they know of. I have difficulty imagining it. I have to end up supposing that in groups where this system "works" the issues must necesarily be peripheral to the lives of the people involved. At least it wouldn't work very well at Twin Oaks.

Take a typical agenda for a week at Twin Oaks, and let's imagine that we had to make decisions by consensus. We would meet, perhaps, after supper dishes, when most people are free from their daily jobs, about 9:00 p.m. First item to be decided: Some member feels that our current rule against marijuana on the premises is unnecessary. He points out that many communities use it constantly and openly and have not been closed down. The group argues about it. The people who have been through the argument several times already present their views regarding the necessity of living as nearly as possible within the civil law. It is not at all improbable that the argument could go on for 45 minutes before some members get restless and someone suggests that we vote.

But no, voting is not part of consensus procedure. We are supposed to discuss the thing until everyone agrees. But time drags on, and everyone does not agree in the least. In fact, some people are getting downright nettled about the whole thing. One group is sick of talking about it, because they just barely defeated the same argument with the last group of newcomers (before they left). Another group is sick of having these decisions made by the same old-time clique, because one of them is a loudmouth who gives them a pain on general principles, and are beginning to rebel just for the sake of seeing them defeated. After 45 minutes, then, we are no nearer decision than before. Somebody suggests we put the matter off until another time. That makes some sense, for at another time some of these members will have gone on to some other kind of life and will be smoking their marijuana in peace in their own pads. Several people can see that putting the matter off is the same thing as agreeing to a "no" decision, for "No Drugs" was the status quo. But everyone is tired of the subject, and there are three more items on the agenda. So there is agreement at last, for no one protests the suggestion to table the drug question.

But what does the agreement mean? Simply that in any issue that anyone is willing to argue about for a long period of time, the status quo will be upheld because of group fatigue.

So let's go on to the next issue. The farm manager (for the sake of simplicity let us assume that the group has at least delegated some authority to individual managers, so that group meetings do not have to be held every night, all night) has suggested that we buy up a barnfull of hay from another farmer at a certain price, and that we try to sell it later when the price goes up. He presents his case. Some other people ask questions, trying to find out whether, indeed, we would be investing well to buy and sell hay. Nobody really knows much about the whole thing; we are short on information. But some people suspect that we don't know enough to be in that sort of business, when we are surrounded by farmers who know a lot more than we do and who aren't speculating in hay. We talk desultorily about it for ten minutes or so. Finally someone with a confident

voice says that it is Perfectly Obvious that we Do Not Know Enough about Farming and about Farm Prices to go in this business. The farm manager is disappointed; but he realizes that this is probably true, so he doesn't argue it. Loud Voice's opinions carry some weight. Nobody else has anything to say on the subject at all. So once again we have reached agreement.

But what sort of agreement is it? All it means is that one person guessed at a course of action, and that nobody else cared enough about the subject to fight his suggestion. Once again, the status quo wins.

But there are decisions that there isn't any status quo to be upheld or overturned. Take the third item on the agenda. There is a man and his wife and baby who want to join the Community. There is a considerable question about their admission. People point out that the labor cost of caring for a baby is very high. A further consideration is that the wife in this case is not enthusiastic about community but is merely willing to join to please her husband. We discuss the wisdom and unwisdom of admitting them under these circumstances. All the evidence we can see points to refusing their entrance at this time. Still, the young man applicant is very enthusiastic, and we are appalled at the idea of turning him down because of mere practical considerations. Besides, he plays an excellent jazz trombone. And the baby is adorable. We discuss the pros and cons. We get nowhere. It is obvious that we all know we are heading for trouble if we accept them. It is equally obvious that we all shrink from refusing them admission. Since it is a decision that no one wants to make, it is highly probable that one person with a strong opinion one way or the other will sway the group. What we would all be looking for is someone else to make a decision. Again Loud Voice pipes up and says, "I suppose we are fools, but I think we all want them to join, and let the chips fall where they may." The chances are that the others will go along with him. So we agree.

But what was the agreement. Merely a group shrinking from taking responsibility for a decision that is difficult to make. It was Loud Voice who made the decision.

Loud Voice can do only so much, though, to help the group come to a decision. There are issues on which there is no possible agreement, and on which a decision is badly needed. Take, for example, the fourth item on the agenda, a discussion of the current financial situation and a suggestion that we send some of our members to find jobs in the nearby cities in order to make ends meet. Status quo will not answer here, for the current practices (we will say) mean ruin to the Community. Loud Voice has opinions and expresses them, but there is no grateful acceptance of his ideas this time, for every member is threatened by the suggestion. There is intense argument. Several members, especially those who know they can easily find work, argue in favor of the Outside Job Plan and say (rather contemptuously) that they will volunteer to be the first to go, but that in good time every member should take his turn. Some other members, especially those who have not held regular jobs for many years and are not sure they could get and hold a job, argue that community is meaningless if members have to hold outside jobs. Someone suggests borrowing money and starting an industry. Another throws in cutting back the standard of living and eating brown rice and honey, having the phone taken out, and letting the automobiles ground themselves as they gradually run out of gas. There are six proposals, all designed by their proponents to keep the Community going and meet the financial crisis. At 10:30 two members get up and announce that they are going to bed, because they have to get up in the morning to milk the cow. Without them, of course, consensus is not possible, for they are full members of the group, and no decision can be made without their support. We adjourn with reluctance. The financial decision hangs in the air.

At this point something happens. Either the volunteers go out and find jobs and just hope that the others will take their turn when the time comes, or the Community has a stroke of luck that makes the decision unnecessary, or the Community falls apart, or else somebody pushes through an agreement to change the form of government to one where decisions can be arrived at.

For "consensus procedure" is hopelessly difficult for a group whose lives are intimately affected by the decisions made. Decisions must, of course, be made; and consensus can stand in their way just so long. What this impractical idea does is push decision-making back to the more primitive methods of individual action, reaction, lead and follow.

PURE DEMOCRACY

The next step up the ladder of efficiency is pure democracy. As soon as the notion of a majority vote comes into the picture, decision-making becomes possible. Meetings may take all night, it is true, but eventually a vote will be taken, and a decision—good or bad—will be arrived at. A brief glance at the same four issues will give us some clues as to whether pure democracy serves the group as well as consensus, or possibly better.

The drug question can be voted on. The answer to whether the Community will abandon its law-abiding position and begin to permit drugs on the premises will be decided by majority vote, and this will depend entirely upon the makeup of the group. Is the majority cautious? Or has there been an influx lately of persons whose desire to use drugs is greater than their concern for the Community's position with the local magistrates? Whichever party is more numerous will win the issue, regardless of whether one course or another would be fatal to the Community. It is very easy to imagine a group with a population made up more than half of people who are not really intending to live all their lives in the Community, anyway, and to whom the legal survival of the Community is of secondary importance. Communities come and go, they say to themselves, and when the police bust one, another one opens up. There will always be a place for me. There is a group to whom the end of the Community would be a major personal tragedy, but they are a *minority*. They are a minority who have the long-range interests of the community in mind, and the

course of action they suggest is the sensible one for the community's survival. But they are overruled — very democratically.

The question of whether to invest money in speculating on the price of hay comes to a vote, too, presumably. Whereas under consensus the decision was made by Loud Voice and an indifferent group, under pure democracy Loud Voice will have only one vote, and each of the indifferent will also have a vote. Since none of them has any idea which way they ought to vote, they will probably vote by one of the following guidelines: whether they generally approve of speculation; whether they like the farm manager; whether they like Loud Voice; whether they wanted the hay storage barn for something else; whether they think that either the farm manager or Loud Voice is generally right about most things; whether they imagine the price of hay ever goes up.

As to the issue of admitting or refusing the couple with the baby, the vote will probably be close, most people either imagining clearly what the additional family will mean to Community resources or identifying with the entering couple and feeling sorry for them. Once again, however, the people who cast most of the positive votes may well not be the people who will be in the Community to take the brunt of the problem when it becomes a reality.

Outside jobs? The majority will almost certainly defeat this measure. The rationalizations will be as varied as the membership, but the end result would be that people who do not want to take jobs will vote against the plan, whether or not there is any financial alternative.

Decision-making by large groups is largely impractical. Too many decisions require careful thought, and no congregation of voters can give sufficiently informed thought to such a wide variety of subjects. Large groups are (of course) made up of people who spend most of their time and energy on projects quite unconnected with government, and the attention they give to government must necessarily be peripheral and therefore careless. They will be influenced by personalities, by superficial aspects of issues, and by their desire to get the meeting over with and get on with their lives. Good government requires close attention and careful weighing of issues. It is necessary that it be done by small, specialized groups.

Most people will follow the argument this far and agree that administration is best carried on by a small group. The thorny question at this point is how to choose that small group. It is tempting to let oneself be influenced by our national government and democratic traditions and just assume that the best small group is a representative group, elected by the people whose lives will be affected by the decisions. Representative government makes good surface sense, for it gives the people the feeling that their voice is being heard, even though they don't personally have the time or ability to deal with the issues directly. Upon closer examination, however, the whole notion of an elected group being "representative" merely because it is elected falls apart.

REPRESENTATION

On how many issues can any one delegate represent any other person, let alone a group of people? All the people can know when they elect a delegate is that he is a liberal, or a conservative, or a radical, or in favor of or against some major issue. He has certain emotional sets in common with the people who put him into office, and they feel that he is likely to vote according to those sets, thus probably agreeing much of the time with his constituents. The fact is, however, that most of the decisions confronting a legislative body are not related to the great liberal-conservative issues and are in fact decided on quite other bases.

Take small community issues once again. Though there are emotional sets in community (the most obvious one is hard-line communal vs. practical compromise), they do not come into play on the question of whether to permit marijuana, or admit a family with children, or speculate in hay, or get outside jobs. Each of these questions may be decided on the basis of other sets (permanent community vs. radical movement as a whole; financial security vs. extending a helping hand; fiscal conservatism vs. speculation). A hard-line communitarian may be a fiscal conservative and still be in favor of allowing families with children. There is no reason at all to suppose that the miscellaneous collection of emotional sets (sometimes called "opinions") of a given delegate will coincide with those of his constituents. People who elect a "representative" have not been defrauded if, after all, they are not represented. It is naive to suppose that representation, in that sense, is even possible.

Representation in another sense, though, is both possible and desirable. What most of us expect of our government is that it deal with issues honestly, thoroughly, and skillfully, without any regard for the private interests of the governors. When we elect a person to office, it is usually with the hope that the person elected will serve as best he can *for the benefit* of the people he represents. In this sense the delegate does indeed have a responsibility to "represent" the people, and it is reasonable to expect that he should do so.

The question then becomes this: Is this person who puts forth his best effort to make decisions for the benefit of the people best chosen by election?

ELECTION

How are people elected to office? Does honesty attract votes? Does caution? Long-range thinking? Most of us know that people do not vote on these bases, even if they sometimes think they are doing so. What most people use as a guide for voting is an intuitive feeling that the candidate in some ways represents their interests. Unfortunately, this feeling is easily generated by a few personality tricks, not in the least necessarily related to the genuine qualities of the candidate. Does he have a "common folks" accent? Or a taste for dirty stories? Is he faithful to his wife? These things will win or lose more votes by far than either his convictions or his character. They are very poor indications

of qualifications for office, but they will indeed be the qualifying characteristics as long as the system for choosing officers remains an elective one.

Election does not work. It does not do what it is supposed to do. In small groups the irrational considerations that make people vote one way or another are different from the ones used in large groups, but they are nonetheless irrational.

But even if we could discard the worry about irrational voting behavior, elections in small groups must face a further argument, founded in the ideals of the group.

GOAL ORIENTATION

The officers of any group have an obligation to the interests and happiness of the people in that group, but the officers of religious or idealistic groups have a further obligation—their obligation to the principles and goals on which the group was founded. If a group has been gathered together declaring its intention to serve God, then its leaders should and must be persons who have in mind to serve God, notwithstanding pressure from the group (however democratic such pressure might be) to forget God and start passing out the consumer goods. Likewise, if a group is formed to promote democracy, or communism, or support the local police or the PTA, it is the responsibility of the leaders of that group to devote themselves to that end, and it is the duty of the group to see to it that persons who take office are likely to bend their energies in that direction.

In intentional community this problem is an extremely crucial one. Nearly every issue either has or seems to have an effect on the membership, and it is natural that the group should from time to time wish for decisions that seem to make life easier, whether or not such decisions are in line with the original intent of the community.

What is needed is a decision-making group that has the strength of character to resist popular pressure and pursue the community's goals, and this kind of government will not come about through election.

Decision-making is a special job. It requires certain specific qualities, like intelligence, dedication to the principles of the group, and sensitivity to the needs of the people. There is no way of assuring that people with these qualities are likely to be put into office by election. The public as a whole is rarely rational and even more rarely objectively dedicated to the group's principles.

The only reasonable alternative is some sort of appointment system, each board of directors being chosen by the board that precedes it. Probably the best way to explain how such a system might work is to describe the one we use at Twin Oaks.

TWIN OAKS' SYSTEM

The overall government at Twin Oaks is in the charge of a three-person team called the board of planners. This board is controlled by a very loose constitution giving the board a great deal of freedom of movement (including the power to change the governmental structure). The constitution does set out the principles on which the group was founded, and these principles cannot be changed without a 2/3 majority vote of the entire membership. (They include the general principle of equality, the community ownership of property, communal child care, a nonviolence clause, and general declarations in favor of the experimental method and non-aversive control.) Within this framework the planners can make any and all decisions in the Community. They can be overruled on any decision by 2/3 majority vote of the membership, but this is an unlikely eventuality, for the board of planners has no force available for enforcing unpopular decisions and nothing to gain by doing so.

What would the board of planners do about the same four issues we have seen through the more "democratic" processes?

On the drug question, the board will almost certainly stick to its no-drug rule until the Federal law changes. Why? Because the board is certainly composed of people who care about the long run. Pressures from the (perhaps large) group who would like to smoke marijuana on the premises and feel deprived of their civil liberties would not affect the board. They have the survival of the Community to consider, and they do care a great deal whether it survives. They would spend time explaining their point of view, pointing out that their reasons were legal, not moral. They might hold special meetings with discontented members to argue the matter out. But they would stick to their decision.

As to the hay question, the probability is that the members of the board don't know any more about the price of hay than the membership at large, but they would have the sense to appoint someone to find out the facts and the caution to withhold money until someone could come up with facts that indicate that the investment would be wise.

The matter of taking the family with children would be decided on the basis of real risks and real gains and not greatly swayed by emotions or guilty feelings. The board makes this kind of decision all the time and develops by experience a sense of probable outcome. It will not always make the right decision, but it is more likely to be right than the larger group.

As to the outside job question, the board will know whether it is necessary, and if it is, they will set up a system and ask the members to cooperate with it.

Of these four decisions, three may turn out to be unpopular ones—unpopular, but necessary. This is where the appointed board is in a better position than the elected one. It can make such decisions without worrying "Will this cost me votes?"

What guarantees does the membership have against tyranny of such a board? Its constitution; its equalitarian economic structure; and the simple fact that any time any legislation becomes too unpalatable, the membership can overrule. The board has no means of enforcing any decision except by the consent of the people it governs, and it has nothing to gain by governing other than for their benefit.

NUMBER 12

May, 1970

GENERAL NEWS

STATISTICS

OCCUPYING THE NEW BUILDING

The new building (called the Oneida Building, in honor of a nineteenth-century successful community) is not yet finished. Its board and batten exterior has all its boards but not all its battens. The living room lacks glass in its windows, but its seven bedrooms on the main floor were completed the first part of February and are now occupied. The Hammock Building (the one we were calling "the new building" in 1967) still has bedrooms in it, but two of them have recently been converted to workshops. We found it very difficult to continue our woodshop work in the old tobacco barn. It was too cold in winter and too far from our living quarters in all weather. Eventually all of the hammock building will be converted to shops, as more and more dormitory space is built.

Not too long ago a visitor who was writing a term paper about us came prepared with questionnaires for Community members to fill out. Before returning the questionnaires to the visitor, we compiled the statistics ourselves. Here they are:

Fifteen males, ten females. The average age is 22.5 and ranges from 17 to 39. Years of miseducation range from 9 to 18 (some members caught on quicker than others). The average is 13.0 (one year of college). Religions don't seem to hold people any more—16 members have rejected their parents' religion, 2 have retained it. There were 2 atheist families, 5 catholics, and 11 protestants. How long have people been here? Average—14 months, ranging from 4 to 34 months. Where do people hear about Twin Oaks? Ten from papers of some sort and 6 from word of mouth. *WIN Magazine* got 4, and the *Leaves* helped 6 to see the light.

TWENTY-FIVE MEMBERS

The membership reached twenty-five and then stopped. This was not because anything happened to the communal movement, but simply because Twin Oaks ran out of room and had to put a lid on its population. With our current facilities, we can reasonably house and feed twenty-five people and no more. Weekend guests crowd us, but not intolerably. Before we can expand much more in population, we will need money for more sewage and a larger dining room.

This does not mean that our membership is absolutely closed. Sometimes members leave or take extended leaves of absence, leaving room for another one or two people. It does mean, though, that we have begun a small "waiting list" of people who want to join and want to be informed when we have space.

PUBLICITY

We are as big as we can get right now, and yet we keep on advertising. Furthermore, some of our best publicity has not been paid advertising but articles about us in various magazines. Grinnell, Iowa's *Pterodactyl* did a long article on us last summer, with numerous photographs and detailed explanations of our structures and policies. The article was largely accurate, presenting us as we see ourselves—a radical alternative; and we were pleased to see that *Pterodactyl* released it for reprint to *Win Magazine* and the *Modern Utopian.* Our correspondence has tripled after these publications.

But publicity has not stopped there. The *New York Times* decided to do an article on Dr. Skinner. When the reporter interviewed him, Dr. Skinner handed him the *Modern Utopian* with the *Ptero* reprint in it, and the reporter drove down to Virginia to see us. A photographer followed, and our name became further known through the *Times'* unenthusiastic but widely circulated Sunday Supplement article.

Then there was the television. A TV station in Washington, D.C. got in touch with us a year ago; and we told them at the time that we would rather wait a year, when we might be in better shape to be photographed. So they waited a year and called back. They wanted to do a fifteen-minute news spot on Twin Oaks. Would we consent? We argued about it and finally told them to go ahead. This turned out to be an innocuous presentation turning on the "hard-working hippie" theme.

Why do we do it? If we have all the members we need, and a waiting list on top of it; if we are turning away visitors for lack of space (and we are), then why keep ourselves in the limelight? Because we want the communal idea publicized. Because we want to stimulate other people to do the same. All we can do with the stacks of mail is to send out printed material and hope for newsletter subscriptions enough to cover the cost of the postage. All we can do with

the visitors is turn most of them away, accepting just those few whom we can have time to talk to and genuinely give a taste of community life. If we can keep only twenty-five members, would it not be to our advantage to select them out of a waiting list of hundreds, rather than dozens?

THE STORE

By far the most absorbing activity for Twin Oaks this spring has been the opening and operating of a nearby country grocery store. The opportunity was offered us by the owner, who found that he could not keep the store open because his family did not enjoy storekeeping. So he rented us his premises and is selling us his inventory on easy payments. In many ways the business is very well suited to Twin Oaks. Working the store in shifts, we can easily keep it open fourteen hours a day. It is lazy, easy work, involving at most dusting shelves and slicing balogna, in addition to waiting on customers. The work is popular, and the labor credit value has already slid down to .7 per hour.

We welcome, too, the opportunity to meet our neighbors in an environment in which both of us are comfortable. We are rapidly establishing a reputation for honesty and reasonable prices and the number of our customers increases each week. It gives the young people of the area a chance to see a communitarian close up and talk to him. "Hey, how come you don't cut your hair?" asked one, and the Twin Oaks member answered him, "Because I like it long—why don't you let yours grow?" "My dad won't let me" was the reply.

We are fairly well stocked for a country store. We sell canned and boxed goods, a frozen food line, balogna and weiners, potatoes and onions, brooms and mops, salted mackerel. But most of our business is in ice cream, potato chips, and candy. We have a full penny-candy line. Children and grownups both take a little paper bag and fill it up with their choice of caramels and gum drops and marshmallow peanuts.

We have gas pumps and cigarettes, too, which account for a good proportion of our sales. There is some possibility that we may get a beer license, which would probably double our gross sales almost immediately. But some of our neighbors don't approve of beer and have circulated a petition to deny us the license. We await the results of the petition with interest, without caring a great deal whether we get it. It is true that we do not make a great deal of money from the store now, and that beer sales would make the place literally profitable to us. But it would anger a certain segment of the local population—mostly whites who don't want the blacks to drink. We let the application ride on to success or failure. . .if we get the license, we can still decide whether we want to use it.

In the meantime we can use the store for other public services. One member makes it a point to show every bread purchaser that the small loaf is a better bargain than the large loaf—a practice doubtless not appreciated by the bread company. We sell the lowest-priced motor oil in the area, too, and the cheapest balogna. We are not greedy in our markups, generally. And we made it a point to tell the Royal Crown people that we would not even consider carrying soft drinks in throw-away containers that would litter the countryside.

Questions of ideology arose immediately when the store opportunity first came up. Were we, by entering the retail business, becoming capitalists? This may seem absurd, but retailing is unlike manufacturing, in that the amount of markup the retailer charges *directly* takes money out of the pockets of his customers. That is, every penny we make is one that one of our neighbors loses. We asked ourselves whether we even wanted to be in that relationship with our neighbors. After a lot of talk, we concluded that a retail grocery store in our present economic system can be and should be a service to the people, provided the retailer does not make more money than the average income of his customers. We live in a poor area, and our customers probably make $1.50 to $2 an hour to support a family of four or five. So we have tentatively decided that when our sales reach the point that we make $1.50 to $2 an hour take-home profit, we will cut back our markup, rather than make more money. This may be a while (depending on the beer license). At present the store is netting us about sixty cents an hour.

CONTRACT TYPING

The more varied we can make our "outside exchange" work, the less aversive will be our work schedules. We are continually striving to substitute on-the-farm moneymaking activities for the detested "outside jobs." Recently we added contract typing to our list of businesses. In order to get the contract, we are having to buy an IBM Selectric typewriter, but a group of twenty-five people really needs two good typewriters around, anyway, and some of us are pleased to have the excuse to buy this super-rapid machine. The contract typing is simple—just names and addresses, then stuffing envelopes. We make a little less than $2 an hour from it—that's a pretty good rate for sit-down, indoor work that can be done at any hour. The contract is not large enough yet to allow us to bring one of our outside workers home, but it is a little extra money in the bank—or will be after we get the typewriter paid for.

LECTURING

Of all the jobs Twin Oaks members have ever done for "outside exchange" (cash), by far the most interesting, as well as the highest paid, is lecturing. After Lafayette College we were invited to William and Mary, then Davidson College in North Carolina, as well as three Unitarian fellowship groups and a high school. In all cases we found the sessions well attended, the audiences interested, the question periods lively, and the remuneration adequate. So why not actively seek such engagements? We didn't quite know how to go about this, so we just sent a letter to psychology departments at various nearby colleges, telling who we were and asking if they were interested. The response to date has been very encouraging. Three invitations were tendered the first month, and more are indicated for the fall.

The lecture itself is very simple. We just tell them in what ways Twin Oaks' life differs from their world and try to give them an idea what it is like to live here. That takes all the available lecture time, and the rest is devoted to questions. Questions range from "How to you justify isolating yourselves on a farm when the country needs you?" to "How can I become a member?"

What everyone really wants to know is what community mating patterns are like, but few people will actually inquire. "Communes are usually associated with free love and orgies—how does Twin Oaks feel about that?" asked a determined interviewer recently. "Our sexual behavior is pretty much like people on the outside, but with the differences that one would expect in a communal situation," we answered him with a straight face.

There are fringe benefits to lecture work. One is the long bus or car ride to the college. Travel time pays only .7 credits an hour, but it is pleasant to have five or six hours in a row to think, entirely uninterrupted by managerial duties. Pleasant, too, are the hotel accommodations provided. It always gives us a sense of waste to occupy alone a room equipped with two double beds, and we feel vaguely guilty having a bathroom for our exclusive use. Every time we leave a college and thank our hosts for the luxurious accommodations, we are always thinking in the back of our minds, "We could house four people in this amount of space at Twin Oaks!"

Best fun of all is being a celebrity for a day and meeting the college professors who have given some thought to the Good Life or Ideal State, and have significant and challenging questions to ask. Speakers are often invited to faculty luncheons or suppers, and talking about community with a small, intimate group is often more fun than the bigger audiences. We always come home feeling refreshed and stimulated. As invitations become more common, more members are training to give the lectures. The trips are fun, but nobody wants to be gone from the Community more than once or twice a month.

DANCING

From the beginning Twin Oaks has had capable folk-dance instructors among its membership. But it has taken us over two years to get a dance group started. One of the problems has been lack of dancing space, but more important was the fact that the dancers couldn't stir up any enthusiasm among the small membership. They just weren't interested in dancing, and that was that.

But a group of twenty-five people is another story. We postulate a theory that where there are twenty-five people gathered together, there will be eight or ten who will want to dance. At any rate, about once a week these days we carry all the hammock jigs out of the workshop and set up the record player. Cramped quarters limit the kinds of dances that can be taught. We started with American square dances and have now added Siberian and Israeli circle dances to our repertoire. Polkas and waltzes will have to wait until we have larger rooms.

THE SLEEP EXPERIMENT

We call ourselves an "experimental community." What we usually mean by that is that we keep ourselves open to changes in our ideas and system, experimenting with different approaches to problems until we get something that works. But from time to time the notion takes hold of us that we are in the position of living quite apart from many of society's restrictive forms, and that we have a unique opportunity to carry on experiments just for the fun of it. It was in this spirit that six members initiated what we call the "three-five-three-five" system.

Participants in the system are trying to find out if they can function happily taking their sleep in three-hour segments rather than whole nights of it at a time. So they have scheduled their days and nights to sleep for three hours, then be awake for five, sleep again for three hours, and so forth. The schedule calls for arising at 9:00 a.m., staying up until 2:00 in the afternoon, then napping from 2 to 5, being up again until 10 p.m., then to bed until 1 in the morning, awake from 1 to 6 a.m., sleeping again until 9. Twin Oaks' labor credit system makes this a perfectly feasible schedule. The participants can arrange their work as they choose; the quiet night hours are perfectly good for weaving hammocks, baking bread, or doing laundry.

At this writing the experiment is still in progress, and no conclusions have been announced. Observers notice that the three-five people have difficulty tearing themselves away from group activities at 10:00 p.m., and sometimes they don't manage to get up at 1:00 a.m. On the other hand, how many other farmers have ever brought in hay from the barn under a full moon?

THE POOH SUBCULTURE

It all started last summer when one of our guests started reading *Winnie the Pooh* to a small child who lived here at the time. The child was really too young for Milne, and it went over his head. But the adults who wandered in and out of the room during the reading were hooked. Some of them had been Pooh enthusiasts from their childhood; others were hearing the stories for the first time.

The child and the guests went away, but not the Pooh readings. They became an institution—groups of five to ten people began to gather in one of the private rooms every few nights to hear Milne read aloud. The influence was felt

throughout the Community as members began to say "bother" instead of "dammit" and to refer to each other as a "bear of very little brain."

The trouble with Pooh Bear, however, is that Milne limited himself to two slim volumes of stories. Even the most ardent devotee becomes sated in time. That's when Twin Oaks' golden age came to the rescue. If Milne was so inconsiderate as to die before writing enough Pooh stories, does that mean that no more can be written? Obviously no. Clem set to work with a pencil and paper and began to create more Pooh. The same group that had gathered to read Milne now gathered to encourage Clem in his new medium.

CRITICISM CONTINUES

Long-term subscribers will remember that last summer we began a project called "Mutual Criticism," in which members of the Community formally request criticism from other members of the group in weekly sessions, a different member volunteering each week. The subject of the criticism sits quietly and listens without replying, and each other member in turn tells him in courteous language what his faults and virtues are and in what ways he would like to see change.

This system has continued now for nine months and is still going strong. Sometimes obvious changes in behavior take place after the criticism sessions — other times no changes are evident, but the person feels more relaxed. We repeatedly hear comments like, "Oh, is that all they found to criticize? I have lots more faults than that!"

M&M'S AND RULE NINE

Item Nine of the Twin Oaks Code says that we will clean up after ourselves. The importance of observing this cannot be overstated. Twenty-five people leaving messes everywhere they eat, smoke, work, and play create a chaos that none of us can tolerate. Some of the group have come here with good habits of neatness, but easily half the group tends to be messy and forgetful. Rules don't help, and neither does angry nagging. What we need is a general consciousness of the problem and our own part in it. And what we need to establish that is, of course, the proper arrangement of contingencies of reinforcement.

With this in mind some of the group have volunteered to participate in a program that reinforces "reminding" behavior. Every participant buys out of his allowance a supply of the classical reinforcer, M&M chocolate candies. Any member of the Community may secure an M&M for himself by noticing any violation of Rule Nine on the part of the participant and reminding him of it. You might say that we are paying people to punish us for messiness. More analytically viewed, however, participation in the social game is obviously reinforcing, as is the sense that we are helping to call the attention of the whole Community to the mess problem.

The extent and direction of Rule Nine are astonishing, once we start thinking about them. Members have forfeited M&Ms for: throwing a cigarette butt on the lawn; leaving a Community book in a private room long after he has finished reading it; failing to scrape his plate after supper; leaving coats on the backs of chairs; leaving guitars on the couch after playing them.

The whole plan is obviously a short-time game, and the problem is a long-term problem. No game is going to be a permanent answer, but any effort is better than no effort. In the meantime, anyway, the house is cleaner.

HOW TO IMPRESS A VISITOR

The following piece was written by Steve and/or Eve Fisher, prospective members who will probably be joining us next fall. We publish it because it is so flattering we just can't resist. We wish we could say that all visitors leave Twin Oaks with the same positive impression; unfortunately, this is not the case. Depending on the individual, the size of the visiting crowd, and just plain chance, a visitor may find us warm or cold, united or disjointed, attractive or repulsive. Anyway, here is what Eve and Steve thought of us.

After reading about Twin Oaks and talking about it and building up our hopes for it and making it into a thousand different wonderful utopian things in our minds, we went to visit. In our heads our arrival was triumphant. But, a couple of members of the Community who happened to be straggling by greeted us casually, almost indifferently. We were shown into one building and then another as the routine tour began. The kitchen was jammed (and peanut-butter cookied). Too many new faces and names to remember. The deserted hammock building was a respite from the farmhouse hubbub. We stood around and talked softly (warmly already) and as we talked, the reality of Twin Oaks took form.

That night we slept in our truck. Twin Oaks was so inundated with visitors that common rooms had sleeping bags for carpets. Because it was dark when we arrived, it was not until the next morning that we actually saw Twin Oaks' land. The hills roll, sharply and gently. Some broader areas are tilled, other open acres are grazing meadows. There is a small creek you can step over in the middle pasture. Beyond the lower pasture is a peaceful river with a dock and rowboat for the Community. The upper pasture leads into the woods, an echoing chamber of crackling and crunching leaves punctuated with total silence. Through fifteen minutes of woods and you are back at the edge of the farming land near the last barn. Here are the inklings of a berry patch. There is a beehive, dormant until warmth is established. We see cattle and milking cows, ducks, geese, chickens, roosters, dogs and cats, and a horse. The row of old farm buildings and rusted plowing and harvesting equipment leads back to the farmhouse and the two new wood-frame buildings that Twin Oaks has erected.

The first building houses in one open space the workshops, library, and living room. There are hammock-making racks and the reels of polypropylene tear-resistant, mildew-proof, bleached-white rope. There is a printing press, a darkroom, a Community clothes closet and shelf after shelf of interesting reading matter from sci-fi to Keats to Skinner to Hesse to how to treat a mastitis infection in your cow's udder. Private rooms are tucked along both sides of the common working and relaxing space. The other new building has two stories, though the second is not yet completed. Private rooms fill the first floor and will fill the second. Twin Oaks currently has about twenty-five members; most are between the ages of 17-22, a few are over 25 and at least two are (gasp) over 30.

Back in the farmhouse, you get the feeling of constant activity. The kitchen is here, the dining space, the Twin Oaks office, the cigarette tobacco and papers, the record player, the food-processing room, and the only bathroom. Some of the hum, we are told, is because Easter vacation has brought twenty to twenty-five visitors a day. More people, more work. (Also more people to do the work, but it is more hectic.) Twin Oaks operates on a labor credit system. Each week the labor credit manager determines what has to be done; he posts a list of the jobs and everybody signs up for his share . . .

We were not there in time to sign up for work. In anticipation of our arrival, the labor credit manager had signed up for us. We did a lot of washing and cleaning, a little bit of work on the hammocks (drilling holes in the stretchers), and some cooking. Because of the glut of workers, the work quota was down to twenty-five hours a week.

Days feel enjoyably long because they are so non-linear. You work an hour or two, and then you are off. You read or rap or go for a walk; then you go back to work, but it is a different job than the ones you did earlier, and then you finish and relax awhile and eat, then go back to work, and later you eat dinner, then work and so on.

Twin Oakers eat well. Lots of eggs, tuna fish, and green beans. We had pork, spaghetti, macaroni and cheese, pork and beans, cole slaw, fried rice, and more. Every day someone bakes biscuits or muffins or cookies. We drank cow's milk and Kool-Aid. We never went hungry.

Each day is filled with accomplished tasks and relaxed pleasure. Even three or four days of rain and three or four inches of mud (as we experienced) could not smother our feelings of freedom and enjoyment or quench our desire to stay and do more. Why is this such a strong sensation? How could we so quickly develop such an affinity for Twin Oaks? It is not just the novelty of farm life, not just the beauty of the rolling red clay central Virginia hills or the forests of oak, not just the sense of accomplishment and freedom created by a labor credit system that works. It is the people.

The people are lovable. They are gentle and concerned. Some more than others, but there is an atmosphere of quiet commitment, a sense of getting something together that no one else has got yet. There is a kind of serenity that comes partly from the overall pace of a rural existence and partly from the knowledge that you and most of the people you are living with have got their heads together. Affection fills the air; affectation is brought in only by visitors, and even they are forced to give it up by the open attitude of the Community. Many of the visitors are great people, too. There is an element of liking people who are similar to yourself, and Twin Oaks did attract us. But this does not mean that everyone who is interested in the Community is alike. Within the broad framework of nonaggressiveness and equalitarianism, the members of Twin Oaks and the compatible visitors have many different interests, abilities, and desires.

There is something more to our enchantment. In daily life, little could be more important than the individual people who surround you. But Twin Oaks has a sense of community. That is significant enough, but there is something further. Twin Oaks was inspired by B. F. Skinner's fictional novel *Walden Two*, a utopian society based on the labor credit system and behavioral psychology. Twin Oaks is exciting in that, because of its ideological sources, it has a scientifically experimental direction. Not everyone in the Community would claim such beliefs for himself, but the core thrust is the belief that answers to social questions come only from social experimentation and scientific observation of the results of these experiments. It is a joy to live in a society that, in the words of a member, "creates people who are committed to nonaggression; a society of people where one man's gain is not another man's loss; a society where disagreeable work is minimized and leisure is valued; a society in which people come first; an economic system of equality; a society that is constantly trying to improve in its ability to create happy, productive, creative people."

Not all of these goals are being institutionally met. People come to Twin Oaks with histories of experiences that sometimes conflict with these values. While adults' behavior may be difficult to alter, children—when the Community can afford them in a few years—will catalyze the institutionalization of these lofty goals. For the time being, several people are engaged in programs of behavior self management, and there is a community awareness and use of positive reinforcement, and that feels good.

Twin Oaks is more than we anticipated, more than we hoped. It is people. It is a spirit and an atmosphere. It is a working system in a lovely place. It is a reality-oriented structure that absorbs variety and supports integrity. It is a society that despises exploitation and other forms of violence; it strives for a deep-seated sense of equality among people of different interests, abilities, and sexes. It is a group of sane people who are willing to experiment with ways of life, and who actively regard positive reinforcement as a fundamental necessity in their lives. Without knowing just what Twin Oaks will grow into, we want to be part of its becoming.

THINGS WE NEED

It has been repeatedly suggested to us that we publish a list of articles that we need, in case our friends who live in nearby cities should have an attic or basement full of things that we would find useful. So here is the current list.

Mattresses; rugs; lamps and light fixtures; drapes for tables; sofas and other living room furniture; drapes for long windows; bedding of all kinds; clothing of recent date for women who work in offices, especially sizes 12 and 14; medical samples (especially cold remedies); drinking glasses; an electric mixer; automobiles in running condition; building materials of any kind; kitchen thermometers (oven, candy, and meat); a secretarial typing chair; tools; and (if you live very close) rooted slips from fruit or flowering shrubs.

TOPIC

Our newest industry is now well under way. It was christened Twin Oaks Programming Instrument Company, TOPIC for short. What are programming instruments? Programming instruments are those gadgets experimental psychologists use to program the stimuli, reinforcement, etc., in their "Skinner boxes." Our programming equipment consists of electro-mechanical modules seven inches high that clip onto horizontal metal "power bars." Each module serves some programming function such as timing, counting, or switching and consists of a Plexiglas plate with electrical terminals protruding from thd front and electrical components mounted on the back.

To date we have sent out and received questionnaires regarding the potential market, designed several of the items we will assemble, printed and sent out 150 copies of a five-page catalog, and built prototypes of the items advertised. If things go as planned, we will eventually assemble a complete line of programming equipment consisting of more than two dozen items. Limited capital will limit the rapidity of the development of the industry.

TOPIC programming modules will compare favorably with those marketed by the four main competitors and will sell for considerably less.

TWIN OAKS AND THE CULTURAL REVOLUTION

Recent years' events in China have familiarized us with the concept of "cultural revolution." What is implied in this term is evaluating your culture in terms of its goals, noting where it falls short, and deliberately engineering changes in line with your highest aims.

Twin Oaks is designed as a radical alternative to the kind of life we left, and it is important to us to make our little society conform to our ideals, even if only to test those ideals. The group being small, cultural change is not only desirable — it is possible.

With this in mind, one of our members wrote the following article. It was originally written not for the *Leaves* at all, but for the Community bulletin board. It was posted for a couple of days, and members read it, talked about it, and began to try to implement some of its ideas.

This does not imply unanimity of opinion on the matters discussed (particularly on the question of doing away with canned music), nor is this an announcement of a Twin Oaks Cultural Revolution. Whether anything creatively radical will come out of this campaign, it is too early to say. But in case it does, we thought you would like to know how it all started. . .

ON CULTURE

Opinion — By Rudy

Societies that have different institutional bases develop cultures. By *culture* we mean the superstructure built up on the economic base. A society that values and is sustained by aggression has children running around with toy guns shooting one another; it attends boxing matches; it thrills at mass automobile smashups on the speedway. A society that has an economic base of competition manifests its values in miniature wars such as football games, intellectually as chess games; its young practice economic exploitation by playing Monopoly (ha, ha—you landed on Park Place and I own it. Pay me $200 and go straight to jail.) If the culture is an advanced capitalist culture to the point of imperialism, the people play Risk (let's see now, I have an army in Latin America. Can I afford also to protect my interests in Asia?) If a society values male chauvinism and sex roles, you find little girls playing house and dolls and little boys playing competitive, aggressive games to fit themselves for the world they will become part of (bang, bang—you're dead. I was, too, safe on third base. You're cheating—it's my ball and bat and so you can't play). If a society is a market economy built on consumerism, then the art smells of it (BUY COKE, BUY CIGS (even if you know they will kill you), BUY SUPER 350H (even if it's illegal to drive over 80 mph and a 50 hp Volkswagen will do that). Clothes that go "out of style" and are built for special situations, seldom functional, and different ones for males and females. If the society is a nuclear-family one, the architecture shows it by wasting great amounts of space and materials on little dwelling units with their labor-wasting (called labor-saving) overabundance of stoves and heaters and irons and washing machines and dishwashers, etc., etc., two cars in each driveway (one of which sits there most of the day). If the society has the value of monogamous mating (pair bonding), then the music constantly moans of "little darling, please be true." This includes the so-called new youth culture, free-swinging "our kind of people"—people such as Dylan, "just you and me, that's the way it ought to be." It is almost impossible to find a song among the "new liberated sound" that isn't just as chauvinist, property-oriented, and jealousy-idolizing as the old "bicycle built for two" crap that our ancestors

grew up on. What if Rocky Racoon went to see his rival and he and the rival and Nancy (who called herself Lil) all dug each other and went to bed together rather than shooting at each other? If a society's values lie in individual action regardless of the effect on the rest of the individuals, then the culture writes stories about super-heroes. Comics, of course, carry it to the extreme with super-human powers (usually males) paternalistically solving the problems of the masses who themselves are powerless. Statues are built and plaques are placed as though *one* person built a building or won a war or singlehandedly brought off a revolution.

Twin Oaks is an island of sanity in a sea of insane, chaotic madness; a new world trying to live up to pure communal ideals while living in the belly of a monster. We have managed to establish the *basis* of the new world—that is, the institutions that will enable us to be an equalitarian, nonviolent, positively reinforcing society in which people come first, in which we produce for use and service and not for profit (at least internally).

But Marx was wrong: economic socialism or even economic communism does not automatically produce the "new people." It is the *superstructure* that is imposed over the *basis* that does this. Russia is a socialist country, with something of the necessary basis, but it has not gone beyond that. There is a bureaucratic classism, elitism, male chauvinism, imperialism, racism, and no indication that it is moving toward the equality of "to each according to his need." In fact, they are moving in the other direction. Basically, to quote Simon and Garfunkle, "they ain't got no culture."

Behavioristically, a culture can be looked at as the problem of surrounding ourselves with the stimuli which elicit responses that tend to take further steps toward our lofty goals. We claim to be concerned about the health and well-being of our members, yet we make a reinforcing game out of cigarettes (bumming them from visitors is fun, roll your own is ethnic, 24 cents a pack wholesale from the store is availability). Even the couldn't-give-a-damn-for-its-members U. S. government has managed to launch some sort of campaign against this form of self-imposed death (and *they* had to overcome the powerful resistance of the tobacco industry).

We claim to be nonviolent, and yet the author of this paper runs around sounding like he approves of "offing pigs" (which he doesn't, but one would hardly guess just by listening to him talk).

We claim to be creating a society of creative people with new values, and yet our recreation consists to a great extent of immersing ourselves in imported music, complete with chauvinist lyrics and property values. Even when we play instruments, the emphasis is on learning to play "outside" music.

We claim to be scientifically, experimentally oriented— but how many experiments are going on? Are decisions followed up to see if the desired effect occurred? Are problems discussed in the form of "what can we do to overcome this difficulty, and how can we know if we are succeeding in doing so?"

We claim to be cooperative, yet out of all our musical instruments we have yet to really get anything together. Sure, our interests are different; but if we were interested in trying it, I see nothing standing in the way of getting group music together. Is the argument of "different kinds of instruments" really applicable? Why not redefine "music group"? Is it innately offensive to combine recorders, guitars, electric guitars, harmonicas, table top drum, banjo, etc.? Why must our cooperative singing group (a really good thing) be reduced to singing religious lyrics? ("A mighty fortress is our God—puke.) There are some damn creative writers in this commune. Why can't they come up with new, more inspiring lyrics? Will members laugh at them? Will people think it is cornball? What would members have thought if someone had come and written a song for members to sing that said "Amazing grace. . ."?

So what can we do? I don't want to start suggesting things here, because I would like for others who are concerned about Alternate Culture to help analyze what it means, so we can really make an all-out effort. Where are we failing? Find the areas—keep lists; think about what we can do more realistically. Now. Let's rap about it at meals, when working, etc. and then move to build a community superstructure on the top of our basis.

Fuck imported U. S. culture! Fuck imported Madison Avenue-controlled "youth culture." Create Community culture. Create Twin Oaks culture.

Chapter Five: Year Four

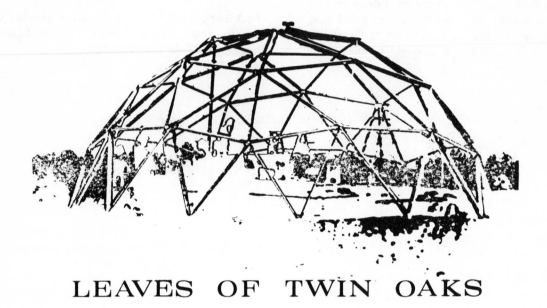

LEAVES OF TWIN OAKS

NUMBER 13

October, 1970

GENERAL NEWS

THE FARM

Once more Twin Oaks is turning its attention toward agriculture. In spite of theoretical questions about the relative profits of farming and industry, two things are causing us to farm again after a year of abandoning it. One is that we once more have members who have a lively interest in farm management. The other is the possibility of a national depression. All of our industries, though promising, are based on a luxury market. Hammocks and crafts are sold to people who have money to spend beyond their basic needs. Even relay panels are dependent on research grants to universities, and those grow slim in money-tight years. The financial mainstay of the Community, outside jobs, would be wiped out as the competition for jobs became

stiffer. Certainly we would no longer be able to drop jobs every two months and expect to find others. Even now this is becoming difficult for the unskilled and the long-haired.

If the whole country should be poor, certainly Twin Oaks would be poorer. If we are to survive at all, we would be wise to have developed the garden skills that will help to feed us.

The garden people this year are interested in the organic approach, though not fanatical about it. We are bringing in load after load of sawdust, woodchips, and spoiled hay to use as mulch. A fully-mulched acre of garden appears to be more than we can manage in our first year of organic gardening, so the garden manager has started with mulching the strawberries and asparagus and will expand as more mulch becomes available. Our soil is very poor and rocky; it will take years to build it up to a rich garden soil. In the meantime we supplement slightly with chemical fertilizer where we have to.

The root cellar, dug in 1968, is finally being put to use this year. We have built a heavy door on it and are building shelves for vegetable storage, cheese curing, and possibly mushroom culture.

COWS

The veal production program that we talked about last January with such enthusiasm failed. There were a number of reasons. The departure of our cattle expert last spring might have been serious if we had had anything to save. Certainly our own inexperience lost us some money through undernourishing our cows through the winter. Two heifers died; others grew too thin. But if we had kept our manager and stuffed all our cows full of grain, we would still have failed in the veal business we were trying for because of one simple piece of misinformation. Premise: We were to buy one-day-old calves and fatten them for veal or beef. Fact: It is almost impossible now to buy one-day-old calves. The dairymen who used to sell them are now into the veal business themselves. They keep the calves. Those few calves we were able to buy we had to pay high prices for, and we couldn't buy enough to keep the program going. So we ended up feeding a lot of cows who didn't have any calves to nurse. We lost about $1500 in feed and expenses alone, not counting depreciation on the animals that was caused by our ignorance and underfeeding.

But all that is in the past. Early this March we consulted with our neighbor farmers about our animals and took their advice. (They would have offered their help sooner if they had realized we were in trouble.) We decided to take our losses and get out of the veal business until such time as we were certain we could handle it. We sold most of the cows we had bought for the purpose. We sold some of the heifers and kept others. We bought hay by the wagonload and put our animals back on a sound nutritional program. We got the vet, learned about parasites, and wormed all the cows, treated minor sores. By summer we had cut back our herd to what our damaged pastures will feed, and all our animals are in good health. We have a few cows now for our own milking, a few yet to be sold, a few more potentially good heifers that we are raising to replace our current milk cows. So far so good.

But not good enough, says our new farm manager, a member who thinks about nothing but cows. (If you want her attention, you have to moo.) Last year, due to machinery breakdown, we didn't put in any hay. This year we must keep the machines repaired and get good hay in. Pastures must be fertilized and cleared of thistles and volunteer berry bushes. Furthermore, our cows aren't good enough. A better bred cow would produce calves half again as heavy without costing us proportionally more in maintenance. We need to get better stock. Also, our fences are in need of a major rehaul; large sections must be entirely replaced. The manager visits prosperous farms and gets ideas. She visits the library of Virginia Polytechnic and reads and reads.

Then she takes what little money is in the farm budget and does the best she can. The aim: to provide our own milk more efficiently and cheaper, then to raise more beef for our table. If, after accomplishing those two things well, there is still pasture and managerial energy left over, we might think of going back into beef farming as a business.

GREAT LEAP FORWARD

We have the feeling that our fourth year (summer 1970 - summer 1971) is going to be different from the three years we've had so far—different and much better. There is an atmosphere of "getting our shit together" and beating our old problems. We are going through a period of very rapid improvement in all directions. We can feel a new spirit taking over. We feel enthusiastic—even proud.

The details? The physical plant is being rearranged for efficiency. You can't go away for a weekend without finding surprising improvement has occurred in your absence. The kitchen now has a stainless steel, triple-well sink; the bathroom has been repainted; someone has built a craft table; the stairway to upstairs Oneida has been installed, the library has been moved to Oneida and appropriate shelves have been built for it; the hammock workshop has been rearranged; the first barn has been painted red; there are two new tables in the dining rooms; construction of a suitable community bathroom has begun.

We ask ourselves why. Why is it that this sudden surge of activity takes place just now, when all of these things have needed doing for many months? The answers are not too hard to find.

First of all the population turnover at Twin Oaks is coming to a slow halt. There are still people who leave after being here a while, and there is still a steady influx of new people; but for the last eight months or so there has been no major, jarring exodus. Even the people who don't settle down for a lifetime are now staying longer than they used to. The average stay is closer to six months now; it used to be three months. With an increasingly stable group, it is possible for managers to learn about their respective fields and give solid thought to improving their areas. This has been particularly true in farm management and food preparation. In each case a dedicated (I'd call it "obsessed," says the farm manager) member has given the time and energy required to study about her area, has herself worked closely with the other workers, and has made dramatic improvements. The milk barn has been paved and made sanitary; the meals are twice as good as they used to be.

Second (though related to the first), our Outside Job contingent has shown a faithfulness in going to work every day (in spite of extremely aversive conditions) and bringing home their paychecks. It is absolutely necessary for us to have a little bit of spare cash in order to make the kinds of "leaps forward" that we have been making. Though our improvements are 9/10 composed of labor, there's that 1/10 cash outlay (lumber and other materials) that we could not have spared last winter when we were having difficulty making ourselves go to work.

And third, we have been free for some months from internal division among Community members. We are all going the same direction, and it is not very difficult to get suggestions implemented. For the first time in our history it is both possible and practical to have numerous meetings of the general membership to discuss problems and policies, to educate, to get public feedback on decision making, because the general good will and mutual trust is such that we can be confident that such meetings will not bog down in bitter wrangles about central theory.

The obvious, tangible nature of the improvements are, of course, reinforcement for the behavior that produced it and the tendency to maintain similar behaviors. It would seem that barring major disasters, as long as the necessary cash for materials comes in, the Great Leap Forward will continue.

EQUIPMENT

Part of this year's progress has been the purchase of some good quality equipment. We have learned that it definitely does not pay a community to buy second-rate tools, for everything we buy gets heavy use. This year's purchases include a drill press, an oxygen-acetylene welding torch, an electric kiln, and an IBM Selectric typewriter.

NEW LABOR CREDIT SYSTEM

In 1967 we devised a labor credit system in which every member signed up for the work he preferred, and credits were adjusted on the basis of competition. That is, if more than one person signed up for a job, it was considered desirable work, and the credits went down; if nobody signed up, we raised the credits and assigned it to someone at random. The system has faults, but it worked for three years, and we were pleased with it.

What we became discontented with as the years passed, however, was the overall quality of the work done. Many a hopeful member would take a managership with the intention of seeing the department thrive under his care, only to find that the other members working in his department just didn't care enough to do a good job, and good projects were continually being sabotaged by indifference. We had some meetings about it and discussed the possibility that the indifference arose from lack of involvement in the department. Under the old system you might clean the kitchen one morning and somebody else clean it the next, while you went on to hammock weaving, which you had only five hours of, and the next day you were mending fences. Most people had a schedule like that. Presumably, most members liked the variety, because they continued to choose it. Nevertheless, its natural results were that if you left a jar of spoiled tomatoes on the counter, somebody on

another shift would have to clean it up, and if you left the saw out in the barn, somebody else would have to go look for it. The most elementary behavioral theory told us that we were not set up to get a good job done. We were not teaching the precious "sense of responsibility" that we all recognized was necessary.

So with a sigh of regret we turned away from the hectic variableness of schedule and began to encourage specialization. The work shifts began to be arranged so that on every meal shift and every cleaning shift in a given week, at least one and preferably two people were assigned throughout the week and were familiar with the work. The system quickly extended to garden work and even office work.

Specialization meant signing up in blocks of 14 to 21 hours, and this made the old competition and random assignment system untenable. For if you lost a 21-hour block at the flip of a coin, you would have to be assigned 21 hours of something undesirable to take its place. Large blocks just did not lend themselves to a signup system at all.

What we are working with now is a simple preference list. Each member has a list of all the job categories and is asked to number them from 1 to 40 in the order of his preference. From there, the labor credit crew takes the preference lists and makes up all the individual schedules, giving each member as much as possible those jobs that he rated high, and assigning all unpopular jobs as much as possible to those who dislike them least.

Another change that has been made, independent of the system, is a new way of awarding labor credits. It is now possible to give labor credits on the basis of the individual preference rather than the group preference. That is, you get .9 credits per hour for your first preference, 1.0 for the next few on your list, and so forth. Jobs far down on your preference list may go for 1.5 an hour. Three people may be mending fences together, and each of them earning different credits, depending on how much he likes the job.

Most members are content with the new system. Their schedules are usually less aversive than they were under the old random-assignment rules. A few people prefer the old system because they didn't mind any kind of work very much, and could take advantage of other people's dislikes by signing up for unpopular work at high credits, thus working fewer hours than the average member. Under the new system this is not possible. The only way to get high credits is to be assigned work that you personally rate very low on your preference list; and when you do this, the chances are that somebody else who doesn't dislike it as much as you will be assigned it. So there aren't any more 3-credit-an-hour jobs.

The improvement in the work itself is very noticeable. Managers are not so discouraged as they were. A lot of members are becoming quite interested in their work. The people on lunch are likely to recognize the leftovers, so they don't become moldy in the refrigerator; the people on cleaning remember that they didn't do any woodwork last week, so it's time to look at it this week. The people on garden know what has been planted where.

This is probably not the last change the labor credit system will ever see. It is interesting to note that we can make sweeping changes in it and still stay within the general framework of the system described in *Walden Two*. The principle remains the same — the more aversive the work, the less you have to do of it.

GROUP RAP

In response to complaints that Twin Oaks members did not have a feeling of closeness, and to accusations that we had descended to being merely an aggregate of people with a common economic bond, we started an institution called GroupRap. GroupRap is nothing but a scheduled conversation. If you sign up for GroupRap (and most people do), you will be assigned to a small group of four or five people, and you will meet with them for an hour or so once a week for six weeks, just to talk. It doesn't matter what you talk about; most groups have taken the opportunity to find out something about each other's past lives, to compare experiences.

It has been suggested that we use GroupRap for sensitivity exercises. Any group is free to do that, of course, but up until now the suggestion has met with shyness and resistance, and so no group has tried it yet. We have not been doing GroupRap for very many weeks, so it is early yet to report on results. Some of us have noticed already, though, that it has facilitated friendships that otherwise might have been slower in growing.

OUTSIDE JOBS

When we planned the Community, we had very little idea exactly how we would maintain ourselves financially. We expected to live off the land as much as possible, and we had some ideas for small industries, which we hoped to develop before we ran out of our original operating cash. But even then we said to each other, "If worse comes to worst, we can always get jobs."

Worse came to worst in March of 1968, eight short months after the Community's inception. Some of us volunteered to take outside jobs. Others stayed home and took care of the house and farm.

Two and a half years later outside jobs are still our major source of income. At one time or another forty different members have sought and found jobs in Charlottesville, Richmond, or their home towns, and brought their paychecks back to Twin Oaks' general account. We long ago abandoned the volunteer method of selecting outside workers and now use a rotation, based on the length of time spent on outside jobs compared to the length of time spent as a Community member. We still get occasional volunteers—people who have a particular opportunity at a given time or couples who want to do their stint together. Originally we needed only two outside workers to bring in enough cash. Our current expenditures require eight workers. Richmond, being a larger city, is better job-hunting ground than Charlottesville, though it is farther away; and these days our red Ford van commutes daily to Richmond, taking eight sleepy, half-dressed people from the Community at 7 o'clock in the morning and returning them, tired, cross, and hungry, at 7 in the evening.

Outside work always has been our least popular job, and there are good reasons why this is so. Getting up at 5:30 in the morning is one of them. Sack lunches is another. For the least skilled, the jobs themselves can be very bad. For many of us the feeling of being isolated in a crowd of insane people who talk utter nonsense all day long is a burden. The worst of it, though, is being away from the Community for long hours, week after week. The outside workers lose touch with Community happenings. It is easy to become estranged and feel left out. It is hard, too, to fight the feeling that you are being exploited, particularly if you come home to find that some inside worker didn't iron your blouse, or the lunch packer has forgotten that you cannot stand pickles in your tuna salad. Inside workers tend to forget what outside work is like, and adjust very quickly to the leisurely pace of normal Community activities.

Suppose, for example, you're the garden manager and are trying to manage the garden in evenings and weekends in spite of your outside job. You make plans, requisition the labor, explain the work to those signed up for it, and then come home to find it undone because "it was too hot to work, and a bunch of us went swimming." This is particularly galling if your outside job is mowing lawns for the city or working in a brick factory. Sometimes the outside workers break down altogether, quit their jobs, and look for better ones. Occasionally a member will leave the Community because outside work is so hateful that he cannot face another twenty days of it.

The problems of the outside worker have been of major concern to the Community for some time. The food manager has loosened the financial limitations on the lunch packer, and snack money is also allowed each worker. The van is lined with mattresses, and some workers can catch an extra half-hour's sleep on the trip in or out. Occasionally a work shift (normally forty work days) is shortened for a member who is having a particularly difficult time bearing it.

Several planners' meetings have been devoted to the controversial question of whether it is right to expect all members to participate in the outside job rotation. The inequalities are gross and obviously so. For some, outside work means air-conditioned offices, perhaps with time to read on the job. For others it may mean working high up on ladders scraping grease off heating ducts at a temperature of over 100° F., or doing factory work under the constant nagging of a foreman who wants the work done faster, or painting bridges out of doors in below-freezing weather and coming home covered with orange paint. Some of us are lucky enough to get work that we can do alone, left to our own methods and our own thoughts. Others work in the midst of gossip or office politics or a barrage of racist talk that they cannot escape. Attempts to adjust labor credits on the basis of aversiveness of outside jobs have to date not been successful. They end in angry discussions, each worker defending his job as being at least as aversive as anyone else's. So outside work credits remain the same for all workers, regardless of the job. It has repeatedly been suggested that we allow certain people to be entirely free from obligation to do outside work—those people for whom it is truly hideous, who "freak out" in a factory or office. There is some justice in the suggestion. Are we not dedicated to the principle "From each according to his ability, to each according to his needs"? But the drawbacks of basing a policy on that principle are obvious. If we made exceptions of that kind, we would find our group of outside workers once again consisting largely of volunteers who have saleable skills, spending most of their time outside the Community supporting an ever-growing group of those who intensely dislike outside work. So we continue to insist that all members of Twin Oaks take their turns working on the outside, and members who find they cannot do it simply leave the Community.

To date we have had only one member who has chosen to work at his profession (teaching) for a whole year rather than take a miscellaneous job for two months, though there are several members who are capable of doing so. Such jobs of course bring in a larger salary and are a real help to the Community. In fact, a member with a "permanent" job easily brings in the equivalent of two salaries and cuts down on the number of workers we have to send.

Occasionally a member will have the opportunity to work in another city and thus escape the early hours and commuting that exhaust those who work in Richmond. Living with a parent or friend who is willing to provide rent-free quarters and an occasional meal makes this possible.

But in some ways this is not desirable. Two months away from the Community make you feel like a stranger when you return. One member, returning from a two-month stint in a Detroit steel mill, came back to the Community, only to be asked by a new member if he was planning to stay for very long. "He thought I was a visitor!" complained the returning member. "And I don't blame him. I feel like one. Everything has changed since I left. People I knew have left—people I never saw before are in managerial positions. I feel like an intruder."

Once the forty days have been completed, though, the sense of relief and freedom are enormous. Some want to take some of their accumulated vacation time immediately and loaf for a week or two. Others sign up for fixing workers' lunches—"because I know how it is." For new members it is the real beginning of Community life, for it means a managership and getting deeply involved in Community work and policy. (The Community always needs good managers for its ever-expanding activities, but does not usually appoint new people until they have finished their outside work shift.) For some it is an opportunity to devote themselves to some project that their outside-worker perspective has inspired them with. One member said, "I

worked in this sparkling clean office every day. Then I would come home and find the Community buildings messy. The job itself didn't bother me too much, but every night when I got home I felt irritated because members at home didn't seem to have done much. Now that I'm off outside work, I want to push a cleanup campaign—sign up for a lot of cleaning myself, get things organized. Why should the outside world be so neatly organized and we be so sloppy?"

But once in a while an outside job will draw a member away. A member will be forced perhaps for the first time in his life to get and hold a job, and will discover that for him it is not so difficult or aversive. Maybe he had joined the Community just for the financial security, because he didn't know how to support himself. Such a member may be tempted by his paycheck and decide to leave the Community in order to have the experience of earning and spending his own money. (The experience doesn't turn out to be so wonderful in many cases, and some have returned afterwards.)

It is discouraging to know that this part of Twin Oaks life—the part that is most hated by the members, that causes some to leave, and that estranges and disorients even those who survive it—nets us less than 75 cents an hour, after we have counted the heavy transportation costs. Richmond is over fifty miles away, and the round trip daily absorbs one member's salary in gasoline and wear and tear, even figuring at a conservative 6 cents a mile. As if that weren't grim enough, rising unemployment is making even these undesirable jobs harder and harder to get.

It should surprise no one, then, that we are happy to manufacture hammocks, though it pays us only $1.50 an hour for our labor, that we gladly run a country store that has perhaps twenty customers in a day, and that we are delighted to do industrial piecework that factories do not find it worth their while to pay hourly employees to do. Typing addresses on envelopes may not be stimulating work, nor is repairing chipped furnace tiles, and the bloom wears off hammock-weaving after you have made two or three. But anything we can do on the premises that will bring in money means that we can keep a member here instead of sending him to Richmond. The same is true of our agricultural labor. It may not "pay" to grow our own beans, but if you have to buy the beans with money earned by outside workers, we have to figure carefully before deciding it isn't worth it.

On the balance, of course, the outside job incomes are worth the pain that goes into them. They have to be, or we would not do them. Each member who successfully completes his shift then turns with confidence to the next member and expects him to do the same. Thus is the Community maintained. If we did not have those incomes, we would not have a community. Two months of gritting your teeth and living through an aversive job will net you from four to twelve months of living honorably on the premises without having to do so before your turn comes up again. The alternative is living on the outside and doing outside jobs the year 'round.

Nevertheless, we continually seek ways of cutting back outside work and of finally doing away with it altogether. A few more industrial subcontracts, a steady supply of lecture invitations, and an occasional professional who actually enjoys his outside job will leave us in fairly good shape. Best of all, if one of our manufacturing projects should find a steady market large enough to support the group, our financial worries would be over.

SHORT-TERM VISITORS

Until recently Twin Oaks had a fairly serious problem with having too many visitors at a time. Though we passed regulations and instructed the correspondence manager to limit the short-term visitors to no more than five at a time, we would get mixed up and invite more than we could assimilate. It was not unusual to have more visitors than members on weekends, and some of the members felt uncomfortable, constantly surrounded by strangers. One day it occurred to the visitor manager to use some simple behavioral engineering in the form of changing the visitor rates. He left the rates at $1.50 a day for people who stay longer than a week, but raised them for short-term people to $3 a day. The effect was immediate. People who cannot come for very long somehow manage to find the $3; more people simply plan for a longer stay. The number of weekend guests has dropped phenomenally, and the week-long visits have increased correspondingly. This suits the Community just fine. When a visitor stays a week, we become comfortable with him. He can help with the work intelligently, too, and he has time to lose the nobody-cares-I'm-here feeling. When he leaves, he takes with him a reasonably balanced, accurate picture of community life.

TWIN OAKS NEEDS. . .

If you're coming this way and have room in your station wagon and are cleaning out your garage anyway, Twin Oaks could use: kitchen chairs, bedding of all kinds, rugs, tools, building materials, hymn books or other three- or four-part choral music, art materials, yarn. . .

NAMES

If you have ever wanted to change your name, the time to do it is when you join a community. Of the current twenty-five members here at Twin Oaks, at least ten are going by names other than those their parents bestowed on them. Sometimes the reason is a practical one: we had three Bills here at one time, and it was a nuisance to refer to them as Bill 1, Bill 2, and Bill 3, to say nothing of the built-in status implied by the numbers. But it was rather a surprise when all three of them changed their names and we had no Bills left at all.

Sometimes the name changes are just a matter of personal taste ("I've always wanted to be named Shannon"). And sometimes the names are really nicknames. There was a period when we had a rash of hick names (Luke, Zeke, Pappy).

What makes it possible to change your name at Twin Oaks is that we have established a precedent that says anybody can be called anything he likes, and you can get cooperation from other members. Twin Oaks membership is a break from the past. We come here committed to changes and expecting them. A new name is just the beginning.

REPORT ON CAMPHILL

Twin Oaks belongs to an organization called the Homer Morris Fund, which has from time to time made some efforts to promote a federation of intentional communities. There are yearly meetings of this group, and we sent our representative this spring, as usual. There he met Helen Zipperlen, the representative from Camphill Village.

Camphill is an intentional community in Copake, New York. Helen introduced herself to Rudy and told him, "I've seen you now at these conventions for three years. The first year I heard you talk about Twin Oaks and I said, 'another one of those fly-by-night things—they'll be done within six months.' The next year I said, 'I'll be darned; there he is again.' Now that I see you again this year I think it's time I made your acquaintance. Now, I personally think *Walden Two* is a ridiculous idea, and anybody who tried to base a community on it must be insane; but then, here *you* are, and you seem to be a very nice young man." Rudy responded as well as he could to this candor, and the conversation ended with a mutual invitation to visit and an intimation that Camphill might be able to help Twin Oaks market some craft items if we cared to produce them.

In the spring a family from Camphill drove up and spent a weekend with us. It was one of those weekends when we had more visitors than members, and the members ran around looking harried. The family from Camphill pitched in quickly with the work, contributed some Camphill-made whole wheat bread to our meal, and made pleasant conversation. "What you need," one of them said as she helped wash dishes in a hasty effort to get drinking glasses on the table, "are some villagers."

We knew in a vague way that Camphill supports itself by caring for the mentally handicapped, that they are divided into a dozen or so households—each with a housemother, her natural family, a visiting college student or two, and half a dozen of the retarded. The "villagers," as the retarded are called, take a full share of the household chores, and always do the dishes.

In July three of us drove to New York and spent three days at Camphill, observing and learning as much as we could absorb. The first thing we noticed was that the "villagers" are not by any means merely a means of support to the community. They are the center of community life, and the members of normal intelligence—with a few exceptions—are there because working with the handicapped in a communal situation is their life work. The relationship is one of mutual dependence. The Co-workers (Camphill's name for what most people would call the "staff") provide the handicapped with security and direction and occupation; the Villagers in turn (through their families) provide financial support for the community, plus a number of special legal benefits that only charitable institutions can get.

The result is a physical plant that made us sigh with longing when we visited. Fourteen graceful modern homes are settled among large trees. A little wood lies in the midst of the community (complete with sparkling stream and rustic bridge). All of their workshops are attached to or are part of the homes. The result is architectural harmony and loveliness. The truck gardens are not all together but scattered, with onions growing in back of one house, and peas behind another. The gardens are centrally managed, however, as is their farm operation, bakery, and dairy. Everywhere were signs of comfortable sufficiency. New construction was going on; there was up-to-date equipment in their shops, new looms in the weavery, modern farm equipment. We felt it even in their hospitality (they did not find it necessary to charge us for our stay). Each of their large homes, they reported, cost between $70,000 and $85,000. That's about ten to thirteen times the cost of a Twin Oaks building of roughly the same size. There are reasons for that wide discrepancy. It is not a taste for luxury that forces the cost of Camphill buildings so high; Camphill homes are lovely and warm and comfortable, but there is nothing ostentatious about them. The cost comes from three things: *1)* the necessity of building to meet the rigid codes for housing the handicapped in New York State; *2)* their preferred architecture shuns right angles and goes in for cornice work; and *3)* they are not in a position to provide their own labor but have to hire it done by contractors.

This last was a surprise to us, but that is because we had never given any thought to what it means to live with the handicapped. Camphill Co-workers devote most of their time to directing the activities of the Villagers, and many of these activities are work activities. The Villagers weave, make dolls, bake bread, do copper enameling, and work in the gardens and farm, and the amount of work that goes into their supervision is enormous. In addition, all of the crafts that the community produces require the Co-workers' skills for part of the work. Only a small number of the Villagers have the manual dexterity to handle saws and kilns and sewing machines. Camphill's population consists of handicapped and people caring for them or taking care of necessary maintenance or administrative work, and there is no practical way that a large labor force could be freed for construction.

But even making allowances for their particular labor situation, Camphill enjoys a standard of living that Twin Oaks does not expect to reach for quite a few years.

We were housed in a pleasant guest room in a house set aside for guests. We were fed breakfast there but had lunch and supper in the various homes of the community. One meal we took with the garden manager, another with the doll maker, and so forth. We asked questions until we ran

out of them and began to feel dull-brained with too much new information. We were taught the rudiments of doll-making and copper enameling and given advice on how to market them. Some of their administrative people set aside an hour to give us advice on technical matters.

Everywhere and always there were the Villagers, calling to us, walking with us, touching us, asking our names and where we came from. We tried to explain—saying that we lived in a place something like Camphill, but without any Villagers. "Then," said a Villager thoughtfully and positively, "then it isn't like Camphill." He was perfectly right. The Villagers were always delighted when we told them that Twin Oaks was not nearly so nice as Camphill.

Then our three days were over. They loaded us down with whole wheat bread and marmalade, and we came back home.

We made our report and decided to go ahead and make an attempt to make and sell handicrafts. Doll-making, we found after brief experiments, is probably too time-consuming to be profitable, but we are experimenting with copper enameling. As it turns out, though, the craft business is a minor part of what we got out of the trip. The major thing was seeing Camphill itself, different from us and vastly more prosperous, but still very much a fellow Community.

ADVERTISEMENTS FOR OTHER COMMUNITIES

Two groups have asked us to print material about their proposed communities, so as to reach possible interested people on our mailing list. Descriptions of their plans and ideas are too long for this paper. The following are brief excerpts only. You can write to them directly to get further information.

Neverland

We are a group of people interested in forming a community similar to Twin Oaks in western U.S. We see the Neverland plan as divided into three stages: Stage 1, individuals, couples, or city communes live in city or suburbs, holding jobs and pooling money towards captial and land. Stage 2, some people move to the country and begin the farm and communal industries. Stage 3, helping others with similar values to establish communities. At present we are in the midst of Stage 1 with two communal houses thirty miles south of San Francisco

Neverland
1074 Del Norte
Menlo Park, California 94025

Community Design

We are planning an intentional community to be established in the spring of 1971. We are considering land in western Texas. We are looking for serious commitment. For this reason we are seeking primarily families. We would like to begin with about twenty-five families and build from there. The community will be set up as a nonprofit, non-equity-holding corporation. We expect to be financed totally by the members. The structure of the community will be based on that of the Israeli and Japanese kibbutzim and the proposed community of Walden Two. Government will be by direct, democratic means, with a minimum of actual structure. Economically the community will be self-sufficient. Part of our land will provide subsistence farming. Another portion of our land will be developed as a camp-site, managed by the community. In addition to income provided by the camping grounds, we would like to estab-lish some craftshops and light industry. We do not envision a back-to-the-soil, live-in-a-tepee community; technology has an important place in our organization.

Community Design

737 South Townsend
Montrose, Colorado

622 Woodbourne Avenue
Baltimore, Maryland 21212

HIGH SCHOOLERS COMMENT

We had a visitor once who taught school and took our pamphlets back to his classroom to stimulate discussion. The class responded with enthusiasm if not approval, and the teacher sent us a copy of their themes. Here are some samples:

This place is nothing but a community of weak-lings. They are a bunch of spineless people who are doing nothing but trying to escape from the rest of the world. They are trying to do away with all those things that are human. There is no incentive, no con-troversy, no titles, no seniority, no personal pride, no nothing. Twin Oaks and others like it can never exist. Evidence of this is that Twin Oaks has a whole 24 members, not many compared with the 200 million already in our present society.

If everyone was equal and if everyone didn't do anything wrong then I think this whole world would be boring. . . But when you can't own your own car that's too much, you have to have something to ride in. I for one wouldn't want people to come up, get into my car, drive away, and maybe even wreck it.

My opinion of this matter is that men will not live together without trying to take advantage of his fel-low man. I also think men who have studied long and hard to earn a doctorate in some field should be rec-ognized by the title of "Dr." and the bit about being two-faced or not discussing someone behind their back is a bunch of baloney. As long as there are people on this earth, people will find things to knock down, cut up, and humiliate his neighbor. No, as long as people exist, it will be the rich on top and the poor in the slums.

Seniority and special privileges should be given to those who deserve them.

Why are you guys always trying to change every-thing? Man, it's little things like this that can pull a great nation apart. Why can't you just let things alone? If you personally feel that if everyone were equal that would make things better or right, I feel for you. As for suggestions of a better program, I have none. I like it the way it is in real life and not in some *fake* place.

I can't say I would disagree with the Twin Oaks but I would say I wouldn't live there. I feel the com-munity is built for people who just want to loaf off in a simple atmosphere with no decisions and no worries. People in this community lack commitment. Twin Oaks still relies on the community of today. I believe the U.S.A. today is on the right track.

LETTERS FROM READERS

"I figured out my average labor credits for life-as-I-live-it. (This is a letter from a friend in Florida who spent two weeks with us and wrote after her return home.) It came out that I do about 75 credits per week, *if* I spent $4 a day to eat out. If I shop for and prepare my own meals and wash my own dishes, I can cut my food costs to $1.50 a day by increasing my labor credits to at least 90 a week! All this is figuring only 1.0 labor credits for programming and 1.1 labor credits per hour for overtime and 1.0 labor credits per hour travel time to and from work.

LECTURES

This is an advertisement. Twin Oaks dearly loves to travel to colleges, high schools, conferences, church groups, or anybody else who will pay us to do it and give talks about life at Twin Oaks. There are several of us who like to talk. We can come singly or in twos, stay overnight, give one lecture or four or five of them. Our rates vary according to the group we're talking to. Colleges generally give us from $50 to $150. Small groups that aren't too far away can hear about us for $20 or $30. In both cases we need transporta-tion, food, and accommodations in addition.

These lectures have been very successful so far. Appar-ently there is something so outrageous about the ideas of community life that people will come to the lectures just to protest vehemently during the question period. At any rate, they have been well attended. So if any of you readers have influence with any groups that customarily schedule paid lectures, put in a word for us—it really helps.

On-the-Premises Lectures

Groups that are within a few hours' drive of Twin Oaks are welcome to get their lecture here on the premises. In that case the charge is $2 a person. Bring your own picnic lunch or expect to eat in Louisa, since we can't feed large groups. We have entertained several such groups, mostly college classes. We show them around the buildings, tell them about our institutions and experiences generally, and then open up a question-and-answer period for as long as the questions keep coming. The whole thing may take two hours or more. Write ahead, so that we can schedule you.

BOOK OF SKINNER

By Josh

And it came to pass that a great nation rose up and held dominion over other nations and oppressed them sorely and this oppression was called Freedom. And the people that dwelt therein did call the name of that nation America and did sing praises unto it, calling it the "land of the brave" and the "home of the free."

And these people did worship the god Money and did build mighty temples unto him, which they called banks. They did labor mightily for their god and bow down to the priest employers, and did purchase possessions of little worth at great cost to shew their faithfulness to their god.

But in the place called Harvard there arose among the scribes and wise men a prophet named B. F. Skinner. And Skinner did speak unto the elders and scribes, saying "your teachings are false. Listen unto me and I will tell thee of the science of human behavior." And they did scoff at him and mock him but he did keep his cool and spake again unto them, saying "Thou lacketh understanding."

And in that time Skinner did have a dream of a place where women and men did live together in peace and did not worship the false god of Money. And he put hand to pen and pen to paper and wrote about what he had seen in his dream. And when he had finished writing he looked at that which he had written and he saw that it was good. And he called the name of it "Walden Two," and also the place did he name "Walden Two."

The multitudes did read *Walden Two* and some of them did lie in apathy and yawn, but others did rise up against Skinner and bore witness against him, saying that he blasphemed the god Money, and cried "Bullshit!" and "Thy system of labor cannot work."

But some did write unto Skinner, saying "Where is this place called Walden Two that I may live there?" And he said unto them, "Walden Two is not, for the time is not yet when men will use the behavioral science to raise up their children in the way that they should go."

And a few of the people said, "Let us gather together to build the place whereof Skinner has written." So it came to pass that seven of them did buy a parcel of land in the place that is called Virginia and they did dwell thereon, and they did call the name of that place "Twin Oaks."

NUMBER 14

April, 1971

GENERAL NEWS

THE BUDGET

The only budgeting experience most of us had before we came to Twin Oaks was household budgeting. That's not too hard—you take the total expected income and divide it among the expected expenses, leaving a little margin for emergencies and recreation.

A similar approach to community budgeting is frustrated by lack of information about income. How much money are we going to have in the month of April? We have very little idea. The first months few of the Community's existence it was impossible to know this, for we were living off subscriptions and donations, plus what we had in the bank from our initial investment. All we could say in those days was that we would spend as little as possible and try to get an industry started as soon as we could to bring in a steady income.

After we started depending primarily on outside jobs as a means of support, the planning job seemed a little easier. Figure $40 a week net per worker, and multiply by the workers. Add a dab for subscriptions and hammock sales, and we have a figure to work with. But it turns out to be an inaccurate one. An average worker may bring in $40 a week, but that average is taken over the year, not over the month. In some months the roads or automobiles have been in such bad shape that we could not even send workers into Richmond to their jobs. At other times sickness or difficulty in finding jobs interferes with our income. Expenses weren't predictable at first, either. Who knows how much doctor bills will cost, or how many pairs of shoes a community has to buy, or whether a new car will break down? We didn't—not in our first two years.

But we did keep books. And from those records of 1968, '69, and '70 we are able to make some generalizations and predictions about 1971. $400 for food, $450 for auto maintenance and gasoline, $150 for medical and dental, etc.

As to income, the uncertainties are mitigated by the credit we have been able to establish locally. If we don't have enough cash today, we can charge things and pay for them at the end of the month, or even next month if necessary. Merchants are patient as long as they believe they will eventually be paid.

In three years, then, we have been able to get our budget up to the level of the average housewife: estimate an income, and divide it among the expected expenses. This doesn't help a whole lot, though, in a group that is constantly building. For expenses are only one side of the picture. At the other are the decisions of what to invest in, what to build. For this, various managers have different ideas. The cattle manager would like to upgrade the herd with the purchase of some superior breeding stock; the orchard manager wants to put in 500 trees. Housing is considering the construction of a small dormitory building that will provide several private rooms for members; and the food department wants a walk-in freezer. Can we do all these things this year? If not, could we buy *some* cows and *some* trees and a smaller freezer? Or should we put off some of the projects until next year? And how do you budget things like that?

Money isn't the only thing that has to be budgeted, either. How much labor will the garden and food processing demand? How much will be left for construction? Considering the number of simple facts that we just do not know, the planning problem is staggering. For instance, we don't know how well any of the vegetable crops will do, and therefore how much food there will be to process; how many members and visitors there will be on hand each week for the work; what skilled people may have joined by then or will be visiting; whether or not unexpected sources of cash may appear. Planning is really just careful guessing.

So here are some of the things we are guessing we are going to do this year.

THE FREEZER

Hand in hand with the large organic garden project that we are doing this year goes the construction of a walk-in freezer. The last time we put in a big garden (and it wasn't as big as this year's), we had to rent freezer lockers to hold the processed corn and beans. The cost of the lockers was high, and their distance from the farm was inconvenient. This year, with an even bigger yield expected, we need to have our own freezers. We thought of buying a number of used freezers at $50 and $100 each, but calculations showed that vegetables and meat enough would require twenty-five such freezers. So it turns out to be just as cheap (?) to build a walk-in, which is what we want in the long run, anyway. This will cost us about $3000, prefab. Construction is scheduled to begin this week.

PRIVATE ROOMS

Almost every year we face, in one form or another, the question of expansion vs. standard of living. The first year there was no question about it. Our sheer survival was such a delicate matter that we did not even consider standard of living. We were determined to become a community. Starting with eight people, not all of whom we could count on, expansion of membership was not only desirable — it was urgent. But as we have become more and more secure, we have allowed ourselves little by little to improve the conditions of our environment. We no longer consider it a luxury to paint the walls of our rooms, or to make lumber available for shelves or bunks. We don't have to restrict the garden manager these days in the number of shovels and hoes he buys, and the auto maintenance people can assume that

there is money enough to rebuild an engine or buy new tires when needed.

The most desirable "luxury" that our members want this year is a room to call their own. We have always lived two-to-a-room. Some people don't mind; most people are not happy about it. In Walden Two, we all recall, private rooms were part of the very behavioral engineering that made everybody happy. We will go along with that: the annoyances and inconveniences of sharing a bedroom space with someone other than a permanent mate are considerable. Even the married couples would like to have a little privacy sometimes.

Nobody quarrels about the desirability of the one-person, one-room arrangement. But everybody has an opinion on the priorities of money-spending. If we build another dormitory building, some of us might prefer to add more members rather than just uncrowding the members we have. There are some good arguments for a larger membership, too. Building any kind of new living space is going to mean putting in additional sewage, a project requiring another large outlay of money.

So we have begun to consider other ways of getting some private rooms. Some members have gone so far as to divide their 12′ x 12′ rooms in half (giving two rooms slightly under six feet wide). Other proposals call for shifting the placement of the walls in one of our current buildings so as to make eight little rooms where there are now five medium sized ones. That plan would involve the sacrifice of two members (which means that we would not replace the next two people who leave, not that we would throw anyone out). Anyway, it looks as if our membership puts a high priority on private rooms, and one way or another we will get them within the next year or so.

THE ORCHARD

We have some trees already planted and hope for fruit from them in a year or so. Those are the ones we put in in 1967 and '68. Drought, flood, and insects have taken a toll, but there are a dozen trees or so that have survived and look promising.

The plan for 1971, however, has a longer range and a broader scope. The orchard manager has calculated the amount of fresh and frozen fruit that our Community would like to eat, and planned for the Community that will be here ten years from now. Cost problems have forced us to buy very young, small trees, many of which will take more than five years to bear. The apple trees, in particular, are an investment in the future; some of them do not bear for ten years.

$400 has bought us four acres' worth of orchard. This is the largest orchard anywhere in our area. The agricultural agent warned us that the last man to put in a big orchard suffered heavy losses from rodents, so we are putting a sleeve of hardware cloth around each of our baby trees. This is a fair amount of labor, but we just close our eyes and think of peaches.

CRAFTS

The challenge of getting rid of outside work has been taken up very seriously by several members, who are devoting their energies to various handicrafts. We started by buying an electric kiln for copper enameling and have been making a lot of pendants and other jewelry. Other people are crocheting hats and purses and making original purses on the sewing machine. Sewing "granny dresses" has been added to our list lately, as has candle-making. The profits are not large, but there is a profit; and the work is not onerous, either. Most difficult is the selling, but some of our members are learning to do that, too. Most of our handicrafts are marketed locally in Richmond, a few in Washington, D.C. We will be putting out a brochure for mail order, too, before very long.

THE STORE DIES

Another business we aren't good at, apparently, is storekeeping. We are closing the store this month because we are not making profit—not even a modest wage.

Part of the problem is simply location. Though the store is on a highway, it is not a heavily trafficked one. We serve primarily the families of the immediate neighborhood, and there are really only about thirty or forty such families. Furthermore, we could not seriously compete with the chain stores for the grocery trade of even these families, for our wholesale price in itself is usually about the same as the supermarket retail prices. We served primarily as a candy, potato chip, and soft drink supply. We also did a brisk business in bread and milk (but there is virtually no markup on either one), and in gasoline and motor oil. On paper, even with these problems, we could have netted a modest $10 a day, and we would have been content to do so. Unfortunately, we were prevented from doing even that, because of the problem of theft.

Nobody who steals from a little store thinks he is stealing much. Running off with $2 worth of gasoline is doubtlessly good fun, and pocketing a package of playing cards and a candy bar, high sport. If we had been in an area where we could accept this as "overhead" and still made a small wage, we would have shrugged our shoulders at the petty theft. The problem was that our profit was already too small to take any cuts at all. We rearranged the store to make shoplifting difficult and cut back on it a great deal, but the gas pumps we could not control. So we are going out of the grocery business, and in some ways we will miss it. In other ways we don't mind. It will free over a hundred credits a week for other labor, for one thing.

WE PLAN A CONFERENCE

Attached to this issue is a bulletin about a conference we are planning for this coming summer. If you want to attend, we suggest you get reservations early. We do not know how to predict the response, but we suspect there may be more people wanting to attend than we can seriously plan to accept because of space limitations.

If you just want to visit Twin Oaks but aren't planning to join a community, this July 4 weekend is not the time to visit. Pick another date and write the visitor manager about arrangements. The Conference is specifically for people who want to live communally.

COMMUNITY CLOTHES

Our institution of community use of clothing has grown entirely without any rules or planning. We never sat around discussing whether using the same clothing would make us feel "closer" or whether it was more "equal," or even whether it would save us money. We left the subject alone and did as we pleased. What many people pleased was full-scale community clothing from a central closet, and that is what we have now.

This is how it works. Every member has clothing he or she doesn't particularly care about. Most of us simply have too much clothing. So we all take our surplus clothes to the big Community closet, the clothing manager sorts it out, puts it on hangers or in labeled boxes. Then anybody who needs something to wear goes and gets it. After wearing, things go to Community laundry, and from there back to the big closet.

One of the things that makes this system work is that it is not compulsory. We all know that Community clothing often suffers from carelessness or ignorance (witness that big box of wool sweaters that have been shrunk in the dryer over the years). If members have things they are particularly fond of, they are more than welcome to mark them with their names and have them delivered to their rooms from the laundry. This option is a completely acceptable norm; you are not considered "less communitarian than we" if you choose it. There are perhaps six people in the Community who do; the rest of us literally prefer communal use.

There are good reasons for that. The big one is that one need not use one's precious bedroom space for clothing storage. One drawer for the next two days' changes is adequate. Next in importance is the fun of having an immense wardrobe, and the satisfaction of seeing something you brought being enjoyed by someone else. Maybe it just confirms your taste, or perhaps it makes you feel that you contributed something of worth. A less positive but very real reason for preferring Community clothing is that it is always difficult to get one's own things back from the laundry. You forget to mark them, or the laundry person did not find your mark, or it washed out. This is particularly true of socks. You have to care a lot about socks to take the time to sew name tags on them — most of us don't. For years now it has been a Community style norm to wear unmatched socks.

What makes communal clothing work is affluence. We have been told that the Israeli kibbutzim long ago gave up the concept because it caused more difficulties than it was worth. Our experience is that in most cases it is private clothing that is more difficulty than it is worth. The difference is probably not that we are more radical than the kibbutzim, but that we have more clothing. America has got to be the world's most superfluously dressed nation! Here at Twin Oaks, with an annual income per capita of about $700, we have more clothing than we can possibly use. We have a box in storage marked "shirts with rips and stains," another labeled "out-of-style shirts we could wear if we had to," and another called "perfectly good shirts we haven't room to hang up." Then there are the shirts that *are* hanging up, most of which hang there from month to month without being used, while a handful of light-blue denim workshirts get worn to shreds by the proletarian style conscious.

There are three boxes of women's dresses that are slightly out of style, plus sixty or seventy acceptable ones in several sizes. There are three cardboard cartons that contain long-sleeved turtle-neck shirts, one for short-sleeved turtle-necks, two for colored T-shirts, three for white T-shirts, and two other miscellaneous knit-top boxes. And so forth. A few days ago we ripped up a dozen whole shirts to make rags out of them. We have a surplus of clothing, but a shortage of rags for the garage and print shop.

Visitors probably notice that communitarians don't dress very well, in spite of this tremendous overflow of available clothing. That is because the visitor's eye is not attuned to inside culture. They cannot possibly know that we feel dressed up in a pair of jeans with a patch on the knee and a clean T-shirt. They certainly do not know that they look rather funny to us in their brilliant, shiny clothing, rather like actors in costume. (When our outside workers change into acceptable town clothing for their outside jobs, they refer to it as "putting on their costumes.")

The keynote for style is tolerance. You can wear absolutely anything. On the same day you will see jeans, short dresses, long dresses, pant-suits, and shorts. Not long ago some of us were discussing Twin Oaks' unconscious dress codes, and we realized that it would probably not be acceptable for a member to set her hair or wear a shirt-waist dress. Now that we recognize it as a taboo, we will probably hasten to violate it as soon as the weather is warm enough to permit the shirtwaist. I don't know about setting our hair, though—it's such a lot of trouble for a pretty small Cause.

Community clothing is not without its drawbacks. Everything you would suspect might happen does indeed happen. There have been times when someone made a perfectly good pair of jeans into cutoffs, or did a printing job in a new blouse, or wore something too small for him and ripped it. But our style norms and enormous surplus prevent these things being a serious problem. So you lost your yellow blouse to someone else's carelessness — take a blue blouse instead. Put your name on it if you want, and take it to your room — there are lots more.

AUTO REPAIR

A year ago this winter our worst financial problem was keeping our automobiles on the road. We depend very heavily on our cars, because most of our income comes from the "outside workers" who commute to Richmond and Charlottesville daily. In addition to the 190 miles a day accounted for by the workers, we of course have to go to nearby Louisa once a day for various purchases, occasionally travel to cattle auctions or wholesale meat cutters or dentist and doctors' appointments. Since Twin Oaks is out in the country, everywhere we go takes gas, oil, and auto wear and tear. The money that goes for auto expense is actually equal to the money we put out for food. We keep a minimum of five cars licensed, insured, and in decent repair, just for our day-to-day driving.

A year ago it was a lot worse. When a car broke down then, it was a minor tragedy. We had to hold a special meeting to decide whether we wanted to have it repaired by a garage or just abandon it and buy another old car. Since the beginning we have been financially aided a great deal by the new members who bring their cars with them. We have not actually had to *buy* more than three or four cars since we got here. Nevertheless, the upkeep has been a ferocious expense. There was a period in the winter of '69-'70 when all of our cars were down at once. Two of them were simply stuck in the mud and frozen there. The tractor that could have pulled them out was in the same condition. Since nobody could go to work, we had an enormous unscheduled labor force on the farm, and we used it to carry hot water to the nearest frozen car, defrost its radiator, and lift it out of the mud with our combined strength, "Chinese style."

Things have changed. The main force behind the change has been the slowdown in population turnover. Our auto maintenance manager joined us last February, has been here ever since, and has no thought of leaving. He wasn't a mechanic when he first came; he was a college dropout philosophy major. He looked around for something useful to do, saw that cars were our biggest problem, and set himself to learn about them. He took advantage of the knowledge and skill of mechanically-inclined visitors, studied repair manuals, and did what repairs he could, gradually accumulating the tools we needed out of our meager budget. Last fall he pointed out the need of an indoor garage to keep the cars running over the winter, and we decided to devote some of our precious heated space to that purpose. We never made a better space-use decision. By this time another experienced mechanic had joined Twin Oaks, and the two of them trained a third previously inexperienced member to work with them. This was Shannon, an enthusiastic Walden Twoer who joined us last June when she graduated from high school. Shannon has attacked the job with enthusiasm and dedication. She knows she has to overcome the mechanical vacuum that her typical female upbringing has left her with. Indeed, it is partly for that reason that she enjoys working with cars.

We have rebuilt three engines in the past three months, also converted a Fairlane with a defunct automatic transmission to a sturdy stick-shift. Also a hundred other repairs that come up all the time. The Community feels completely relaxed about automotive breakdowns these days. When we get a call that the VW bus has broken down in Charlottesville, we don't think a whole lot about it—we just go tow it home. Our mechanics will have it back on the road next week.

PAPERS ON THE BOARD

The perrenial question, *What do you do for recreation?*, can be answered, for some communitarians, by the statement, "We talk a lot." Certainly the community atmosphere is very reinforcing for those of us who enjoy controversial discussion. Controversy can be made out of anything, and usually is. Arguments about Community policy are usually not bitter or angry. After all, we are all going the same general direction, and the differences that we argue about are small enough so that, if no compromise is possible, the losers can live with the legislation that they don't quite agree with.

Items currently being discussed, for instance, are: *1)* whether we can determine someone's "need" for a private room better by asking her reasons for wanting one or by offering her a room so small that only a person desperate for privacy would be willing to live in it; *2)* whether people who leave the Community and then change their minds and want to come back within a short time (two months?) should have to make up the labor they missed while they were gone; *3)* whether the appointment of planners and managers properly takes place in a closed planners' meeting or whether the general membership should participate in such discussion.

When there were only three or four people who cared about such subjects, we could talk them over among ourselves and agree (or disagree) without misunderstandings. But as the group has become larger, it becomes obvious that there are a great many people who want to know about policy-making while it is going on, and who want to have a say in how it goes. We need better information than chance conversations give us; that is probably why the Opinion and Idea Board became important.

If a member writes a paper on an idea and posts it on the bulletin board, the idea is available to every interested member of the Community. Someone may "answer" the paper with a counter-paper. More likely, several people will discuss the idea with the person, agreeing or not, expanding or contradicting it. The value of the bulletin board paper is that it does not get garbled as it passes from person to person. What the author of the paper said is open to every member's interpretation, but at least the interpretation is in all cases of the original idea. This is quite different from trying to find out what someone said at some meeting that one didn't attend, where one has to filter one person's opinions through the prejudices of another.

Not all these papers are suitable for printing in the *Leaves*, partly because their subjects are too in-group to be interesting. Some, however, are sufficiently universal to be printed — for instance:

TWIN OAKS AND THE REVOLUTION

Opinion — By Erik

Twin Oaks and the *Walden-Two* oriented part of the community movement seeks to achieve and maintain a total environment that maximizes the happiness of every creature on earth. The priority in our minds goes to humans, but we shall some day reach a stage where it will be pertinent to consider the beasts of the field and what we can do to make their existence more reinforcing for them.

I present now a minor theory of world history that has occurred to me recently and is interesting to me. It is: systems of government that are not reinforcing do not and will not last; that to the extent people are unhappy with a government and have reason to believe that change will improve their lot, they will work to institute that change. I won't offer any examples, for I'm not very convinced myself; but the implication is one of optimism, for, unless the world is destroyed through some catastrophe such as atomic war, this theory would indicate that history's inevitable course is, as Marx said, destined to reach a state of maximal reinforcement, temporary revisionist setbacks notwithstanding.

Our goal, therefore, is worldwide. We should not forget that fact. This is our ultimate Long Range Plan. There are two lesser levels of concern, however, with regard to long-range plans. One of them is our affiliation with nationwide and worldwide alternative systems and organizations. The other is our plans for the future of our own physical plant.

We are in sympathy with the ultimate goals of various nationwide and worldwide revolutionary groups. Our goals of maximizing the quality of life for everyone seems to be, at least according to our degree of awareness of their nature and aims, fairly similar — particularly with regard to the present establishment of U.S. class, race, and sex oppression. We are against American imperialism and militarism abroad, too. The remarkable movement in the last few years — the marches of protest, the demonstrations, the persecution and consequent growth of such organizations as SDS and BPP, the books about revolutionary people's governments in China, Cuba, Vietnam, Korea, etc. — all of these have sparked an interest among various members and a verbal show of support.

My analysis leads me to differ with some persons about the relationship of the community movement and the revolution. The active revolutionaries tell us that we are not helping the revolution by being here—and perhaps are holding it back. If this is indeed the case, then we must face the question: is the revolutionary method of reaching our common goal the best? If so, we must also either leave the

Community and join the revolution or admit that we are indeed copping out.

We should not blithely assume that the revolutionary method of reaching our common goal is actually the best. There is an alternative, and we are it. We usually do not think of ourselves in those terms, and are thus easily attracted to the revolution's daring and glitter.

The idea of the community movement as opposed to the revolutionary movement is to change the existing social structure through positive reinforcement, as opposed to punishment. It is to make people join because ours is a better way of life and not to spend hours trying to convince factory workers that communism will improve their lot in life. For mark this: a revolution is not a *coup d'etat*. For the revolution to succeed, the broad mass of people must be either sympathetic or apathetic. And this is very, very far from being the case now. On the contrary, despite the feelings you may get from attending demonstrations where there are perhaps thousands of hip folk with raised fist, America's population is overwhelmingly conservative or middle of the road, and is antagonized by long hair, drugs, and Black Panthers. It may seem that the revolutionary movement has made much more progress than we have, but the gain they may have on us is acutely small when compared with the distance we both have before us. I predict that the U.S. revolution that people we know are working for will peak before the people are actually ready—that is, go off half-cocked—and that repression will set in proportionate to the threat presented by the unsuccessful revolution.

Let us remember that anger is not a useful thing in solving problems. It tends to get in the way of a rational approach. We are all angry when we first become aware of the existence of the ruling "one per cent," the extent of bigotry, corruption, and injustice, and the lies told us from childhood about America's role in the world, and about life under communism. We can sympathize with those who wish to use force to achieve the common goal. But let us hesitate and think carefully and rationally before we join them. Let us ask ourselves: what was wrong with our original idea?

The original idea was to form communities that satisfy the needs and desires of the members, that maximize the quality of life of the members, and that will grow because it is a better way. At times Twin Oaks has had members who poo-pooh the idea that social change could occur in this way. They felt that repression would definitely wipe us out within a very few years, because we would be a threat to the capitalist colossus. They laughed at our naivete in thinking that we could simply grow and grow. *But what was that thinking and those conclusions based on?* They were not based on fact, or even any logical presentation of figures and historical precedent. They were based on the personal convictions of one or two intelligent and thoughtful members.

My conviction is an opposite one. It is that communities will indeed be able to grow, that we will not represent an economic threat to capitalism for a very long time. It is true that we risk repression; but that repression risk stems from other than economic factors. It could come as a result of local antagonism. We are, in fact, a cultural colony; and we are afraid of the natives and afraid of integration. This situation leads us to react in natural but unfortunate and irrational ways. We could, with some effort, become friends with our neighbors.

Risk also stems from our association with and sympathy for revolutionary forces that do, indeed, frighten the Establishment. Thus hateful as it may sound, our interests and the interests of the revolutionary forces conflict when our safety is considered.

As we turn from the forces of revolution, we find that we are no longer alone on the frontier. Around us are friends and new communities, communities that are very sympathetic to our goals and methods and that take themselves seriously, such as Neverland, Community Design, East Street Gallery, and Walden Three. For a long time our efforts have been turned inward almost exclusively, in contrast to the days before the summer of '67, when tons of verbiage was expended on long-range plans and federations, etc. We discovered that things were harder than we imagined, that federations and Walden Two were much further away than we thought. But three years of internal concern and little contact with the movement have enabled us to get ourselves together, to establish through trial and error various systems dealing with internal coordination and management. This past year has, to my eyes, been one of significant growth and physical advance.

Now is the time to establish firm lines of communication with new communities, and with existing communities that are sympathetic with our methods and goals.

WALDEN THREE

We are very close to a group called Walden Three. At one time these people considered joining Twin Oaks, but they decided to try to start an independent community, because of some minor differences in theory and practice. Here is what they say about themselves:

Walden Three at present is comprised of eight individuals residing in a large house in Providence. We are based principally on behavioral, cultural, and environmental design as presented by B. F. Skinner in *Walden Two*. We have also been influenced by other writers in the behavioral and environmental sciences, such as Ruth Benedict, Ashley Montague, and Bucky Fuller.

Although small at present, we would like to expand to a community of five hundred to a thousand members on a rural location with facilities for light industry, such as a foundry, woodworking, metals fabrication, hydroponics, etc.

We are preparing to publish the *Communitarian,* a magazine concerned with the intentional community/commune movement with regular articles on the scientific-technological communities. The *Communitarian* will discuss both theory and practice as they apply to communities. Through this magazine we hope to reach individuals wishing to join efforts like our own and aid those with other philosophies in finding communities best suited to them.

Anyone interested in visiting and/or joining Walden Three or subscribing to the *Communitarian* should write:

Walden Three
Annex Station Box 969
Providence, Rhode Island 02901

REPORT ON A CNVA CONFERENCE

In January we sent a representative to Volunton, Connecticut, to attend a conference on communes. She reports:

"It was a weekend conference. Friday night representatives from the Bruderhof spoke. Unfortunately I arrived too late to hear them. I heard later that the speakers had been cirticized from the floor by the women's lib contingent for calling themselves a "Brotherhood," but that a young girl who had recently visited them defended them, saying that their women were indeed treated as individual people, not in terms of their sex roles.

"Saturday morning several of us who had something to say about the places we had come from or the activities we were engaging in spoke briefly and then answered questions from the floor. Twin Oaks was the only real commune represented. A lot of people came to hear about communes, but the number of resource people available after the Bruderhof left was small. Partly for this reason, I was much in demand. People asked me questions about Twin Oaks most of the day. I just sat in one corner of the hall on a mattress (the place was practically lined with mattresses), and little groups came and went, trying to find out if Twin Oaks was the place for them or not. In most cases I would say that it is not. The feeling I got was that most of the attendees at that conference were people who wanted a life somewhat more communal and certainly more rural than the one they were living, but that Twin Oaks was too radical for their taste. Either that, or they had children and we couldn't take them anyway. But they were certainly interested and stimulated. Several people expressed pleasure or gratification that Twin Oaks had sent a representative—someone who could talk from actual experience instead of just theorizing.

"The Walden Three people were there. They spoke right after me and said something like, 'Well, we're similar to Twin Oaks, only smaller.' The question was asked why they didn't just join Twin Oaks, and they explained that they felt they had what it took to get a second Walden Two community started and that anyone who could, should. Also, they have their own ideas about different labor and behavioral systems and other experiments that might be

easier to effect in a beginning group than in an established one. I think they are mistaken about that. I think that it is easier to do experiments with a group accustomed to experimenting with their structures, but that is their affair.

"There were three people there who represented a *garin,* a group of Jewish young people about to start another kibbutz in Israel. Their project was interesting to us. Most conference participants knew little about kibbutzim except what they read in Bettleheim's *Children of the Dream,* a book held in contempt by the Jews I talked to. These particular people were very dynamic and attractive. I felt drawn to them, and so did the Walden Three people. The six of us ate together and generally sought each other's company. I urged the "kibbutz people," as they were called, to visit Twin Oaks, and they are eager to do so. The conference was a new experience for them. Heretofore they had spoken only to Jewish people who understood their longing for Israel but perhaps questioned the communal life style. At the conference they met a group that took communal life for granted but wondered why they wanted to go to Israel.

"The conference was well handled. The CNVA people got around the touchy food question by serving vegetarian meals, some of which were very good. There was a seminar on bread baking, and the bread that came out of that class was served to the conference participants later. The simple plan of having a huge stack of mattresses available in a large hall, rather than bothering with chairs, struck me as ingenious and practical. Sleeping arrangements were also simple: you brought your own sleeping bag, and they provided a roomful of mattresses. They had bedding there for people who hadn't brought any.

"One part of the conference that is more fun to talk about than it was to live was a supper of raw food, prepared and presented by some organization of people who take their eating habits religiously seriously. It was a bitterly cold day, and the supper of four kinds of raw bean sprouts, plus a salad, lacked a great deal in terms of satisfaction, plus making a lot of people's stomachs ache. Along with the supper came a lecture by a Believer, who told us—among other things—that eating raw foods had healed boils on his feet and made his hair grow back in. We unimpressed six sat in a circle and munched our sprouts and tried to think about Experiments and Domes and Israel. As for me, I thought about hamburger.

"We met two people who had tracts of land that might be available to communities. We even rode out into Connecticut to see one of them—a lovely spot. We do not at this time know of a community that is ready to move onto the land, but we have those addresses for then the time comes.

"In general we got the feeling that such conferences are definitely worthwhile, and we mean to send someone every time we can afford the transportation. CNVA is planning another conference on communes in April. Write CNVA, Volunton, Connecticut, for information and reservations."

GROWTH, PHASE TWO:

Leveling Off at Forty

An Overview, as seen by Bob

A community develops like a single human being. Long before it existed, Twin Oaks was conceived in theoretical formlessness—a psychologist's notion expanded into a novel. Only the protective womb of the urban commune fore-runners, Walden Pool and Walden House, could give it substance. But its umbilical cord remained securely tied into the web of urban America—the nine-to-five rat race, the boss, television, and the tranquilizer. It took the trauma of the 1966 conference, spurred by the giant University quest for that panaceic green research grant, ascending the lofty peaks of great intentions, and then falling into the pits of commitment, to set in motion the mechanisms for muscle contractions, the real labor behind the delivery of the embryonic community, almost premature, but precocious, upon the foothills of central Virginia.

And a contraction it was: from a thousand speculations to a mere handful of Rube Goldberg farmers.

Agricultural conditions had changed significantly since *Walden Two* was written (1945): buying up rundown farms no longer offered the advantage of instant prosperity. Our undernourished infant was left on its own to hit upon a method of supplanting its resources, something easy to develop and halfway rewarding. And it did—the hammock industry.

In the beginning the hammock was Twin Oaks' diaper pin—it held everything together. Getting the crew of pioneers coordinated may not have been an ordeal, but neither was it a Garden of Eden. Membership turnover was high. Some backed out. Other over-eager members, their expectations in the clouds, left disappointed.

Farming was not a communitarian forte. The first summer crop, tobacco, was too much work for what you could get out of it—a broken back, a little (too little) bread for survival, and knowledge you were feeding the industrial cancer machine. But most of the members, those who were here to stay, were determined, almost fanatically, not to be undone. There were no doctors, architects, plumbers, dairy herders, carpenters, electricians, or marketing-sales experts. But the "do-it-yourself" attitude began to permeat the membership. They read up; they wrote away; they asked neighbors. And they "did it."

Thus the infant community survived, and slowly its untrained eyes began to focus on the world beyond the driveway, on those people looking for a world, not in which to hide, but to create. Over a three-year span the population took a tumultous upward surge.

Despite the astronomical turnover in membership (70 per cent per year), the surge never slowed until recent months. Now even the turnover has plunged. Reason? We have reached a spatial plateau. Although blue-prints four years ago called for expansion up to 500 or 1000 before splitting into a multi-community, our present size (give or take ten members) has been temporarily fixed by three basic material factors: food, shelter, and technology.

Please excuse the oversimplification. By food I actually mean dining facilities, not our capacity to supply a healthy country three squares for all. The main problem is this: the farmhouse will not hold enough ovens, sinks, chairs, and tables to feed very much more than the present membership plus visitors. The dishwashing, bathroom, and septic tank systems are already working at capacity. Various modifications—like installing a larger sink, tearing down a wall, or rearranging the table space—extended accommodations in the past. But the enclosure of the farmhouse porch to seat an additional twenty hungry members this fall stands as a landmark in community growth. We have reached a turning point. The next expansion will be a giant step to house and feed the community of the future. A geodesic dome to accommodate eating and meeting facilities for more than a hundred has been proposed. But the construction manager remains to be convinced of their practicality. Other plans are being researched. But all this will have to wait until the residence and technological facilities catch up.

The pioneer communitarians lived in the farmhouse until Harmony was built. The next step was putting in the first floor of the Oneida Building. Then gradually over the last summer, the second floor was finished. And we are now full, two to a room. One proposal provides for fifteen or twenty more "Oneida type" buildings (pole support, two-story, V-roof, duct-heated, asphalt ground floor) arranged in spokes around the proposed dining complex. Other people are in favor of modular construction that would permit the population to expand a little at a time, as money became available. In either case, we first need the bread and better building techniques. For instance, we have discovered that water leaks into the Oneida living room during heavy rainstorms due to inadequate drainage on the surrounding land. Drainage ditches have alleviated the problem for Oneida, but we will want to raise the floor above flood level for future buildings. Furthermore, in mid-winter we noticed that Oneida does not get heated uniformly—icy winds suck the heat out through the exterior on the windward side, especially on the second floor. We will also want to watch for long-term wear and tear on the asphalt, and efficiency of our present oil heater versus other methods. You might say that we are structurally in a period of watchful waiting.

Meanwhile, even when we are ready for our next building, the population growth will be buffered by the rising desire for single rooms. Not that we never wanted them before — just that now that there is a sufficient population to guarantee a reasonable stability, we are less pressured into sacrificing ideal environmental conditions in order to take new members.

Our long- and short-term growth potential has thus been sketched. To what degree and how long it will take to meet this potential will be contingent upon our success at attaining a viable self-sufficient economy. Simple? Ah. . .also the crux.

We can expand our hammock industry only to a point, the point that balances between what rate of production feels comfortable and what maximum rate of sales can be reached. We are now beginning to increase production from twenty hammocks per week (about eighty hours) to almost three times that. The emphasis will be on making the work more enjoyable by piping music or readings into the work area, and having a lot of people weaving at the same time. We have learned from our experience with planting and harvesting that morale is high in large, informal groups where there is laughter, singing, and a strong feeling of accomplishment as each member gazes at the enormous output of the group. This decision to put out "hordes of hammocks" was made and felt by the entire membership—a Community first in the hammock industry.

As for marketing, our advertising is becoming much richer in quality, and we are stepping up our efforts to make better contacts.

So the emphasis for this new growth period seems to be digging in and getting our products out. Anyone who completes an outside work shift quickly becomes a crusader for self-sufficiency. The motivation soars. The task is to get the technology off the ground. We will need something besides hammocks to support the Community of the future. The printing press netted us $4,000 since the last semester, another Community first. But as a heavy, steady industry, this will require some investments and risks we are not quite ready to take. We are working successfully with small craft industries—copper enameling, hand-crocheted hats, dresses, and candles for starters. The crafts don't net us very much, but their high sales success is reinforcing, and we are working our way slowly into other industries. There seems to be a lot more leeway in the budget and attitudes of the group to promote them. In the next few months you may see us developing stationery, silkscreen, photography, free-lance writing, pottery, and loom weaving, to name a few.

Just as a human being's attitudes and activities may shift in relation to change in growth, so may a community's. The rising desire for single rooms, turning out ears to the outside for advice, digging in to get our products out, and more room to experiment with industries reflect only a part of an overall shift in attitudes concommitant with leveling off of the population. Up until last summer the prevailing attitude was "The most important way to strengthen the community is to increase membership, be it at the expense of some degree of life quality, technological development, and leeway for experimentation." The expense was not felt so much as a denial as much as an acceptance of more rewarding conditions. That is, when there were only twenty members, it was a relief to have another member join, lower the labor quota 5 per cent, supply added skills and learning ability, intellectual impetus, and human warmth. Unable to predict the early growth potential, it wasn't worthwhile to research better construction techniques, make commitments to long-range land, cattle, or industrial development. The priority was to accommodate as many members as could join by getting low budget buildings up as fast as members could fill them. The varnishing, curtains, better roadways and paths, trimmings, doghouses, etc. were postponed.

However, things got a little hairy this summer assimilating so many new members, with so many visitors parading through, and overnight changes in Community buildings. You got a strange feeling when you'd wake up one morning, dash into the farmhouse for some breakfast, and discover two members had removed a wall while you were asleep; or that the two rooms next to yours at the end of the hall had suddenly been transformed into a mammoth indoor garage. It was even strange for a member doing outside work away from the Community for two months to return to so many changes. "Where's Community clothes these days? What happened to the library? How does the new labor credit system work?"

Now that there are enough members to fill all the basic skills, and now that energy can be channeled away from basic construction to enhancement, and now that conditions are more conducive to having managers stick around, and their corresponding managerships branch out in a clear-cut, continuous stream, the movement to get the existing membership closer to its idealized vision of Community has intensified. For all of us this includes eliminating outside work. For most of us it means more time for recreation, creativity, and experimentation; making labor more enjoyable, encouraging group cohesiveness and spirit. For many it means single rooms. For others it is planting a fruit tree orchard or researching architecture and landscaping.

The most profound change in attitudes is notable at Community meetings. At one time people would argue at great length about what they thought was right, or ethical, or realistic. For a while there was a preoccupation with defending, paralyzing rebukes, monopolization of discussion, and endless moralizations—all on a high and fast-pitched intellectual level. People unable to compete in the great debates would either get bored and leave the meeting or sit and ponder whether a pound of sweat was really worth an ounce of decision.

People know each other now. There is more awareness of "group process." There is more room for individuality, more acceptance of differing viewpoints and alternate suggestions. "People don't barrage you with criticisms any more; they encourage you to think creatively," says one member.

Further along the road to Community togetherness, a lot of things have been tried and a lot abandoned. We have initiated a weekly "utopia class," for instance, that began to discuss group process. Enthusiasm for Group Criticism seems to have died. Either members don't go to the sessions or they have little to say. For a while people were signing up for "private criticism" (on a one-to-one basis), but even this is on the way out. Apparently people are exchanging feedback more spontaneously. We have progressed from moralization to communication.

"GroupRap" was another institution that was at its peak last summer, then tapered off. It was for members who were having a hard time finding each other among all the new faces and hordes of visitors. But things have settled out, and it is much easier and natural to assimilate a new member.

Our visitor policy has also undergone change. There was a time when there were so many visitors flying around, looking for something or other, that many complained they found only confusion and coldness. Members were admittedly backing off from the hordes, trying to establish some regularity and fullness in their personal involvements. We finally decided to restrict ourselves to ten visitors at a time, discouraging short-term visits, visits from people coming out of sheer curiosity, for a weekend diversion, students doing field research for their term paper on communes, and generally people who show little promise of joining or promoting the community movement. Members still do a double-take when they see a busload of visitors coming for an afternoon lecture tour. But for the most part, members are more sensitive and open to visitors, encouraging a disintegration of the distinction between member and visitor, as long as things don't get too disruptive.

Nowadays there is definitely a different feeling one gets just being around the Community. As I lie on my hammock underneath the apple tree near the farmhouse in the center of things, taking in the scene, I can hear Mayflower, Angie's

calf, mooing away in the barn behind me. I remember how we all stood around in the chilly December winter, watching her slide out of Angie's womb—the way she struggled for an endless twenty minutes to stand on her own four feet, and the way she knew right away where to find Angie's udder. She has grown. And she'll make a fine dairy cow—a virtual milking machine. But if you get too close to her now, she'll nip out her tongue and affectionately lick the shirt right off your back.

To my left I can hear shop noises from Harmony. Cars, hammocks, saws, sewing machines, offset press. Two voices are singing in harmony.

To my right I can smell dinner in the pot—chicken and dumplings—and dessert, chocolate cake, a Twin Oaks speciality. In front of me Judy is planting grass for the village lawn. Beyond her is Oneida, and beyond, some members are planting strawberries while another is fertilizing the peas. And beyond, the tree orchard, amidst gleaming green barly, invoking a feeling of permanence and prosperity. And beyond, toward the South Anna River, fields, endless fields and forests. The daffodils and crocuses are already up. Apple blossoms will soon be scattering in the April breeze. The air is fresh with spring and the future.

REPORT ON TWIN OAKS' SUMMER CONFERENCE

THE INTENTION

Is Twin Oaks anything more than just a groovy place to live? Perhaps a good place to live is its own justification for being. A commune that makes its own members happy — happier than they would be elsewhere — has made a social contribution. It makes the world just a tiny bit better than it way, by improving the lives of a handful of people. That's better than nothing.

But it isn't what we started out to do here at Twin Oaks. We meant to make the good life available for large numbers of people, and to give some solid evidence, while we were at it, that communal living might make sense for the country as a whole. The suggestion in *Walden Two* was that this might be accomplished by a "grow-split" method. First we accept members up to a population of a thousand people; then we divide down the middle like an amoeba, then each of those halves fills up to its capacity again and divides, etc.

The difficulty with this plan is that it isn't easy to get up to that first thousand. There is no lack of potential members! But before we can accept more members, we must

have ways of supporting them and places to house them, adequate sewage, dining, and public rooms. This is an economic problem that will take some time to solve. In the meantime, hundreds of people are writing to us and asking for advice about how to get started living communally.

While we are getting our money and organization together for eventual expansion, other groups could be getting started. There are going to be plenty of members to go around. What people need is a way of meeting each other, so that people with similar ideas can pool their resources and get communities started.

Twin Oaks undertook this July Fourth weekend to help get people together. Ours was not the first conference on communal living, by any means; but it was somewhat unique in that we made a deliberate appeal to communal-minded people who are not afraid of organization and who take a common-sense rather than mystical approach to problem-solving. We advertised in places like *Mother Earth, Alternatives*, the *Green Revolution*, plus our own *Leaves*, and we stressed that we were inviting people who are serious about joining or creating a community within the next year. What we hoped for was that at least a dozen people who really had the determination to see such a project to completion would attend the conference and meet each other.

PREPARATIONS

It was with some trepidation that we made the decision to hold the conference on our own land. Certainly there are other conference facilities (CNVA in Connecticut, for example) that we could have rented and that would have had dormitory space and a large hall to offer. Twin Oaks has neither—nor adequate bathrooms, nor a separate kitchen. Our decision to invite people here was based on the idea that prospective communitarians need to get a realistic idea what can be done with a small amount of money and a small group of people. Let them (we said) look at Twin Oaks and judge whether or not our ways of doing things would suit them. The concrete example (good or bad, depending on their points of view) would help them keep their feet on the ground and talk about real problems.

Having a lot of people on Twin Oaks' property meant that the conferees would camp out. We needed to provide them with a place to camp, accessible by car (a lot of people camp *in* their vehicles), a water supply, outhouses, and shelter for dining. None of our buildings were anywhere near big enough to feed such a crowd.

THE DOME

We did a lot of arguing about whether to build a big dome or whether to build some sort of shed that would have a permanent use. We decided at first on a big implement shed. We would build it for conference dining, then use it afterwards to house the tractors and other farm equipment. It was to be pole construction. But finding poles turned out to be a problem. We bid on some telephone poles at an auction, but we didn't win the bid. As the time drew nearer (by the time we knew we had lost the bid, it was June 15), we realized that we had to change our plans and construct a dome after all. It was not at all clear what we would use the dome for afterward. It isn't at all suitable for an implement shed, but it was cheap and fast to build.

We had never built a dome before, but *Dome Book One* told us we could do it. We constructed it of two-by-fours fastened to slices of metal pipe by means of metal straps. It is about 32 feet in diameter, 16 feet high. Originally we meant to make it bigger than that, but a simple arithmetical error forced us to cut the struts shorter than we intended. Moral: When you build a dome, check your multiplication.

Inside the dome we put eight picnic tables, also constructed for the conference out of rough oak. We covered the dome with black polyethylene except for the bottom row of triangles. It provided shade from the sun and mediocre shelter from the rain. It leaks in a hard rain.

ORGANIZATION

In addition to the physical construction, a great deal of preparation went into the scheduling of conference activities. We used a modified labor credit system, asking each conference participant to do a share of the work. Everybody who attended was assigned to one shift of work, varying among cooking, dishwashing, child care, lifeguarding, and attending the snack bar. Conferees were assigned to the tasks for which they declared themselves qualified and which they said they preferred. Actually, we assigned more people than were necessary on most shifts, knowing that some registrants might not show up.

We thought of scheduling workshops, too, and asked conferees which of several workshops they would be most interested in attending. (We offered workshops in construction, health problems, legal and tax structures food planning, government, economic base, labor distribution systems, issues in child care, marriage and sex roles, and membership selection.) But almost everybody said they would be interested in almost all of the workshops, so all we did was schedule each workshop two or three times, and let the conferees try to fit them in the best they could.

HOW MANY PEOPLE?

In our first conversations about having a conference, we envisioned a thousand people; and we had some talk about public address systems and such things. But a day's worth of sober consideration threw out that idea. We resolved to limit participation to that number whom we could reasonably find parking spaces for, feed, and address in one building as a group. This last consideration, especially, made us set the figure at 125. We did our advertising accordingly, deliberately avoiding the huge-circulation media.

Parking turned out to be no problem. We set aside a hay field and measured it. It would easily hold more cars than we intended to accept. We worried a lot about our capacity to cook for large crowds. We decided to invite people to cook for themselves in their own campers if they chose. As to a building for public meetings, our largest has a capacity of less than 100. Maybe some people wouldn't want to attend public meetings??

THE SHERIFF

Registration forms came in slowly at first. When we had received a scant twenty registrations, the Louisa County Sheriff came to visit us. He had heard rumors, he told us, that we were holding a "love-in rock festival" on July 4. We straightened him out on the purpose of the conference and assured him that our outhouses would meet health department regulations. But he still worried about numbers. Sometimes people didn't realize what size crowd they could handle, he said. At the close of our conversation we agreed that we would let him know when our registration reached 75, and that for their part, the Sheriff's Office would be on call in case we were inundated by undesirable types expecting a rock festival.

THE NUMBERS MOUNT

The last week before conference the registrations poured in. We thought of cutting them off but did not do so. One day the correspondence people posted a little note on the bulletin board telling us "Conference registration has just passed 200—gulp!" Some of us began to be frightened. If 200 registered, how many would appear without having preregistered? Still we did nothing but chew our nails, worry, and increase the food buying a little bit.

As a matter of fact, the numbers worked out very well. 194 adults and 62 children attended the conference, besides the 34 members and their assorted regular guests. True, there were people who came without having preregistered, but there were others who had preregistered and didn't come, so it worked out all right.

THE CONFEREES ARRIVE

We felt less jittery when the first people began to arrive. The first arrivals were old friends who had visited before. Then came the first trickle of campers and station wagons. Tents began to go up in our hay field. By evening the field resembled a carnival, with over fifty vehicles and tents.

THE PEOPLE

We couldn't have asked for a nicer group of people. They were typical of Twin Oaks visitors in general—intelligent people on the fringes of the middle class, disillusioned with what the Outside has to offer them, but a little timid about taking the big step to community. A lot of them were young marrieds with small children, though a good number of single people also attended. The people being considerate and easy to talk to, administration problems became light. If one arrangement didn't work out, the conferees easily adjusted to another.

WORKSHOPS

The object of the workshops was two-fold. First, there are some things that Twin Oaks has information on that other people would be interested in learning. Second, and more important, we hoped that the workshops would give people a chance to sound off on their favorite theories, thus helping others in the workshops to begin aligning themselves. They could begin to think about whether they wanted to live with those people who have those ideas. It was in this way, after all, that the original Twin Oaks members found each other at the Walden Woods conference in 1966. To a certain extent both aims were fulfilled. Certainly a lot of talk went on.

Twin Oaks set out to avoid giving the impression that we were trying to force our ideas onto new communities, and our workshop leaders were instructed not to preach about Twin Oaks' methods. But often they found themselves spending much of the session answering questions about Twin Oaks.

THE GENERAL MEETINGS

There were two general meetings, one for listening to a Twin Oaks member talk about the problems Twin Oaks has met or failed to meet during its four years, and the other for introducing the various small communities that were represented at the conference. The latter was highly informative. At least ten different groups were represented. Each told of its general aims, its current status, whether they were looking for members and—if so—what kind, and whether or not they would accept children. Each group was allotted ten minutes to speak.

After this meeting it became evident that there was a need for still another kind of meeting—meetings for like-minded people to meet each other and begin to plan for living together. We hadn't scheduled anything precisely like that, but there was plenty of free time, and the conferees scheduled for themselves. By Saturday evening there were several groups sitting around in serious discussion, feeling out each other's beliefs and commitment. The folk dancing that we had planned for recreation was poorly attended; conferees had more serious business to attend to.

EATING

The only Twin Oaks people who really had to work hard at the conference were the two cooks. Although they had plenty of conference people to help them, they had committed themselves to be on hand for all the cooking, and it was hot and steady work. The food was in general good and plentiful. For Twin Oaks members, accustomed to very little meat and fruit, it was a four-day royal feast. We had meat twice a day and all the fruit we could eat. Breakfast each day was orange juice and granola. The granola was prepared ahead of time by Twin Oaks.

And then there was the snack stand. Pepsi Cola provided a snack wagon free of charge, and a local dairy did the same with an ice cream freezer. We decided to let all the Twin Oaks members have free treats during the conference and sell to the conferees at wholesale prices. So we took a small financial loss, but it was worth it. Gorging oneself on ice cream once a year doesn't cost so very much.

MONEY

The conference cost a total of $2,200. Half of that was food; the other half was lumber and other materials to make the dome, the outhouses, water supply, shower, improvements in the swimming dock, swings and seesaws, and so forth. Our aim had been to break even and to donate our labor. We charged adults $15 each and children $4 each if they ate with us, and $7 each for adults (children free) if they provided their own food. The figures are not complete yet. We may come out as much as $200 over or under, we don't know which. It doesn't matter much — if it cost us a little, we don't begrudge it; and if we made a couple hundred dollars, I seriously doubt that the conference participants would resent it.

THE RESULTS

What everybody wants to know, of course, is whether the conference worked. Ok, so it was a big success. Everybody got fed, met a lot of nice people. The child care went smoothly. Nobody was bitten by a dog or even by a bee. The infirmary, for all its preparations, served only one upset stomach and a cut hand from a motorcycle accident en route.

But did we foster another community? That's what we want to know.

Probably we will not know the final answer to this question for several months, or even years. We must remember that it takes time for people to gather, talk things out, make plans, and come up with money and land for their community. However, there are some preliminary plans to report:

1) Most of the established groups represented at the conference attracted at least one member or potential member, or made contacts that will probably increase their membership later.

2) A group of young married people with small children (known currently as the "extended family group") is meeting this weekend on a farm belonging to one of the families. Their intention: to set up immediately a community loosely like Twin Oaks but retaining parental autonomy over the affairs of their biological children. They want to settle in Virginia and keep in close touch with Twin Oaks.

3) Three of Twin Oaks' members are splitting from Twin Oaks and met others at the conference with whom they hope to set up another community, also in Virginia and fairly close to Twin Oaks. They hope to have a small group (twelve-fifteen people), grow slowly, and place their emphasis on improving their environment rather than being a large group.

We are very excited about the possibility of three communities being within cooperating distance of each other.

4) A group who call themselves "a splinter from the splinter group" is meeting this week in Washington, D.C. This is generally a younger group than either of the above. Their spokesman told us that they shy away generally from heavy structure and want something "looser" than what the splinter group seemed to have in mind.

5) A couple on their way to British Columbia attracted others interested in doing the same. Several people have agreed to travel in that direction together and find out if they are sufficiently compatible to form a community.

And there may have been others. These are the ones we heard about. The probability that all of these groups will actually set up communities is perhaps small. We don't have much experience to base any predictions on. What are the ingredients of success? Money? Skill? Determination? Perhaps a degree of rashness? A dash of innocence and naivete? Who knows?

REGULAR
COMMUNITY NEWS

A NEW BATHROOM

The sign on the bathroom door said "Please do not run water or flush toilet. Josie is in the septic tank." In the back yard, an unsavory odor greeted our noses as we went to investigate. Sure enough, there was Josie, knee-deep in sewage, squinting into the sunlight that came through the manhole, and from time to time shoving the garden hose still deeper into the clogged drain.

We discovered the blockage when we tried to hook up the new bathroom. Water that should have gone into the septic system kept backing up onto the bathroom floor. Investigation with a plumber's snake seemed to indicate that the blockage was somewhere near the septic tank itself. First we had the tank pumped out ($75, but we got the sludge for our fields, with the blessing of the health department). Next job: find a communitarian willing to climb down into the empty but reeking tank and try to unblock the pipe. The construction manager put the job up for bids. We did not lack bids — 100 credits an hour was the highest, then 42 credits (about a week's work); some people tentatively offered to do it for 10 or 15 credits. The maintenance manager nearly got the job when she offered 5 credits an hour. Then Josie said she would do it for 2.0. The offer was snapped up instantly, and Josie was in the septic tank before you could say *Ikkggh!!*

Progress was fast at first, as sludge came out of the pipe; and Josie shoved the hose further and further into the opening. Then it began to slow up, and the work got dull. To make it pleasanter, Gerri got a book and read to her.

We don't have many poetry readings at Twin Oaks, and a small group gathered around the septic tank with Gerri as she read, "Were there but world enough and time. . .," aiming her voice in the general direction of Josie's curly head in the murky depths.

In the end the job turned out to be futile. The blockage was not near the septic tank at all. In fact, it wasn't a blockage, properly speaking, but a completely broken pipe, the broken ends of which failed to meet by about two feet where part of it had sunk and part had not. The contractor who had originally put the pipe in came out eventually and repaired it without charge, and Twin Oaks has its second bathroom in operation at last.

DANCING

Dancing at Twin Oaks has always been an off-and-on business, because of space problems. We have everything else—experienced teachers, good records, and people interested in learning. But we have never been able to spare a large open covered space to dance in. Any indoor space we build has had higher priority activities (like workshop or sleeping space) clamoring for it. This year the interest in dancing got high enough to try to do it on the lawn. Dancing on grass is not as satisfying as on a good floor, but it is better than nothing. We have been dancing twice a week, specializing in Israeli and Yugoslavian circle dances, with an occasional square dance thrown in.

CHEESE MAKING

Some seasons of the year our cows produce more milk than we can drink. We turn the surplus into cheese. The techniques we learned from a department of agriculture bulletin. It is not very difficult: we pasteurize the milk, add buttermilk and let it form a curd, cook it just a little, drain it through a cloth, then press it in a home-made cheese press. When it comes out of the press it is aged for three months before we eat it. Actually, flavoring is a problem we haven't conquered yet. Most of our cheeses have not tasted good enough that we would want to snack on them. But they are excellent grated and used in spaghetti or lasagne.

Sometimes we consider trying to make cheeses as a potential industry. There is certainly a market for a home-made cheese, probably through the natural food stores. Like most cottage industries, however, this one cannot seriously be done in our current buildings. We would need a dairy building, and we don't have the space to spare.

ARTS AND CRAFTS

Space is also a major problem in the way of our encouraging the arts. Our work load at Twin Oaks is not so heavy as to preclude many of our members' taking part in artistic things, but space problems place a severe limit on the kinds of arts that we engage in. We did a survey recently on the artistic activities that have taken place here in the Community. We collected a long list, covering a wide range of crafts, but it is noticeable that the kinds of art that require indoor space are conspicuously missing—i.e., oil painting and sculpture, pottery, etc. Here are some of the things we listed, followed by the number of people who have been involved in them:

Painting and drawing—5, graphic art—5, candle making—4, macrame—2, needlepoint—5, patchwork—7, knitting and crocheting—8, wood carving—6, Dutch barn charms—1, lace tablecloth—1, puppet-making—1, copper enameling—9, dressmaking—6, furniture-making—3, lamp-making—4, leather craft—2, playwriting and production—3, poetry—9, stories—5, original double crostic puzzles—2, cartoons—3, songwriting—4.

In addition to those items conventionally called "arts and crafts," we listed a number of creative activities that are related to work of the Community, like planning and construction of Community buildings, the organization of the kitchen, the garden and orchard, the Community clothes closet, visitor rooms, etc.

Then there are the musical activities: folk dancing, playing the guitar, flute, and recorder, singing in the choir.

And the technical arts—four of our members set up their own radio network to pipe music into their rooms from a central station.

Even with the list as complete as this, there were people who protested that the distinction between "artistic" and other activities is a false one. A number of people here are creatively involved in the Community itself. Theoretical articles on the board have been written by at least twelve people that we can recall offhand. That doesn't count all the energy that has gone into inventing and changing the labor credit system or struggling with Community policy in public meetings. (Meeting behavior can be an art in itself.) Then, isn't the effort some of us are putting into learning to get along with others a creative thing? How about the art of friendship, and of love?

We don't seriously place any value judgment on this list of Community artistic output, but it was fun to collect the list. Maybe it isn't the Golden Age, but it answers the recurring question, "Is there any art in Community?"

CLOTHING

"Look," says Linda, the clothing manager, "any new members who want to join Twin Oaks have got to come in nude. I cannot deal with any more clothes!"

Community clothes in indeed flourishing, and there are still boxes of excess clothing that is perfectly good (or was, in another era); but we haven't room to hang it up. Nevertheless, some articles of clothing are much in demand, and we don't have enough of them. Especially scarce are loose, pretty cotton dresses for hot weather. They are very simple to make, and we have already made several. Linda says we would make more if we had more cotton materials, and suggests that there might be readers who have some around the house that they would send. Appeals like this have been very successful in the past, when we wanted rug wool. So we try again. What we need are yard goods, big enough to make a garment—not scraps (we have lots of those).

MORE NAME CHANGING

Changing one's name has become epidemic since the last time we reported the custom. The girl who started out as Susan, then became Sally, is now Josie. Eve became Shawn and then changed her mind and wants to be Eve again. Even visiting children are changing their names. One child went so far as to change her age while she was at it. She is a four-year-old her parents call "Charlon." "I'm five years old, and my name is Jane," she tells us.

AWARENESS GROUPS

This spring saw the birth of a new form of dramatic entertainment. It was a play in which everyone was audience and performer. Everyone knew a short part and a cue, but only the narrator and the playwright knew the whole sequence. The performance was not smooth, because there had been no rehearsals, but it came off quite well nonetheless. In addition to being entertaining, this proved to be a very effective method of uniting the whole Community.

The play was in the form of narrative with interspersed scenes, mostly evoking events in the history of Twin Oaks and illustrating our shortcomings and successes in terms of interpersonal relations. There was no end, per se, to the play; rather it evolved into a discussion of the need for a "social revolution" at Twin Oaks. The next night, a meeting was called for all interested in pursuing the matter to discuss practical steps to be taken; and this resulted in the formation of three encounter or "awareness" groups, which began to meet weekly and have been doing so for about a month.

Twin Oaks has tried various forms of encounter or sensitivity groups in the past, with little success. Yet this time we are still optimistic. Living in a small community has, for many of us, stifled or made us pessimistic concerning our original utopian dream, the vision of how things could be, which brought us together. We find that in spite of our best hopes, we are still the unfortunate victims of a sick society and we become easily discouraged in attempting to change ourselves. We get angry, we are punitive in very subtle ways; we see people who are lonely, and neglect to ease their situation because it would put us in an uncomfortable situation—it is too much to ask for. We believe in equality, yet we are unable to face the staggering implications of total and real social equality.

Yet for many of us this play rekindled our enthusiasm for the venture of "getting closer," of being honest with ourselves. What does it mean to be honest? It is easy to talk about; it is hard to do. We do not normally see so much as a fragment of the real reasons for our behavior, for we have never been trained to do so; how much harder to face them! Even when we can be honest with ourselves, what an immense task to become honest with others! For we do not wish to hurt them, nor do we wish to be hurt by the reality of what others think of us. And yet, a true level of closeness and love must be based on truth. It is hard to do, but it is something that must be done.

In these awareness groups, we have cast about for exercises that can help us. Many books have been written, but few are really helpful. What is required is new behaviors; the old ones will not do. Sensitivity and encounter have not often been applied to communal living situations. Certainly there are people who could help us, but they are not here; and we must learn by experience. In our groups we are faced with the necessity of making something happen, of changing the others in the group, and all our old behavior patterns don't fit the bill. So at times it is frustrating and all we can do is scratch our heads.

But we sense, by and large, that what we are looking for is indeed there and can be achieved. It won't happen over night; it is a long process. But once it begins happening, we will know it—we will feel it—we will see changes that will surprise us. At times it will be traumatic; we all have little vicious traits of character that stand in need of reform, and we can feel how much it is going to hurt, how much effort it will require, to change. The process doesn't really seem to have started yet; people are dubious, but not skeptical.

For each of us there is a different vision of what things will be like when the transformation, the social revolution, is finally under way. For me (Erik), it means that problems will be confronted and resolved more quickly; interpersonal tension will dissolve; people will not be intolerant, or moved to anger—or if they are, the responses of the people around them will be radically different. No one will be lonely or unloved. Even visitors will be welcomed and will see and feel the effects of our transformation. Because we will be on a better schedule of reinforcement for successful interpersonal interaction, we will be more energetic and outgoing, while at the same time more peaceful and meditative inside. We will smile more. We will be freer in touching and loving. We will, in fact, be happier. We will not construct issues to hide interpersonal conflict.

Those are the goals. What are the results to date? I asked several people what changes they thought there had been as a result of the awareness groups. In talking with them, I realized that it is hard to say for sure whether some behavior changes are actually the result of the groups or not. We do know that these changes in behavior have at least coincided in time with the group meetings.

GROUP ONE

Josie—

I am changing, though it's hard to know if it's because of the group. There also seems to be an aura that surrounds the groups; we are learning that Twin Oaks' systems and set-ups are not all there is to helping people to live together in harmony. One specific result of the group is that I now talk to someone whom I could never think of more than two sentences to say to before. I found out that he's a real person like me.

Kat—

Most of the people in my group were already my good friends. But I chalk up one improved relationship and one deteriorated one. The others are just the same as before. We play interesting games in our group, and I am not bored. But I can't help feeling it is a waste of time. We almost seem to be committed to staying on the surface. I don't think we'll get very far unless we develop a leader among us, and nobody is interested in the role.

Steven—

More people are getting into more open discussions of interpersonal relations. The groups have occasioned a lot of self-analytical behavior. In some cases, we are more critically self-conscious than receptively self-aware, though.

Peter—

The groups are fun while we are there, but new behaviors don't seem to have carried over.

GROUP TWO

Will—

Since the play, interpersonal relations have become an important topic of Community concern. There seems to be more open discussion among Community members about their feelings. I understand the other people in my group better. I wouldn't have gotten to know some of them otherwise. The groups have given me added strength to do what I want to do but couldn't otherwise do; they've increased my willingness to be out front and get rid of some of the games.

Piper—

Personally, I am much more comfortable with some members of my group than I was. It has been a way of multiplying good feelings. As a group, I'm sure we've given strength to a couple of members. I might not otherwise have felt comfortable about asking the individual about what was bothering co.* Also, it's a fun thing; something to look forward to. And it's been my first opportunity to try out all positive and no negative discussion, and the group is helping me.

Leah—

I got to know people better. I developed tolerances and understanding for some members of my group because I understand their needs and behaviors. Also, a couple of hassles between me and some members were worked out. Now I feel I can talk to the people outside of the group when they feel bad. I've also gotten more feedback from people about how they feel about me.

Luke—

I have become more aware. I feel I was aware of people before, but there's a difference between being aware and acting accordingly. I felt before that nobody else was acting a certain way, so why should I?—but now that they are, it's easier for me to.

GROUP THREE

Sara—

I have gotten closer to the people in my group. Some overt behavior changes that I have noticed are that some people are more affectionate. I take that to mean people are feeling closer to each other. Sometimes people seem to say things more openly and honestly now.

Lorien—

I understand the people in the group better, but I don't know that I'm any friendlier with any of them.

Karl—

It is a groove talking with all the people in the group because I usually don't get a chance, but I don't necessarily feel closer. But I still dig it.

Linda—

A norm is becoming established in the Community to be able to be honest. It is not there yet, but people are working at it. People will listen more and not laugh. They'll respond honestly. More people are talking openly about themselves and their feelings.

I also talked to some people who chose not to join the groups. Here are some of their comments:

Shannon—

I've noticed that one person has become friendly with people in her group.

Aidan—

I don't notice any changes in people I talk to who are in groups. Though some of these people have said they found out things about themselves that they didn't know, and were glad to find out. At first I felt some pressure because I wasn't in a group, but this isn't true any more.

Ken—

It seems that only positive things have come out of the groups. It's good that people in groups don't talk about their groups, thus leaving others out. A neat thing that happens sometimes is that everyone who's not in a group seems to end up in the same place on "group night" and we have our own "group."

Barny—

I see people trying to deal with things more. But there is an oversaturation of some people trying to work things out in a blatantly honest and straightforward manner. People may continue it, and then not get reinforced and cut off this behavior altogether.

ERIK REPORTS ON HIS TRIP

MEETING OTHERS

Early this spring I left Twin Oaks on a leave of absence in order to travel around the country and visit other communes. My trip was curtailed due to unforeseen circumstances, but I was able to visit several places in New England and attend several conferences in the month and a half that I was gone.

The purpose of my trip was to establish contact with other communal groups, get a better idea of what they were like and how they were doing, and to discuss the question of intercommunity relations—how we can help one another.

HOMER MORRIS FUND

Late in March the annual meeting of the Homer Morris Fund took place at Pendle Hill. This is a somewhat dry, business meeting of representatives from many different communities, which have in common that they are "intentional." Thus they run the gamut from middle-class Tanguy through religious communes to communal pads. The meeting on Saturday was to discuss intercommunity affairs and raise the question of the relevance of the former Federation of Intentional Communities (of which only the Homer Morris Fund remains) to present-day activities. There was a good spirit of friendliness and cooperation, but little or no concrete progress was made, due to shortness of time and variance of expectation.

CNVA

New England Committee for NonViolent Action at Voluntown has regular conferences on "communes and co-ops" (report in last issue of *Leaves)*, and this quarter's conference took place the weekend of April 12. Here the purpose is different from the Homer Morris conference: This is a time for people interested in communes and co-ops to come and discuss issues and learn about existing communities. At the same time, it is a good opportunity for people from different communes to meet and learn about each other. It was quite a hectic weekend, and it is difficult to assess the progress made; but certainly a vast amount of beneficial informal contact was made.

BROTHERHOOD OF THE SPIRIT

One of my first visits was to a large commune called Brotherhood of the Spirit. It is little known in the media of the alternative life style, but it is very interesting. They number between 150 and 200, living in very crowded dormitories. Brotherhood is a religion unto itself. Their leader is Michael Metelica, and he is reputed to be a medium of some stature. A rock band of about twelve members, called *Spirit in Flesh*, is hoped to become a major source of income. *Metromedia* is doing a large promotional effort on them, and their first album has already appeared, I believe. It sounded good but not exceptional, although I only heard it once, in a noisy dining room.

I tried to catalog some of the beliefs that were held in common. In my short overnight visit I was approached unceasingly and preached at. They don't use the word *preaching*, but it is very clear that all members desire to be teachers of the faith and practice at every opportunity, using the same earnest style of fundamentalist evangelists. It is clear to me that they have come upon some valuable principles of interpersonal relations, even though their understanding of those principles is superstitious. Here are some of their beliefs:

There exists the highest form of energy/vibration, called Vishna, and this energy has taken carnal form in order to express itself creatively. We are all part of this energy, which enters the world through mediums, one nearby in Massachusetts; and apparently Michael can also introduce energy now. All about Brotherhood there is a field of energy that you are supposed to feel as you come into it, produced by the interactions and expressions of the members. Members came together because they agreed in a previous incarnation to do so. Members want a "real connection" between each other, they wish to "spark" something between each other.

The future is grim; the crust of the earth is going to shift, causing cataclysmic events, and these events will cause some people to come together in brotherhood, which will be necessary in order to survive. Everyone really wants "brotherhood." Any one who says co* does not deceives coself.* Brotherhood is the greatest thing happening on this planet. In days to come, when the turmoil is upon us, some will live in groups of "brotherhood" and the others will revert to savagery, marauding, etc.

The concept of "brotherhood" is the hub of what is happening there. I am quite sure that to live there is to live a perpetual "encounter" session, perhaps similar to the Fort Hill Commune in Boston, where they say they "destroy and rebuild each other every day." Behaviorally speaking, Brotherhood is quite exceptional. The members appear happier than usual; they are outgoing, openly loving, excited, smiling. Visitors are practically attacked; when you have finished talking with one person, another will begin. There is a hodge-podge of religious talk, mostly mystic. Some of their basic precepts are quite interesting, and they are really put into practice. Perhaps the most important is the insistence on honesty in all things: honesty in expressing oneself creatively. Work is perceived as creative expression. Good feelings as well as bad are encouraged. It is expected that all matters between people will be dealt with immediately; confrontation and encounter. Obviously this gets very heavy, but one gets the feeling that with several years experience in this many members are very qualified at handling a plethora of situations with success. One is struck by the forcefulness of character and the self-confidence of the older members. My general impression was that Brotherhood of the Spirit is in fact "getting closer" by increasing honesty. Fears and inhibitions are viewed as challenges to be attacked, charged into. Here is an example of the superstitious justification of what is probably a very valid behavioral precept: they believe that fears and inhibitions are acquired in previous incarnations.

While I was excited and impressed by my observations of the Brotherhood, I was naturally turned off by other aspects. The standard of living would not please many; there is little concern with social equality, in fact there appears to be a rigid social hierarchy with Michael at the top. People in New England who are familiar with them are less ambivalent about them, more turned off by negative aspects, less impressed with positive aspects, than I was. I heard many allegations and charges but of course was unable to tell how much was accurate. It is clear to me that the Brotherhood is a potent and forceful thing, but I am not sure I like the direction it seems to be applying this force. This is difficult to verbalize; it is more an intuitive sort of distrust. While I was there I did catch a vision of the kind of society we need to create for the future—one of honesty and love—taken seriously.

FREE VERMONT

We had been hearing interesting things from Vermont for some time, and I caught a glimpse of it in the few days

I was there. I visited Packers Corner, a small group that thinks of itself in terms of a family, where Ray Mungo and Marty Jezer live. Ray has left, but the members are convinced he will return. This was a refreshing change from the Brotherhood—relaxed, homey. There may be a dozen or more people there, no children. There is obviously a lot of love and trust between the people. Again, the contingencies for work are more "natural" than ours, and there is a correspondingly low standard of living, although one in which I felt very much at home.

Free Vermont is an intercommunal organization that keeps nearly all the elements of the alternative life style in touch. They are working on various inter-communal cooperative efforts, such as a free book exchange, free seed exchange, a medical traveling group, etc. There is also a nascent Organic Farmers Association that holds much promise. The newspaper has, I feel, slightly more revolutionary sloganeering than is useful or tasteful, but the intercommunity newsletter, *Free Family Notes*, is a very informative and practical tool for its purpose. All in all, the development in Vermont justifies the rumors and speculation I had heard elsewhere.

HIDDEN SPRINGS

Twin Oaks had heard from Hidden Springs a year or more ago, but had not had any contact with them. My visit of about a week brought me back to an atmosphere more similar to Twin Oaks. They are currently in the process of defining themselves as a community, and it is difficult to talk about them in other terms than the individuals living there and the facilities. They are an intentional community with a good deal of practical but not theoretical communism, and lots of dreams and lots of doubts, lots of problems. The land is very beautiful, and there are 418 acres of it.

WALDEN THREE

We had rather extensive contact with the group known as Walden Three, due partly to a similarity of views between us. I stayed and worked with them in Providence for three weeks. Currently they have two bases: some are working on the large dairy farm of Hermann Patt, which will probably see the development of the eventual community; some are still holding jobs and living at their apartment in Providence. Things look very hopeful for them. Right now their most urgent need is more people to help them accomplish the vast amount of work necessary. Hermann Patt has had a difficult time working out the conflicts between his family and the Walden Three group, but things look hopeful at present. Two members of Twin Oaks are at Walden Three right now.

OTHER GROUPS

Apart from these groups, we have been in contact with a few other new groups who are building communities with largely the same aims as Twin Oaks, although using a variety of techniques. We have not heard much from Community Design, a group that plans to settle in Colorado. They have

sent several prospecti, but either mail service from Colorado is poor or they are too busy to write, for we have written several times—and so have Walden Three—and gotten only one response. From their literature it is apparent that their goals are similar to ours, but they are "more eclectic in approach," influenced by the Israeli kibbutzim, and concerned about having a wide age range, stability from maturity, and a firm economic base. It is likely that there are only a few people presently, but they look forward to up to 100. Almost all of their literature is concerned with plans rather than with current activity.

Neverland in California will probably have moved to a piece of land in Oregon by now. Their first newsletter was a cheery affair, giving a glimpse of what they are in a variety of ways: social blurbs, land scene, visitor policy, letters received, personal profiles, opinion about communal birth pains and larger matters. They have selected three spots in Oregon and are temporarily based in Eugene. Last word said they should be moving the first of July. They number about twenty, mostly between 20 and 30 with an average near 25; into yoga and meditation pretty heavily. Vince has visited Twin Oaks, and there is good rapport there.

East Street Gallery is located in Grinnell, Iowa, and consists of four to six people. They have been friends of Twin Oaks for a long time, although they are only getting together as a commune now. They have been busy establishing their industry, production of a film development unit, and will put together definite plans for a community in the next few months. Along with Walden Three, they were her for the conference on community, looking for members. They will probably have a labor distribution system and want people in particular who are interested in engaging in experimental sociological change.

Llano -- Another item of perhaps great importance to us in the future has to do with the defunct Llano del Rio Colony. Llano was a large community formed in 1914, which moved from California to Louisiana, where in 1936 internal political strife broke the community up. Land whose value was assessed at the time at $17,000,000 was sold for a trifle by fraud and conspiracy involving local officials, it is maintained by many members. Most of the Llano people are dispersed and too old to seek to come together again, but some are still interested in recovering the funds or land if possible, so that the money can be used for the purposes of civil rights and the community movement. In particular they want to create some sort of shelter for communities so they will have protection from the kind of attack that brought an end to Llano.

Recently Llano was sued by a former member for some $37,000. A black attorney took the case and won it. Llano planned to pay him by selling a tract of forty acres to which they have title, but it has been impossible to sell the land. Steps must be taken now to sell the land and pay the lawyer, and then to pursue the larger case in court. It is said that the case was practically won back in 1936, but for various reasons was not pursued through appropriate channels. Twin Oaks will be making a trip down to Leesville, Louisiana to perform some chores for the Llano people with respect to this case in a few weeks. As soon as this lawyer can be paid, we will be free to begin work on the larger suit. This will require promotional work and research into the case. Money will be needed, in all probability, and there will undoubtedly be bureaucratic complications in the courts. But if this could be successfully accomplished, it would be a great boon to our movement.

INTER-COMMUNITY COOPERATION

Soon, if not immediately, the commune movement will be at a stage where it is desirable to reach out to each other in cooperation. At present communication is tenuous, and cooperation practically nonexistent. The recent join effort between Twin Oaks and Heathcote to produce a commune directory is the only such effort we know of in this region.

Dealing only in the area of information/research/education, there are many things that could be done right now to further our alternative life style and assist new groups and interested people. These concern chiefly facilitating the flow of information in three ways: *1)* between communes, *2)* from resources (information) to communes, and *3)* from communes to the public. Here are a few possible projects:

COMMUNITY EDUCATION PROJECT

A project that would produce informational pamphlets and booklets on a number of topics for use by new communes. It could include topics such as Incorporation and Other Legal Organization, How to Do It and Why; Industries: Production and Sales for Communes; Interpersonal Problems: Some Methods and Solutions; Local, State, and Federal Governments: How to Coexist; Practical Health for Communes; Communes and Internal Revenue; How to Buy Food; How to Get the Work Done; etc. These pamphlets should contain valuable, authoritative information in a practical, usable form.

CONFERENCE ORGANIZATION

To organize conferences and workshops *a)* for the benefit of the public interested in communes as an alternative, and *b)* between communes on a regional and national basis. This latter is a vital step in regional organization: All the inter-communal cooperation we have heard of stems from such "tribal" gatherings of all those in a given area who live and pursue the alternative life style.

INFORMATIONAL CLEARINGHOUSE

To gather and coordinate information on communes. Properly executed, this would relieve communes of a large amount of clerical, routine labor, since it could have for mailing the informational brochures and other material that the group itself produces. This project would need to be accepted in its role by most of the communes and would have to become well-known.

PREPARATION OF MATERIAL FOR MASS MEDIA

To ensure good, fair coverage by the press and TV and to forestall development of an undesirable image and build-up of fear through ignorance or sensationalist reporting. An interesting possibility for the immediate future is for a good writer and photographer from our own ranks to produce and free-lance articles on communes. This would kill two birds with one stone: present our views rather than those of a liberal (or not so liberal) middle-class reporter, and the money would go to the movement rather than to the Establishment. This effort is a vital one. Ignorance or biased information can do us a lot of harm. Once in operation, communes could decline requests by straight TV, radio, or press to do reports on their own, telling these latter that articles and reports are already available and ready for print, videotape, or studio.

MICROFILM LIBRARY

To operate an extensive free library of microfilm with educational, technical, and entertainment material. Apparently microfilm readers are not difficult to make with a price range most communes can afford—$20 to $30. The microfilming equipment also is within reach of our combined efforts. For some groups, such as urban communes, this service would be of little value; but for communes that have only small or distant libraries available, it would eliminate hassle and extend the range of materials available.

FILM LIBRARY

To build up a library of films for use by communes that have projectors.

SKILL BANK

To make contact with sympathetic lawyers, doctors, and other professional people and organize ways for them to make their services available to communes.

JOURNAL

To publish an intercommunity journal, a means of sharing news, ideas, and maintaining morale.

These are possibilities of the future. Presently we are limited in both finances and labor, for we are all busy with internal and survival problems. I feel that most organizational effort at present should be oriented towards regional matters; in every state there are scores of small communal groups that are not in touch with alternative media, nor wish to be, who perhaps are not interested in the national scene but who would profit by regional organization similar to that which is being done in Vermont.

I hope to continue to publish news of the movement as a regular feature of the *Leaves;* I would greatly appreciate hearing from anyone about these ideas, but in particular from other communal groups.

[Erik]

REQUEST FOR SHEET MUSIC

Our recreation budget does not extend far enough to buy much sheet music for our musicians. We would particularly like to have music (if you have some lying around you don't need) for the following instruments: classical guitar, piano, recorder, and flute—especially flute and recorder duets.

LETTER FROM A READER

[This was addressed to Erik after his article in the last *Leaves:*]

"I am writing you about your thoughts on the role of communities, life styles, and 'revolution.' [Your article] reflects some common misconception of young dedicates...

"People don't *make* revolutions. They only find themselves in a revolutionary situation and have no choice but to struggle through...

"Revolutions don't fail. To fail is evidence that it was only a rebellion...

"You seem to think that a revolution comes as a choice like a fork in a road: you may choose to take either one or the other. Instead, when a revolution is imminent you have *no* choice; you are in it and must deal with it. You strongly imply that those who "start" revolutions will and should be leaders. You should read up on the history of revolutions, their origins and compositions.

"Supporting your theory you mention an alternative—'we are it'. It is quite plain that you are unaware of what happened to the co-op movement in Italy when Mussolini took over. His first act was to stomp out the co-ops. In doing this he found absolutely no resistance. Co-ops by their very nature fail to provide a guide to action when the going is rough. Particularly they are unaware of their most important allies, so they are short on counsel when they need it most...

"The role of co-ops, communes, or whatever, today is to provide schools of political understanding, along with all the benefits of mutual aid, ethics, and brotherhood, etc. I content that you underestimate our enemies and overestimate what you symbolize in 'we are it'.

"Let's work for peace, plenty, and a classless world where the human race can progress to whatever they are worthy of."

— Bernie Stevens

ABOUT "CO"

Co means *he, she, his, hers, him,* and *her.* It was invented by a women's liberation group in New York who felt that the generalized *he* referring to both sexes should be done away with as part of our language. Many Twin Oaks members agree and write their articles accordingly.

SUBSCRIPTIONS

The price of the *Leaves* is going up, mostly to reflect the rise in postage rates. $3 still covers a subscription, but it will now be for six issues and will run for one year.

Appendix—Twin Oaks Behavior Code

1 We do not use titles of any kind. All members are "equal" in the sense that all are entitled to the same privileges, advantages, and respect. That is the reason we shun honorifics of any kind, including Mrs., Dr., Mother, Dad, etc.

2 All members are required to explain their work to any other member who desires to learn it. The purpose of this is to insure the opportunity to learn any available and appropriate work. Observing this rule makes it impossible for any member to exert pressure on the Community by having a monopoly on any certain skill.

3 We do not discuss the personal affairs of other members, nor speak negatively of other members when they are not present or in the presence of a third party. This rule is both unusual and difficult. Most of us find a certain pleasure in gossiping or grumbling about other people. We here feel this kind of talk is harmful to a community. If a member is unpleasant, or lazy, or gross, let each other member discover this for coself. It is not fair to damage another member's reputation, nor to encourage others to dislike another member. We are constantly trying other means of dealing with interpersonal problems and complaints. Gossiping about them with each other does not help the problem; it only spreads the discontent.

4 We do not publicly grumble or gripe about things we think wrong within the Community. Complaints are best taken up with the appropriate manager. Public bitching is bad for morale; it imposes on those persons who overhear it and may find it unpleasant; and it never substitutes for positive concern and constructive suggestions.

5 Members who may have unconventional or unorthodox views on politics, religion, or national policies stay clear of such topics when it is prudent. Most of us probably disagree on many issues with our neighbors and residents of this county. We need the good will and friendship of these people, and it is our policy to be discreet and stay clear of controversial topics when we converse with them.

6 Seniority is not discussed among us. This is because we wish to avoid the emergence of prestige groups of any kind.

7 We try to exercise both consideration and tolerance of each others' individual habits. This means that we don't play the record player at full blast in a public room when there are people trying to have a quiet conversation. It also means that if someone *is* playing the record player full blast when someone else wants quiet, we try to put up with it for a little while or go elsewhere. There is nothing absolute about this rule—it's just a guideline.

8 We do not boast of individual accomplishments. We are trying to create a society without heroes. We are all expected to do our best, so making a big fuss over some accomplishment is out of place.

9 We try to clean up after ourselves after any private or individual project; we try not to keep articles longer than we need them but return them to their proper places so that they can be enjoyed by other members. Cleaning up after ourselves includes washing out the tub after a bath, cleaning up our own pans if we make popcorn or cookies, and clearing our dirty dishes from the dining tables.

10 Individual rooms are inviolate. No member enters another's room without that other member's permission. We all need a place to be alone. It is the aim of the Community for all members who so desire to have private rooms as soon as possible.

Index

Industries:

* denotes articles from *Walden Pool*
** denotes articles from *Walden House Newsletter*
(Both of these publications were forerunners of Twin Oaks Community and its newsletter, *The Leaves of Twin Oaks*.)